T0339465

PUBLIC RELATIONS AND COMMUNICATIONS

This book provides an introduction to public relations (PR) that employs pedagogical experiential learning models to assist students in developing the skills and competencies required by the PR industry.

The book takes the reader on a journey from the theory and origins of PR, through to the structure of the PR profession and the more practical elements of how PR is practised today. It devotes attention to the common competencies necessary for success as a communications professional, such as communication skills, critical thinking skills and business acumen, while giving due focus to the rapidly evolving new technologies and media that impact how organisations communicate. Featuring example cases from around the world, chapters include discussion topics and scenario-based questionnaires to encourage learning and assist students in developing key competencies.

This book is ideal for undergraduate PR modules, particularly those with experiential and/or blended learning pedagogical approaches. It will also be useful to those in business seeking to gain a deeper understanding of communications.

Situational Judgement Tests and sample press releases, presented as online resources, also accompany the book. Please visit www.routledge.com/9781032170435.

Aoife O'Donnell has been working in communications in Dublin, Ireland for over 25 years. She lectures in public relations on both undergraduate and post graduate programmes and holds a masters in education and training.

Public Relations and Communications

From Theory to Practice

Aoife O'Donnell

Routledge
Taylor & Francis Group

NEW YORK AND LONDON

Designed cover image: gremlin/E+ via Getty Images

First published 2023
by Routledge
605 Third Avenue, New York, NY 10158

and by Routledge
4 Park Square, Milton Park, Abingdon, Oxon, OX14 4RN

Routledge is an imprint of the Taylor & Francis Group, an informa business

Library of Congress Cataloguing-in-Publication Data
Names: O'Donnell, Aoife, author.
Title: Public relations and communications : from theory to practice /
Aoife O'Donnell.
Description: 1st Edition. | New York, NY : Routledge, 2023. |
Includes bibliographical references and index.
Identifiers: LCCN 2022061905 (print) | LCCN 2022061906 (ebook) |
ISBN 9781032182902 (hardback) | ISBN 9781032170435 (paperback) |
ISBN 9781003253815 (ebook)
Subjects: LCSH: Public relations. | Interpersonal communication. |
Business communication.
Classification: LCC HM1226 .O36 2023 (print) | LCC HM1226 (ebook) |
DDC 659.2--dc23/eng/20230302
LC record available at https://lccn.loc.gov/2022061905
LC ebook record available at https://lccn.loc.gov/2022061906

ISBN: 978-1-032-18290-2 (hbk)
ISBN: 978-1-032-17043-5 (pbk)
ISBN: 978-1-003-25381-5 (ebk)

DOI: 10.4324/9781003253815

Typeset in Bembo
by MPS Limited, Dehradun

Access the Support Material: www.routledge.com/9781032170435

Contents

Figures

Tables

Contributors

Mark Campbell, Mark is a Lecturer on MSc and MBA programmes in Ireland. He is also a Member of the Science, Technology, Engineering and Maths Board of Studies and a Director of Upgrade Education Ltd., which provides consulting, writing lecturing and training services to educational institutions and students.

Dr Robbie Smyth, is Head of the Journalism & Media Communications Faculty at Griffith College. He lectures in research methods, media and culture studies, political communication and the business of media, particular the area of media regulation and compliance.

Aoife Farrell. Thanks to Graphic Designer, Aoife Farrell for the design of the figures in this book.

Acknowledgement

This book is a culmination of my experience of working in the PR and communications industries and my teaching and training experience to date.

From my early days working in in-house positions to my time spent in agencies, I have worked with many people who mentored and supported me, to whom I owe thanks, and to all the amazing colleagues I have worked with over the years who have helped to make me a better practitioner and teacher.

In recent years, I have become more involved and interested in the academic side of public relations and have received much support from experts in this area, most notably Dr Robbie Smyth, who has contributed to this book, and Dr Fiona O'Riordan, to name but two. I also owe a debt of gratitude to the students who I have taught over the years, whose enthusiasm and energy have energised me in writing this book. Thank you to all of them.

Thanks to everyone in the Public Relations Institute of Ireland for their support and use of information from their website. Thanks to communications professionals, Cathy Riordan, Maeve Governey and Róisín Reilly, who helped compile the online situational judgement tests associated with this book. Thanks to Gini Dietrich for the permission to reference her invaluable PESO Model.

Thanks to everyone at Taylor and Francis for their patience and assistance along the route to the publication of the book. It was a pleasure working with you.

Finally, to my friends and family, and most notably to Darach for his unwavering support and to Jack, whose determination and strength of character has given me the focus I needed to get this book over the finish line.

1 The History of Public Relations

Chapter Contents

1.1 Learning Outcomes

On finishing this chapter, the reader should be able to:

- Have a critical understanding of what public relations (PR) is and the role that it plays in the modern world.
- Demonstrate an awareness of the origins and history of PR and how they impact on contemporary practice.
- Understand the diversity of the public relations professional's role and develop a deeper understanding of the relationship between PR and media professionals.

1.2 Public Relations in Action

Modern-day public relations (PR) comes in many shapes and sizes. The roles of its practitioners are diverse and could be explained in a variety of different ways. For example: understanding public behaviour, counseling organisation leaders and/or developing strategic two-way communications programmes that can resonate with a specific public or audience. This might make perfect sense to those who have been working in the profession for many years. However, for students and those new to PR, the diverse duties and descriptions of the roles of

DOI: 10.4324/9781003253815-1

its practitioners can be hard to grasp. The best way to begin is by demonstrating PR in action in recent times.

In late 2019, news emerged of the breakout of a serious respiratory disease in China. The disease became commonly known as the Coronavirus and eventually as COVID-19 as it spread from east to west throughout the world. For communications students, the response of the World Health Organisation (WHO) and the individual responses from national governments to the pandemic presented an ideal opportunity to study an international communications crisis as it unfolded in real time. A communications analysis of this period offers insight into political communications, lobbying, corporate communications, crisis communications and the power and challenges of persuasive communications.

As COVID-19 began to establish itself as a pandemic, the WHO released guidelines for countries advising them on their communications strategies. The document offered advice as to how to proactively engage in two-way dialogue with citizens. It recommended that communications should happen through multiple channels to inform the public of the public health measures they needed to take. The plan clearly highlighted the important role that effective communication is required to play in a health crisis to enable governments and public health officials to engage with the public, with healthcare providers and with other stakeholders in order to inform, educate and reduce stigma (WHO, 2020).

In every country throughout the world, communications played a major role in the response to the pandemic. In some countries, chief medical officers and public health teams became household names and faces as they presented regular press conferences to the media to inform the public of the prevalence of the disease in the community and instruct them as to how to stay safe. Clear and not so clear public information campaigns were rolled out across the world using various slogans and words that became part of the common vernacular such as 'Stay Safe', 'Stay Home', 'Lockdown', 'Social Distancing' and 'Quarantine'.

In other countries, the pandemic was politicised by leaders. For example, in the weeks following the first diagnosis in the UK, British Prime Minister Boris Johnson undermined the advice of the scientists and medical professionals by stating that he had recently met and shook hands with many COVID patients while taking no precautions to reduce transmission. Within weeks, Boris Johnson himself was admitted to hospital after contracting the virus. By June 2020, in a report in *The Guardian* newspaper, less than a third of the UK public were reported as approving of the UK Government's handling of the pandemic (Savage, 2020). In the US, the then President Donald Trump initially described the virus as merely like a flu and used his initial press conferences as opportunities for blame and speculation. As is common in his rhetoric, he used racist language and attempted to instil hatred and racism in those who followed him. In one now infamous utterance, he speculated at a live press conference, if there was any merit in people consuming household disinfectant to treat the virus. Immediately manufacturers of such products were active on social media cautioning the public against ingesting their products. A poll by Reuters/Ipsos quoted in *Forbes* in June 2020 reveals that 58% of Americans disapproved of Trump's handling of the pandemic. The article states that this was Trump's lowest rating since public opinion was first sought on his handling of the crisis in March 2020 (Porterfield, 2020). In Brazil, President Bolsonaro repeatedly flouted the advice from the health experts by contradicting recommendations on social distancing and attending mass events. Brazil then reportedly overtook the UK as the second country to have lost the most lives by June 2020.

Lobbying played a huge role in the pandemic. In Ireland for example at the outset of the pandemic, organisations responded and mostly adhered to the restrictions and closures imposed upon them by the Government. However, by the time the first wave of the disease and lockdown had passed, the public and organisations had grown weary. As Christmas approached businesses began to lobby hard to re-open in an attempt to recoup some revenues lost. Leaders of organisations from the aviation industry to the Irish Hotels Federation, the Licensed Vintners Association and so on, appeared in the media to advocate for their industry. In the end, multiple industries including retail and hospitality were opened up for Christmas. Unfortunately, this period coincided with the emergence of a new variant of the disease and this combined with the increased mixing and socialisation of the public led to a huge growth in the trajectory of the disease and the longest lockdown the country had endured.

In the business world, organisations went into crisis mode. Worldwide, businesses, schools and universities were forced to shut down as countries entered 'lockdown' to stop the spread of the disease. As a result, businesses were suddenly faced with individual mini-crises of their own. How were they going to operate? Should they continue to sell their products and services online? How would they communicate this with consumers? How would they communicate with their staff most of whom were now working remotely? How would they protect the staff who were still on site? Organisations were suddenly faced with multiple problems in unison with the imminent threat to their revenues and survival. Crisis communications were required and demand for online crisis communications from PR practitioners grew. The emphasis that organisations were now placing on communications is clear in a survey conducted in March 2020, by Provoke Media. In this survey, PR practitioners worldwide both in-house and in-agency were asked what services their clients were seeking most frequently. 82% cited crisis communications. The following year, corporate communications was cited as the most in-demand service at 78% with crisis communications following suit at 65% (Sims, 2021).

Arguably, the most significant communications challenge of the pandemic was the requirement to change attitudes and behaviours. Populations around the world were encouraged to stop socialising with one in other for business or pleasure and to change their behaviours when it came to personal health. The communications around mask-wearing became a huge challenge for public health teams in the Western world. At the beginning of the crisis, the communication on face masks in some parts of western Europe was not clear and in some cases, the message was conflicting with some medical professionals advocating for their regular use and others citing a lack of evidence as to their efficacy. In Ireland, a couple of months into the pandemic, the Department of Health found that only 41% of people were wearing face masks in public (O'Shea, 2020). Perhaps the lack of clarity played a part in this low uptake and maybe stigma had an impact also. In a study conducted by researchers from Middlesex University in London and the Mathematical Science Research Institute in Berkeley, USA, the researchers found that men and women self-reported negative emotions when wearing a face covering such as shame, feeling uncool, feeling face coverings to be a sign of weakness and a stigma. In its communications guidelines, the WHO emphasised the need to reduce stigma in communications when trying to change attitudes or behaviours related to public health. It stated that *'regular and proactive communication with the public and at-risk populations can help to reduce stigma, build trust and increase social support and access to basic needs for affected people and their families'*. Departments of health around the world were then tasked with the significant challenge of persuading large populations to change their attitudes and behaviours to public health.

Analysing the communications activity of the COVID-19 pandemic offers an insight into the and the diversity of knowledge and skills required by its practitioners. Communicators during this time were required to think fast, to act quickly, to be more creative, to lobby governments, to protect the reputations of leaders, brands and businesses, to manage multiple crises and to communicate to mass audiences to persuade them to change attitudes and behaviours.

This is a modern example of PR in action. To truly understand PR, it is important to start with its history as a profession.

1.3 What Is Public Relations?

In an in-house poll conducted in Ireland amongst third-level students, on their first day in a PR class, when asked to describe PR in one word, the students referenced words such as 'reputation', 'image', 'spin' and 'narrative'.

These words, while appropriate and relevant, also serve to summarise the reputation problem that PR itself has as a profession. In the industry, words such as *'spin'* or *'propaganda'* are considered to be undesirable characteristics of the profession. However, these are words that are commonly associated with PR and the reasons for this lie in its often cited story of origin, in the Western world.

In the late 19th and early 20th centuries. It is widely reported that politicians began to see the value and impact of persuasive communications during World Wars I and II. This version of its history then follows its trajectory from the battlefield to the business world in the United States with 'Big Business' such as the mining, coal and tobacco industries using PR to counter the accusations of the 'muckraking' journalists. This is an exciting modern incarnation for the PR field and one that will be discussed in more detail in Chapter 2.

At this time, businesses were skeptical of media attention and did not proactively seek it out as they would do today. The media generally only came calling if there was a negative story brewing and businesses tended to try and hide these stories from the public as far as possible. In the years between then and now, such businesses and industries have become famed for their misleading communication which have had a detrimental effect on public health. In 2011, a report published in Nicotine and Tobacco Research UCLA revealed that the tobacco industry had known since 1959 that particles in cigarette smoke could cause lung cancer but concealed this information from the public (Jaslow, 2011). Communications from the tobacco industry continued to insist that this was not the case.

Comparisons between the manipulative and deceptive tactics used by the tobacco industry in the early days and industries in modern times could be made.

In 2017, the CDP Carbon Majors Report outlined how only 100 companies in the world, including Shell and BP, have been responsible for more than 70% of the world's greenhouse gas emissions since 1988. In 2019 a report from the Climate Accountability Institute revealed that 20 fossil fuel companies have been driving climate change through the exploitation of oil, gas and coal reserves and these companies were aware of the dangers of their work for the planet. These companies do not communicate this with their audiences and in some cases, as with Shell for example n Nigeria, they spend considerable effort mitigating against the environmental damage with significant corporate social responsibility activity. Michael Mann, one of the world's leading scientists said: *'The great tragedy of the climate crisis is that seven and a half billion people must pay the price – in the form of a degraded planet – so that a couple of dozen polluting interests can continue to make record profits'* (Taylor and Watts, 2019).

In October 2021, technology giant Facebook was compared to the tobacco industry during a committee hearing into its practices. In the hearing, Facebook was criticised by Senator Richard Blumenthal for failing to address the mental health impact of its *'Instagram'* app on teenagers and concealing the information from the public. The Senator said: *'In truth, Facebook has taken Big Tobacco's playbook. It has hidden its own research on addiction and the toxic effects of its products, it has attempted to deceive the public and us in Congress about what it knows, and it has weaponized childhood vulnerabilities against children themselves'* (Rodriguez, 2021). Facebook's CEO, Mark Zuckerberg denied this and defended Facebook's practices in the media.

It is worth noting the communications activities of large industries, such a the tobacco industry as they form an important part of PR's history. Their man-impuative sencretive tactis and purposes and their use of PR to achieve their objectives are the causes of the cycnical view that many have the public relations and the image problem that the profession itself has to this day. In many cases this view can be rightly founded, especially when you consider the history and the practices of some of the industries' earliest practioners. However, there now exists an alternative trajectory for the field of public relations and an opportunity for modern practitioners to create an exiting and potentially altruistic history fir the profession alternative trajectoy for public relations. Those that argue against the most commonly cited version of PR history would proffer that PR professionals are not merely representatives working on behalf of 'Big Business' but are activists who use their skills and knowledge to fight for worthwhile causes.

This is an exciting incarnation for the field of PR and one that will be discussed in more detail in Chapter 2.

Regardless of the purpose of the practitioner, be it to protect and further the reputation of 'Big Business' or to assist a public in advocating for a cause, PR professionals are required to adhere to international codes of ethics as discussed in Chapter 3. This chapter will look at the history of PR from countries in the Western world and also from other markets where PR is growing as a profession with the aim of assisting the reader in understanding the context to the theories discussed in Chapter 2.

1.4 The History of PR

If we consider PR as a form of activism, then it would appear to have its origins at the beginning of time. For example, the word propaganda originates from the Catholic Church's purpose which was to 'propagate the faith'. The cave drawings from the Chauvet Caves in France date back to the Stone Age over 30,000 years ago. Egyptian Hieroglyphics, one of the earliest known forms of writing date back to around 3,300 B.C. and the orations of the great great philosophers, Aristotle, Cicero, date back to c. 400 B.C. However, for purposes of this book, we look at the origins of public relations as a profession mainly in the business world. It is in the mid-19th century as the Western world was becoming more industrialised, political unrest was mounting, media was becoming more accessible and psychology was just emerging as a scientific discipline, that persuasive communication became more organised and the much-cited Western story of the profession of PR begins.

In the late 18th and early 19th centuries, the United States ploughed its resources into the development of industry, railroads and utilities (Cutlip, 1994). The growth of these industries and the big businesses within them coincided with the emergence of mass media and the establishment of the first national press association in the United States. Prior to the 1900s, organised communication to the media was mainly coming from publicists who were to be found working in the entertainment. P.T. Barnum, the creator of the 'Big Top' circus experience, is probably the most commonly cited example of such a publicist. Barnum is thought to have coined the phrase: 'there's no such thing as bad publicity' due to his penchant for using stunts to attract people to his shows

(Butterick, 2011). Barnum found the more publicity the show received, either good or bad, the more people who would arrive to watch. Publicists are still in action mainly in the entertainment, arts and sports industries' today right throughout the world. People in the public eye, including musicians, authors, sports stars become brands in their own right requiring publicists to manage their public image and reputation. A prime example of such stars are former footballer David Beckham and his wife, fashion designer and former Spice Girl, Victoria Beckham, who have built their own luxury *'Brand Beckham'*. As reported in *The Guardian*, *'they have evolved beyond mere celebrities into a fully-fledged brand, a household name as familiar and comforting as your daily breakfast cereal or family car'* (Hinsliff, 2019). Other examples include the musicians Ed Sheeran and Rihanna, the soccer star Cristiano Ronaldo or the tennis star, Serena Williams. Any person who has a public profile will most likely have a publicist on board to manage their personal image as we will discuss in the next section in this chapter.

Barnum and others like him were active in the United States during a period of early investigative journalism, commonly referred to as the *'Muckraking Era'*. In this era, businesses or *'Big Business'* as it was known at the time, did not speak willingly to the media. If the media came calling, it was usually because there was a negative story in the news. The *'Muckrakers'* were tasked with uncovering scandals from *'Big Business' and as a result of their work*, powerful organisations in the steel or railroad industries for example would find themselves at a centre of an image or reputational crisis brought about by a negative newspaper article from the *'Muckrakers'*.

It is against this background that the two men, who are often referred to as the 'fathers of PR' entered the professional scene – Ivy Lee and Edward Bernays. Their stories are important to document as it is on their practices and the practice of Barnum that Grunig and Hunt later based their *'Four Models of PR'* that is still used today to explain and categorise how PR is performed. This model is further discussed in Chapter 2.

In the early 1900s, Ivy Lee, a former journalist is thought to have set up his PR agency in New York. Lee was hugely influential in the development of PR as a profession. However, together with his paternal PR counterpart, Edward Bernays, as influential as they were in setting standards and creating a framework for practising PR, they also contributed to the creation of a lifelong reputational issue for the profession itself that exists to this day.

Lee began his career working for the *New York Times* amongst other newspapers. On exiting journalism, he worked in political PR and eventually in business. At the time, businesses in the United States favoured a secretive approach and were keen to avoid the attention of the *'Muckrakers'* who had the potential to destroy their reputation through their negative media reports. Lee believed however that secrecy generated suspicion and that there was a market for businesses to tell their stories and position themselves in a positive light. To this end, he famously drafted what is known as the *'Declaration of Principles'* which became an early ethical framework for informative communications between organisations and their publics. In the *'Declaration of Principles'*, Lee set out guidelines for how his agency would operate, identifying honesty and transparency as markers of his role and making clear distinctions between his activity and the activity of advertisers. For example, the *'Declaration of Principles'* states:

> *This is not a secret press bureau. All our work is done in the open. We aim to supply news. This is not an advertising agency; if you think any of our matter ought properly to go to your business office, do not use it. Our matter is accurate. Further details on any subject treated will be supplied promptly, and any editor will be assisted most cheerfully in verifying directly any statement of fact …. In brief, our plan is, frankly and openly, on behalf of business concerns and public institutions, to supply to the press and public of the United States prompt and accurate information concerning subjects which it is of value and interest to the public to know about.*

> (Cutlip, 1994)

Lee developed quite a reputation for himself as a professional communicator who had the ability to help large organisations to turn the tide on the negative publicity generated by the *'Muckrakers'* and as a result of many of the large workers' strikes that were common at the time. For example, in 1906 when the Pensylvannian Railroad Company was involved in a large accident in which 50 people were killed, Lee made PR history by communicating openly with the media and inviting them to travel to the scene of the accident, an action that was unheard of at the time.

Ivy Lee made a big impact on the PR industry. His *'Declaration of Principles'* has stood the test of time and his transparent and informative style of communications was later used by Grunig and Hunt as an example of how PR is practised in their *'Four Models of PR'*. However, by the time Lee died at the age of 57, he was shrouded in controversy. He was accused of being a Russian propagandist and his work with the company, I.G. Farben, led him into an association with the Nazi party, which damaged his reputation permanently.

As mentioned earlier in this chapter, big businesses in Germany and throughout the Western world were beginning to thrive at this time. However, in Germany, the profits of these businesses were being negatively affected by the activities of the Nazi party prior to the outbreak of World War II. In 1934, Farben hired Lee to try and improve the image of Germany in America. Over the course of his work, it is reported that Lee even met with the Nazi party and its chief propagandist, Joseph Goebbels. As a result, Lee was brought before a U.S. House Special Committee and accused of being a propagandist for the Nazi party and of disseminating pro-Nazi communication in the American media. He was referenced in the Nuremberg Trials in 1947 when Brigadier General Telford Taylor, Chief of Counsel for War Crimes, acting on behalf of the U.S. said: *'In 1933, Farben's American public relations expert began to disseminate Nazi and anti-Semitic propaganda and literature throughout the United States'*

(Cutlip, 1994). In Lee's defence, the true atrocities of the Nazi party had not yet been realised. However, history indicates that Lee's actions were at best naive and at worst blindly ambitious. As the US Ambassador to Germany, William Dodd put it at the time, *'It is only another of the thousands of a cases where love of money ruins men's lives'* (Cutlip, 1994). Over the course of his career, Lee succeeded in cementing the reputation of PR as a vehicle for businesses to communicate positively with their public but also as a 'dark art' in which its experts could use their skills to manipulate public opinion for propagandistic purposes.

Lee's paternal counterpart, Edward Bernays was operating in New York around the same time as himself. Bernays was hugely influential in the birth of the PR profession in the United States and was the only PR practitioner to be listed in Life Magazine in 1989 as one of the 200 outstanding Americans of the 20th century (Cutlip, 1994, p. 159). Like Lee, Bernays made a huge contribution to the PR profession, establishing a framework for two-way ethical communications and writing the first academic book on PR. However, also like Lee, Bernays's activity succeeded in tainting the profession owing to his association with propaganda, his links with the Nazi party and his work for the tobacco industry. Bernays' story demonstrates the powerful forces at play in PR and the close ties between PR and behavioural science.

Bernays was the nephew of renowned psychologist, Sigmund Freud, which gave him instant recognition and led to his own interest in the science of persuasive communication. He had a close relationship with Sigmund Freud and worked with him most notably to publicise the publication of his famous book, *'A General Introduction to Psychoanalysis'*. Freud's influence on Bernays is evident throughout his work. He was referred to by Henry Pringle in the February 1930 issue of 'The American Mercury' as a mass psychologist (Cutlip, 1994, p. 171) and according to Irwin Ross who interviewed him in the 1960s, *'Bernays liked to think of himself as a kind of psychoanalyst to troubled corporations'* (Cutlip, 1994, p. 170), a description many modern-day practitioners could no doubt empathise with.

Bernays began his PR career during the publicity/press agentry era of the early 1900s and worked as a publicist for the arts and entertainment industry representing many actors and musicians. The advent of World War I had a significant impact on the growth of PR, bringing with it an increased need for political communications. Bernays moved into this field when he joined the US Committee on Public Information (CPI) and during this time he came to the realisation that the communications activities that were implemented during wartime could just as easily be used by organisations in peacetime and he set up his own agency. Whereas Lee's initial work in PR was centred around issues management amidst the various crises that *'Big Businesses'* found themselves in, Bernays brought his interest in psychology and his proactive persuasive wartime communications skills to his work as a PR consultant or *'counsel'* as he referred to himself. He used his knowledge of psychology and understanding of how the public thinks to develop innovative strategies for clients that sought to humanise big brands and indirectly persuade people to buy their products by developing narratives for their brands, a strategy that is popularly used in PR to this day. An example of this is the work that he did for General Electric (GE) in the promotion of its *'Light's Golden Jubilee'* in 1929. The concept for the event was devised by GE to honour the inventor of the lightbulb, Thomas Edison. Bernays together with Henry Ford organised a huge event, attended by dignitaries and celebrities, including President Hoover. The Jubilee was described in The Atlantic Monthly three years later as an event that masqueraded as a honorary tribute to the inventor of the lightbulb but was in fact a successful publicity stunt for GE (Cutlip, 1994).

Bernays' reputation suffered further down through the years due to his work with the American Tobacco Company. In the 1920s, the damage done by cigarettes to human health wasn't as widely known to the general public as it is today. Competition was fierce amongst the cigarette brand producers and Bernays was retained to promote Lucky Strike cigarettes to increase sales amongst the general public and particularly amongst women. Bernays invented a campaign slogan for Lucky Strike, *'Reach for a Lucky Strike instead of a sweet'* encouraging women to smoke rather than eat sweets and using images of slender women to accompany the slogan. In 1930, he famously marched young women down Fifth Avenue in New York lighting cigarettes, which he dubbed *'Torches of Freedom'* in protest at women's inequality. At the time, it was frowned upon for women to smoke in public and this campaign succeeded in associating smoking with female empowerment and beauty, reducing the stigma associated with cigarette smoking for women and ultimately in encouraging more women to smoke.

In his book, *'Crystalizing Public Opinion',* the first academic public relations PR book ever written, Bernays helped to set a framework for the evolving profession, coining the term, *'public relations counsel'* to describe the activity of a public relations PR professional and replacing the terms, *'publicity'* or *'press agentry'*. The book was a huge success and raised his profile significantly across the Western world. However, *'Crystalizing Public Opinion'* was also allegedly used extensively for reference by the Nazi party. Its chief of propaganda, Joseph Goebbels reportedly kept a copy of the book in his desk referring to it to leverage the propaganda of the Nazi party and disseminate their anti-semitic rhetoric throughout the world.

Regardless of the views on Bernays' work, there is no doubt of the influence and shape he put on PR as a profession. His interest in persuasive communication led him to introduce the concept of two-way communications and he was the first to make the case for PR as a management function, something that Grunig and Hunt developed further around fifty years later in their Theory of Excellence which will be discussed in Chapter 2.

In many ways both Lee and Bernays profiteered from and were victims of the era in which they operated in the early 1900s. Industry was growing rapidly and large corporations were becoming finely tuned to the power of the media and were keen to have their voices heard to counter the negative publicity dragged up by the *'Muckrakers'*. Mass media was evolving enabling these businesses and organisations to communicate more quickly with a wider audience. Political instability was leading to an increased need for skilled communicators to disseminate information to a public on behalf of political parties and World Wars I and II had demonstrated the power and influence of propaganda. This created a gap for Ivy Lee and Edward Bernays to operate in. However as much of the activity undertaken by these professionals was unprecedented, naivety, inexperience, ambition, curiosity and perhaps greed may have exposed them into developing associations either directly or indirectly with unethical causes and campaigns that mired the reputation of the PR industry to this day.

For Outside of this version of PR's origins, there are many less cited histories of PR as a profession. As early as the 1860s, there is a record of major companies in Germany such as the steel company, Krupp and the technology giant, Siemens having established press offices or communications departments to manage media relations (Puchan, 2006).

In Nigeria, the most populous country in Africa, there is a record of PR emerging around the same time with the publication of the first newspaper, the *Iwe Irohin*, in 1859. The newspaper was published to inform people of the Christian activities within the church and included *'news about colonial administration, some foreign affairs, advertisements and public announcements'* (Salawu, 2004b as cited in Amujo, 2009).

Today in Nigeria, PR is a young and growing field. In a recent report on the industry by BlackHouse Media (2020), it found that only 9% of agencies in Nigeria have been in operation for over 20 years.

In the UK, the first record of PR being used professionally is around the time of World War II (Butterick, 2011). Today, the UK PR industry is valued at over £15 bn British Pounds and there are approximately 97,300 PR practitioners working in the industry (PRCA, 2020). The history of PR is colourful and there is no doubt that an understanding of it provides insight into how PR is perceived and practiced today.

1.5 Conclusion

This chapter has set out to inform the reader as to what PR is and how it performs in action It begins with an analysis of the various responses from governments and the WHO to the COVID-19 pandemic. It continues with a look at the various professional bodies for PR within countries and offers a description as to how PR is practised and similarities that can be found between these. The Mexico Definition provides us with an internationally relevant definition of PR that sets out its role as a means of two-way communication between an organisation and its publics, to analyse trends and predict consequences that enable organisations to communicate effectively. A look at the history of PR as a profession offers an insight into its origins which are aligned with the advent of World Wars I and II when communications were used extensively by wartime strategists and then adapted by '*Big Business*'. The growth of 'Mass Media' offered more access to the public to the news and more channels for businesses and governments through which to communicate to reach wider audiences. This growth has continued to this day with the emergence of the internet, online and social media. Communication from organisations and political leaders as has been demonstrated in history has not always been used for the greater good and an acknolwedgement of this is key to the continued successful practice of ethical PR.

Post-pandemic, the value the PR practitioner plays is still being recognised and the demand for PR services appears to be growing. In November 2022, the International Communications Consultancy Organisation (ICCO) reported that PR agency leaders throughout the world expected increased profitability in 2023. The participants in the survey reported a growing demand for a range of services that were termed by ICCO as 'beyond traditional PR' with a greater focus from companies on corporate purpose and reputation (ICCO, 2022). This is a paradigm shift in the role historically that public relations has played in organisations and may be the turning point that the industry itself needs to create a new and more meaningful chapter in PR's colourful history.

1.6 For Discussion

To follow are discussion points on the key topics raised in this chapter:

- Do you consider PR to have its origins in the US in the 19th century or further back than this?
- Would you view PR professionals as activists or as representatives of Big Business?
- Can you think of a modern-day activist campaign?
- Can you think of a modern-day Big Business campaign?

References

Amujo, O. C. (2009). *150 Years of Modern Public Relations Practices in Nigeria*. Available at 10.2139/ssrn.1372704 [Accessed 3rd September 2021]

BlackHouse. (2020). *Media Nigeria PR Report 2020*.

Butterick, K. (2011). *Introducing Public Relations*. Sage: London.

Cutlip, S. M. (1994). *The Unseen Power: Public Relations. A History*. Routledge Taylor & Francis Group: New York and London.

Hinsliff, G. (2019). *20 years of the Beckhams: how they ushered in our era of personal branding*. Available at https://www.theguardian.com/fashion/2019/apr/18/20-years-david-victoria-beckham-personal-branding

Jaslow, R. (2011). Big tobacco kept cancer risk in cigarettes secret: Study. Available at https://www.cbsnews.com/news/big-tobacco-kept-cancer-risk-in-cigarettes-secret-study/

O'Shea, C. (2020). *Are face masks mandatory in Ireland? Current laws and proposals for public transport.* Available at https://www.irishmirror.ie/news/irish-news/face-masks-mandatory-ireland-current-22251557

Olisa, S. (2021). 'Why PR in Nigeria Needs PR'. Available at https://govandbusiness journal.ng/why-pr-in-nigeria-needs-pr/

Porterfield, C. (2020). *Trump's coronavirus approval rating sinks to new low as cases surge.* https://www.forbes.com/sites/carlieporterfield/2020/06/24/trumps-coronavirus-approval-rating-sinks-to-new-low-as-cases-surge/?sh=2fec3ec268ef

PRCA. (2020). PR Communiations Census 2020.

Puchan, H. in L'Etang J. & Pieczka, M. (2006) *Public Relations. Critical Debates and Contemporary Practice.* Lawrence Erlbaum Associates Publishers: New Jersey and London.

Rodriguez. (2021). *Facebook used Big Tobacco playbook to exploit teens and children, senators say at hearing after WSJ series.* Available at https://www.cnbc.com/2021/09/30/senators-say-facebook-used-big-tobacco-playbook-to-exploit-kids.html

Savage, M. (2020). *Poll: UK Government losing public approval over handling of virus.* https://www.theguardian.com/politics/2020/jun/14/poll-uk-government-losing-public-approval-over-handling-of-virus

Sims, M. P. (2021). *Provoke Media Study: Corporate Counsel Demand Continues to Rise As Pandemic Enters Second Year.* https://www.provokemedia.com/latest/article/provoke-study-corporate-counsel-demand-continues-to-rise-as-pandemic-enters-second-year

Taylor, M. and Watts, J. (2019). Revealed: The 20 firms behind a third of all carbon emissions. https://www.theguardian.com/environment/2019/oct/09/revealed-20-firms-third-carbon-emissions

WHO. (2020). *RCCE Action Plan Guidance. COVID-19 preparedness and response.* Available at https://www.who.int/publications/i/item/risk-communication-and-community-engagement-(rcce)-action-plan-guidance

2   The Theory of PR

Chapter Contents

2.1 Learning Outcomes

On completion of this chapter, the reader will be able to:

- Demonstrate a critical understanding of pubic relations theory.
- Have a deep understanding of how theory of public relations (PR) impacts on modern-day practice.
- Understand how the various systems, rhetorical and communications theories impact on PR.
- Think critically about the communications activities of organisations and individuals.

2.2 Introduction

In February 2022, Russia began the biggest European invasion in Europe since the end of World War II with its war of Ukraine. As the fighting began so did Ukraine's President Zelensky's, media onslaught.

DOI: 10.4324/9781003253815-2

Zelensky has become a prominent and ever-present figure in the media and in particular on social media channels since, using these channels, to communicate the news from Ukraine and to debunk mistruths being spread online and elsewhere. In the first few months of the way, he was seen regularly broadcasting in combat clothes from the streets of Kyiv. He was then frequently beamed in to address parliaments and universities throughout the world via online media channels.

As reported in CNN at the outset of the War, 'Zelensky is wielding a modern-day slingshot in the form of social media tools and modern communications skills that are helping him gain an upper hand in what is also a crucial battle: the struggle to control the narrative of war' (McGowan 2022). In his address to the British House of Commons, Zelensky quoted former British wartime Prime Minister, Winston Churchill, when he said that Ukraine people would fight the Russians *'in the forest, in the fields, on the shores and in the streets'* (McGowan and Silva, 2022). In Churchill's day, the tools may have been different, but the tactics were the same. Churchill placed great emphasis on the use of rhetoric and media to control the narrative in war. At one point, he reportedly said that *'of all the talents bestowed upon men, none is so precious as the gift of oratory. He who enjoys it, wields a power more durable than that of a great king'* (McGowan and Silva, 2022). Churchill used the media tools that were available to him to communicate his rhetoric.

Both Churchill and Zelensky could be referred to as propagandists who used a certain ideology to persuade people to change their opinions or to take a course of action. Both understood the power of rhetoric and how media and publics can be used to promote rhetoric to a mass audience.

Both men are prime examples of public relations (PR) practitioners, albeit from different eras. Both understood the power of rhetoric and used it regularly in their communications activities. Their communications was thought out and progressive in terms of the type of media that they used and how they managed wartime communications. It is interesting to compare both in the context of the theory of public relations and the evolution of the practice of PR.

Some theorists would argue that PR as a profession was born out of the industrial revolution and became particularly popular following its emergence of commiunications and in particular propagandistic communications in World Wars I and II. Others would argue that PR is a communications tool that developed as early as 200 B.C. but was hijacked by large corporations in the western world who honed its use as a reputational management tool. Others, and this group has been growing in numbers in recent years, would profer that PR is a skill that can be used for the greater good to assist minority groups or organisations in fighting for a worthwhile cause.

This discussion of PR Theory will look first at systems theory with Grunig's Excellence Theory, arguably the most cited theory of PR in the Western world.

We will then look at the evolution of rhetoric and communications through the ages to the Modern and Postmodern eras and how this has impacted PR.

2.3 PR Theory

PR theory offers students and practitioners an explanation as to how communications activity has worked for organisations in the past and how PR could be used effectively in the present and into the future. Reading about relevant theories on communications, rhetoric and postmodernism will assist the reader in formulating their opinion on the role and modern-day practice of PR in today's society.

2.3.1 Systems Theory

Systems theory was developed by Katz and Kahn (Miner, 2011) and is the name given to the group of theories that are most commonly used to explain how organisations react to the environments in which they operate.

PR's most referenced systems theory is the Theory of Excellence designed by Grunig. This was developed by Grunig during the 1980s and 1990s during the period that is commonly referred to as the Modern era. This era is considered to have commenced around the time of the Industrial Revolution in the 17th century and continued to the 21st century when it was replaced by the Postmodern era in which we are allegedged to be now living. Some would also argue that the Modern and Postmodern eras are in fact running presently in tandem (Borchers and Hundley, 2018). This will be discussed further later in this chapter.

2.3.1.1 The Four Models of PR and Excellence Theory

2.3.1.1.1 THE FOUR MODELS OF PR

The Theory of Excellence was an evolution of Grunig and Hunt's 'Four-Models of Public Relations' which was a result of Grunig's research in the 1960s on the nature of publics and how they develop. He found that when companies sought to engage that sometimes communications activity was unsuccessful, not because publics were unwilling to listen but because some organisations engaged ineffectively with their publics. Grunig then, together with Hunt, went on to investigate why organisations practised PR differently and the result was the development of the four models of PR.

The four models are regularly referenced in PR in an attempt to explain the different ways in which PR can be practised. The premise is that there are four ways or models for practising PR: Press Agentry/Publicity, Public Information, Two-way Asymmetrical Communication and Two-way Symmetrical Communication Often, each of the four models of PR is aligned with the practices of some of the first documented PR practitioners including P.T. Barnum who represents the Press Agentry/Publicity Model, Ivy Lee, the Public Information Model and Edward Bernay's style of practice could be linked to the Two-way Asymmetrical Model. The model is commonly referenced in the Western world, as best practice in communications between organisations and their publics (Waddington, 2012). However, this is a subject of much debate. For example, University of Westminster Professor Trevor Morris stated in PR Week that *'the idea of totally unbiased public information with no persuasive intent is naïve'*. He went on to say: *'the two-way symmetrical communication model is not really even an ideal. PR people will always consider the views of the people they communicate with, but ultimately they must do so to serve the best interests of their paymasters – be they government, business or charity'* (Morris, 2014). Morris is indicating that the core objective of any PR practitioner's communications, regardless of the input received from its publics, is to persuade and assist an organisation in achieving its business objectives. PR as a profession has a reputation problem as discussed in Chapter 1 and it could be that the Two-Way Symmetrical Model of PR is more of an aspirational objective for the profession for those seeking to distance themselves from the propagandistic side of PR.

The other models of PR are still regularly practiced however, eventhough, they may not be as attractive to those who dislike certain aspects of PR's reputation. For example, the Press Agentry/Publicity structure is a widely practised model with many communications professionals operating as agents for example for celebrities, movie stars, sports people or well-known high-profile individuals. The Two-Way Asymmetrical Model plays a huge role in political PR and public affairs where messages are regularly communicated with the public to achieve a response that fulfils the needs of the communicator or where the communicator is in a more powerful position than the receiver. The Public Information Model is one used regularly by charities and in public health communications campaigns where the purpose of communications is to inform and educate rather than convince a public to vote or make a purchase. It could be that the different PR models can be aligned with different types of PR such as corporate, consumer or public affairs for example and further research into the practice of PR throughout various cultures and industry sectors would help determine this and perhaps establish new working models for the profession of public relations. The four models of PR in the meantime, is an important starting point for a discussion on PR Theory and how it is practiced and lays the foundations for the Excellence Theory, the main systems theory of PR.

2.3.1.1.2 THE EXCELLENCE THEORY

The Excellence Theory states that organisations are effective when they have the expertise needed to respond to threats and opportunities in their environment (Grunig et al., 2002).

The Theory was developed in 1984 following an extensive review of relevant literature and studies and an empirical study involving over 300 organisations and thousands of employees across the United States, Canada and the United Kingdom. The objective was to analyse how PR was and should be practised in order for it to add value to an organisation and to society. The result was the identification of four specific characteristics that the study found to be required in PR programmes or departments in order for them to be effective for an organisation

a The four characteristics are: empowerment of the PR function, communicator roles, organisation of the communication function and its relationship to other management functions and models of PR.

2.3.1.1.3 EMPOWERMENT OF THE PR FUNCTION

This considers the relationship of PR to the overall business management and requires that communications are recognised as a critical management function. The theory states that communications or PR executives should be part of the strategic senior management team within the organisation and that two-way symmetrical communications programmes are designed to reach out to specific publics that have been identified in the organisation's business objectives. Campaigns should be built on formative research and have measurable outputs. Communications tools and tactics should be varied and activity should be evaluated and demonstrate that objectives have been met and relationships have been improved between an organisation and its publics. Diversity is recognised as important to empower the PR function and is required to ensure that the organisation's workforce reflects that of its environment. This benefits the practitioners and assists the organisation in building relationships with its publics and stakeholders.

2.3.1.1.4 COMMUNICATOR ROLES

The Excellence Theory identifies four roles that a communications professional can play within an organisation: a manager, senior adviser or communications liaison, technician and a media relations role. The research revealed that in less excellent departments, all the practitioners are incorrectly operating as technicians and carrying out day-to-day communications activities. The theory proffers that the PR professional must be operating at a strategic managerial level in the organisation in order for the PR function to be effective. It states that the communications unit should be headed up by a strategic manager rather than a technician or an administrative manager and that team members should have acquired the required knowledge through education to progress in the department. Interestingly, The Theory proposes that men and women must have equal access to the managerial communications role within organisations.

At the time of the research, the majority of PR professionals were identified as women and should have been therefore more likely to possess the required knowledge to progress to managerial roles. However, this did not prove to be the case.

A study on the PR industry in the UK over 30 years later indicates that major challenges still exist when it comes to equality in the sector. The European Communications Monitor (2020) found that despite the fact that three out of four communications departments and agencies in Europe employ more women than men, only one out of two top leaders are women. Furthermore, in the 2019 census from the Public Relations Consultancy Association in the UK, it found that the industry in the UK is female-dominated (67% female and 33% male). However, there is an industry gender pay gap at 13.6% with the pay disparity between female and male employees reported to be at £6,412 (PRCA, 2019). The high percentage of females in the industry and the identification of this pay gap would indicate an inequality between the experiences and trajectory of men and women in the PR workforce despite the assertions made in Grunig's theory. This is just one issue related to diversity in the PR industry. The topic of diversity is discussed in more detail in Chapter 15.

2.3.1.1.5 ORGANISATION OF THE COMMUNICATION FUNCTION AND ITS RELATIONSHIP TO OTHER MANAGEMENT FUNCTIONS

The third category identified in the Excellence Theory focuses on organisations having an integrated communications function. The theorists explain that in some organisations, they found that there were separate departments aimed at different publics and in some instances, organisations placed communications under another discipline such as marketing, human resources or finance. Organisations were also found to work with external consultants only for specific communications requirements such as the announcement of an annual report. In the Excellence Theory, these specific components are integrated into and coordinated by one department, the ultimate purpose of which is communications. The Theory specifically addresses the issue of the relationship between marketing and PR and states that PR should not be sublimated to other functions such as marketing as this will prevent it from strategically managing the organisation's communication with its publics.

2.3.1.1.6 MODELS OF PR

This characteristic is concentrated on the four models of PR and the role it plays in Excellence Theory and specifically the Two-Way Symmetrical Model of PR. The theory states that this model is the most effective in managing relationships with an organisation's publics. This model is also specified in the theory as the most desirable model for internal communications within the organisation (between management and employees). According to this theory, Two-Way Symmetrical practitioners are loyal to the organisation and to its publics, they are concentrated on balancing the interests of organisations and its publics, base their strategies on research and use communication to manage conflict. A characteristic of an excellent PR programme or department according to Grunig is a Two-Way Symmetrical one that focuses on activism and the environment. Such a programme will have worked with activist groups within the community to listen to their concerns, will have conducted risk assessments and will be prepared for a potential crisis that could impact on the reputation of the company.

In general, opponents of the Excellence Theory profer that the theory is over-simplified and is too centred on consumers and on organisations as opposed to the environment, cultures and markets in which organisations operate. Postmodernists would argue that the theory is too narrowly based on western Modernist society and is not relevant to other and emerging markets in a post-modern world.

The Excellence Theory however is a large and possibly the only such sized body of research that is specific to the PR industry. It therefore holds merit and value for today's PR practitioners in that context. However, the world has changed considerably since the original research was conducted and in the context of communications, the evolution of technology has broadened the reach for many companies enabling them to communicate with a global audience quickly and efficiently. This has impacts on the formation of publics which are now global in a way that would not have been considered in the original research. The communicator roles identified in the Excellence Theory have also evolved with content creation becoming a vital role in the PR department.

The Excellence Theory does a service in that it makes an attempt to explain PR and to evolve the profession from one that is focused solely on persuasion, propaganda and tactical media relations to one that is a recognised function of strategic management that operates ethically and adds value to organisations. It is an important reference point in establishing functional communications departments and in developing excellent or effective communications strategies. The Theory lays the foundations for further research as the PR profession ma-tures and evolves in an increasingly digitised, diverse and globalised market. Further research and analysis of the PR activities of organisations in different countries across continents would build on this systems theory and provide a more accurate basis for modern-day PR practice.

2.4 Rhetorical Theory

Rhetoric is concerned with the art of communication and the persuasion of others through language, visuals and symbols. Borchers and Hundley (2018) define rhetoric as: *'the use of language and other symbolic systems to make sense of our experiences, construct our personal and collective identities, produce meaning and prompt action in the world'*. The role that rhetoric plays in communication and particularly in PR is evident from this definition when we understand that the core function of PR is to persuade an audience to change its opinion, to reinforce an existing opinion or to encourage the taking of a course of action.

Rhetoric is commonly considered to have its origins in c. 200 B.C. (the Classical Period) in ancient Greece and Rome in the theories of Aristotle, Cicero, Plato, Isocrates and Quintilian. Rhetoric has developed over the ages in tandem with the evolution of cultures and communications technologies. Scott (1975, cited in Borchers and Hundley, 2018, p. 19) categorised the various time periods in rhetorical history according to the emphasis of the theorists. He identified three potential focuses for theorists: speaker, world and listener. He suggests that in different time periods, theorists place more emphasis on one focus over the other. For example, A theorist that is speaker-focused will use evidence or emotional appeals. A world-focused theorist will use rhetoric to convey an external, objective truth and a listener focussed theorist will involve the audience in the rhetoric by presenting them with several ideas from which they form their own beliefs (Borchers and Hayes, 2018).

Scott's time periods of rhetoric are detailed as follows:

2.4.1 200 B.C.E.–5 C.E. Pragmatic-Dominant Rhetorical Theory

This period, which is also called the Classical Period, includes the ancient Greek and Roman philosophers with the principal theorists being Isocrates and Cicero. These philosophers utilised rhetoric for democratic and judicial purposes and gave little consideration to the audience. They saw speakers as influential in world events and became teachers and scholars of rhetoric with enduring influence to this day.

2.4.2 1400s–1500s Aesthetic Rhetorical Theory

This is the period of the late Middle Ages and early Renaissance, during which Scott states that rhetoric was predominantly used to as Borchers and Hayes (p. 20, 2018) state, *'to embellish the truth or ingratiate the rhetor to a very small audience'*. As the name suggests, most of the emphasis on this period was on the style of the oration rather than the content. Examples of rhetoric from this time include sermons and letter writing.

2.4.3 1700s–1800s Pragmatic-Subordinate Rhetorical Theory

This period refers to scientific discovery where rhetoric would be used to communicate what scientists had found but would be seen as of lesser importance than science.

2.4.4 1900s–Present Social Rhetorical Theory

The audience is the primary focus in this period. Social rhetorical theory concentrates on how audiences perceive a speaker's message.

Famous modern poitical figues provide us with ideal examples of rhetoric in use in the present era. In President Obama's famous *'yes we can'* presidential election campaign in the US, he used a common tool of rhetoric-repetition with the use of the slogan *'yes we can'*. He delivered numerous speeches to large audiences where he garnered votes through his oration style involving gestures, slogans and powerful words that aimed to unite and empower people.

President Trump used the same techniques in his presidential election campaign although his motives and goals were different. His rhetoric used the slogan *'Make America Great Again'* which implied that there was something wrong with America that needed to be fixed. It was a particularly negative style of rhetoric aimed at a specific audience.

The UK's Brexit campaign used a similar style of rhetoric that aimed to instil feelings of injustice and cause unrest amongst a disgruntled British public. The slogan, *'take back control'* developed by the Brexiteers urged Britons to believe that immigrants were stealing their jobs and in order to protect them, they needed to vote for Brexit. The word *'Brexit'* itself is an example of modern-day rhetoric. It came into being as a hashtag, a new use of language or symbolism, which has its origins in social media. Brexit is now a commonly used word that can be found in the English dictionary.

Ukraine's President Zelensky used rhetoric in his online speech to the House of Commons in the UK where he made several references to Britain's former wartime Prime Minister, Winston Churchill in order to evoke empathy and action from his audience.

Rhetoric has and will continue to evolve through the ages as cultural, social and political changes occur. Technology has and is continuing to play a huge role in the evolution of rhetoric by facilitating mass communication on a worldwide scale through online and social media.

2.5 Modernism and Postmodernism

Postmodern theorists proffer that we are now in a contemporary era or the 'Postmodernist' era which commenced in the late 20th century. The term 'Modernism' is associated with the emergence of a new society which is different to those that went before it. It is defined by liberalism and humanism and the enablement of new developments in science, technology, industrialisation and improvements in living standards and life expectancy (Holtzhausen, 2011). However, Holtzhausen states that the Modernist approach also led to many problems such as the rise in bureaucracy, standardisation and capitalisation of society. Holtzhausen identifies the United States as the *'ultimate modern society'* due to the widespread bureaucratisation of society.

Postmodernism refers to deep and long-lasting political and social changes in society. It is an evolution of modernity with its roots in the 1960s and 1970s and is typified by globalisation, the rapid expansion of technology and the challenging of power and dissensus. Hottzhausen explains that postmodernists continuously question long-standing positions and the power motives behind them. In this context, Holtzhausen proffers that the post-modern agency of PR is activism, stating that all PR is political because the aim of all communications is to influence, assert or affect.

In Grunig's Modernist Theory of Excellence, communications are viewed as a symmetrical two-way process where the organisation and its publics are equal. In a Postmodernist society, Holtzhausen argues that practitioners need to accept that relationships between organisations and their publics are in fact asymmetrical, in favour of stakeholders. Boundaries within organisations have broken down and this forces the PR practitioner to recognise the viewpoints of the organisation and its stakeholders and speak out often in favour of the stakeholders.

Holtzhausen challenges the Western version of the history of PR that concentrates on its establishment in the 19th century. She offers an alternative historical foundation for PR as activism and claims that the profession was hijacked by big business and academics which have positioned this ideology as history and as a result have damaged the reputation of the profession.

To support this theory she references the work of English woman, Emily Hobhouse in the Anglo-Boeer War (1899–1902). Holtzhausen describes Hobhouse as an early example of a PR activitst. During the Boer war in South Africa (1899–1902), Hobhouse acted as an activist for the Boer people by writing letters in British newspapers, lobbying political figures in both England and South Africa, establishing a network of women's organisations to support the lobbying activity and often citing the law in her arguments.

A more modern example of such activism could be taken rom the war in Ukraine. In 2022, in response to the war, Airbnb, the short-term international rental company, partnered with international and regional not-for-profit organisations and governments to house refugees fleeing Ukraine. The organisation also provided accommodation for those who stayed behind to defend the country. Over 28,000 people signed up to offer housing to Ukrainians through Airbnb and the company committed to donating up to $10 m to the cause. The campaign from the organisation followed a user-generated social media campaign in which people all over the world started booking rooms in Ukraine through Airbnb to provide financial support to people during the war. This type of activity could be classified as activism by Airbnb on behalf of the people of Ukraine.

Whether considering PR as a tool for *'Big Business'* or as *'Activism'*, it is clear that language and rhetoric are important tools in Post modern PR. However, the over-saturation of media and consumerism in the Postmodern world makes for greater challenges for Postmodern rhetoric.

2.6 Communications Theory

The culture in which communications are being conducted influences how rhetoric or messages are likely to be received and therefore presented. For example, during the COVID-19 pandemic, health officials in some Western world countries had difficulty in persuading members of the public to wear masks. In densely populated cities in Asia, mask wearing was commonplace following repeated threats to public health and these populations have needed as much persuasion. In Ireland, for example, a survey conducted for the Department of Health on almost 2,000 people at the beginning of the pandemic, revealed that only approximately 55% of people were self-reporting to be wearing face coverings. This was quite low considering the mounting evidence from studies in Britain, Germany and the United States that indicated that face coverings were extremely effective in curbing the spread of Coronavirus. The culture in the west was not positively disposed to mask wearing so communications regarding mask wearing needed to be tailored around this to persuade people to change their behaviour.

Evolutions in communications technologies also have an impact. For example in ancient Greece, Aristotle would have relied on a speech directly to an audience, to get his point across whereas President Obama or indeed his predecessor, President Trump in the United States, may have used a social media channel such as Twitter. In the case of the recent of communications technologies, in the classical era, the communicator would be required to get the message out there in the presence of a physical audience relying solely on the words that were being uttered. In today's world, this message could be communicated via many channels, such as news media, Instagram and Twitter and using a variety of tools including photography and videos.

PR as a discipline has evolved in tandem with the changes that have occurred in communications technologies. It is important therefore to understand communications theories to fully understand how PR practitioners can channel rhetoric to ensure the message is received by the intended audience and the desired result is achieved.

2.6.1 Laswell, Shannon and Weaver, Lazarsfield

Times of crisis such as war have been the catalyst for many of the developments in communications. As discussed earlier in the book, in the COVID-19 pandemic, major communications challenges resulted in interventions that have changed how communications are carried out forever more. For example, during this time, the world turned to online support systems such as Zoom or Microsoft teams to conduct meetings and face-to-face contact when real physical contact with other humans was prohibited. The use of these technologies is now commonplace across the working world.

During the period around World Wars I and II, people were forced to communicate across countries and in a particular manner to connect with one another, and to inform and influence publics. During these periods telecommunications technologies evolved significantly and radio and television emerged and eventually resulted in what we now know as mass media. Many of the communications theories including those of Laswell's and Shannon and Weaver's developed around this time.

Harold Laswell and Shannon and Weaver were concerned primarily with communication as the transmission of information during World War II. Laswell developed his Communication Model in 1948 following a study of Nazi propaganda during World War II and how it was successful in generating support for Hitler. His model poses the questions: Who is the communicator? What is the message? In what channel is the communication happening? To whom is the communication being directed? What is the effect? The theory hints at persuasion by proposing that the 'sender' intends to have an 'effect' or influence on the 'receiver'.

Shannon and Weaver's model in 1949 was developed following a study of telecommunications during the war. As a result, this model is process driven focusing on the linear transmission of a message from sender to receiver with minimal consideration of the psychological or social aspects involved. In Shannon and Weaver's model they purport that a sender thinks of a message, translates it into signals and transmits it over a channel to the receiver. Shannon and Weaver's model is interesting as it initiates the concept of 'noise' in the communications process. 'Noise' was understood by Shannon and Weaver to be any outside interference to the transmission that is not intended by the receiver. In modern times, this 'noise' could be identified as commentary on social media. For example in a public health vaccination campaign, the department of health in a country might communicate the attributes of a vaccine and explain to people why they should take it. However, 'noise' from anti-vaccination campaigners with disinformation on social media might affect the receiving of this message by those for whom it is intended and cause them to change their minds and their responses as a result.

Both these models are linear indicating that the communications process goes one way from sender to receiver and that both sender and receiver are equal. Little acknowledgement is given to the role of behavioural psychology in the communications process.

The Two-step Model of Communication was developed by Paul Lazarsfeld at the beginning of this period of media explosion. In 1940 following an analysis of voting patterns in New York in the United States, researchers found that voters were influenced by the opinions of their friends and by opinion leaders. The model proffers that during communications, a message is sent to mass media that is then transmitted to an audience. However, it also demonstrates that messages can be blocked from reaching certain audiences and require a trusted individual or *'opinion leader'* to assist with the communication. This model demonstrates the importance of having strong advocates on board for an organisation who can be trusted to become 'opinion leaders' and explains why many brands opt for this form of communication in today's world.

A clear example of this theory in action today is in the role an influencer on social media might play in helping to promote or communicate the merits of a product or service. These influencers essentially provide the 'word of mouth' on a global scale allowing information to be communicated immediately and quickly. A public health campaign run by the Irish Health Service in 2017/18, demonstrates this theory in action. At the time of the campaign, the health service was having difficulty convincing people to avail of the Human Pampolova Virus (HPV) vaccine for their teenage daughters after a negative 'anti-vax' campaign had been run by an activist group. Only a small percentage of people had taken the vaccine despite it being free and that it was proven to help prevent cervical cancer. An opinion leader came on board as an amabassador/opinion leader for the health service in the form of a young lady called Laura Brennan. Laura had been diagnosed with terminal cancer and wanted to raise awareness of the importance of the vaccine. Following a high-profile campaign with Laura acting as a strong and visible advocate for the vaccine programme, misconceptions were debunked and uptake on the vaccine increased significantly. Laura tragically passed away since. Her advocacy work has lived on as young people continue to get vaccinated and help reduce the prevalence of this type of cancer.

2.7 The Evolution of Media

Around the same time as Ivy Lee was beginning his career, America's first national press association had launched along with the first mass-circulation newspaper, bringing news for the first time to a mass audience (Cutlip, 1994, p. 24). Since the advent of printing in the 17th century and the use of machine printing and railways in the 19th century, access to media has been increasing in speed and thus the communications opportunities and channels open to organisations has increased. Film, radio and television, followed print in the 19th and 20th centuries and with them came advertising and the world's first television ad for an American watch brand called Bulova, which aired before a major baseball game in the United States in the 1940s. These advancements enabled organisations and politicians to communicate with a wide or mass audience.

Since then, mass media has also grown significantly to include also, the internet, smartphone and online and social media. An organisation can now communicate with a wide audience immediately and the audience can now access that communication immediately no matter where they are. The intended recipient of the message no longer has to wait until a big sports match airs on television or a new film is launched in the cinema to be advertised to or com-municated with. Communications from multiple sources are accessible imme-diately on the various media channels through mobile phones. This has implications for communications in that people are consuming information differently and organisations are thinking differently to communicate with them.

2.8 Conclusion

The theory of PR provides us with an insight into how PR has developed as a profession and explains why it is performed today, in the way that it is. It also offers insight into how PR is evolving and its potential trajectory in years to. There is no doubt that the profession of PR has evolved in line with the cultural, social and economic evolution through the eras. It will most likely continue on this trajectory as we enter the post-pandemic world following the considerable social and economic shock that the COVID-19 pandemic caused. In its European Communication Monitor 2022, the Euroropean Association of Communication Directors studied over 1,500 communications professionals across 43 European countries to ascertain the impact developments in societies and organisations have had on the communications profession. The research found that empathetic leadership in the communications industry is on the rise.

Further research will lead to the development of new theories and demonstrate how the societal and behavioural changes that were forced upon society during this period will impact on PR in the post-modern era and beyond.

2.9 For Discussion

The following are some discussion points to consider for further learning. These topics can be considered on your own or discussed in a tutorial setting, with peers or with colleagues.

- Think of two examples of PR activities – one following a more modernistic approach and the other from the postmodern school.
- Analyse the elements of rhetoric used in both.
- Explain each and how the tasks of and the media channels used by the PR practitioners differed.
- How do you think this activity would be best carried out today and how might it evolve in the future in your opinion?

References

Borchers, T. and Hundley, H. (2018). *Rhetorical Theory: An Introduction*. Waveland Press Inc: US.

Cutlip   (1994). *The Unseen Power*. Routledge: New York.

European Communications Monitor (2020). Eurprera and European Association of Communication Directors. Available at https://www.communicationmonitor.eu/wp-content/uploads/dlm_uploads/ECM2020_Facts_1_Standard.pdf [Accessed 15th April 2021].

Grunig, L. A., Grunig, J. E., and Dozier, D. M. (2002). *Excellent Public Relations and Effective Organizations: A Study of Communication Management in Three Countries*. Lawrence Erlbaum: Mahwah, NJ.

Holtzhausen, D. R. (2011). *Public Relations as Activism: Postmodern Approaches to Theory and Practice*. Routledge.

McGowan, B. and Silva, J. (2022). Putin's PR game is falling flat. But in Zelensky's hands, the pen is mightier than the sword. Available at https://edition.cnn.com/2022/03/21/opinions/zelensky-wartime-speech-communications-pr-mcgowan-silva/index.html

Miner, J. B. (2011). *Katz & Kahn's Social Psychology of Organisations*. 1st Ed., Routledge.

Morris, T. (2014). Are Grunig and Hunt still relevant? PR Week. Available at https://www.prweek.com/article/1291832/grunig-hunt-relevant [Accessed 15 April 2021].

Public Relations Consultants Association (2019). PR and Communications Census, 2019. Available at https://www.prca.org.uk/sites/default/files/PRCA_PR_Census_2019_v9-8-pdf%20%285%29.pdf [Accessed 8 April 2021].

Shannon and Weaver https://www.toolshero.com/communication-skills/communication-cycle-shannon-weaver/

Waddington, S. (2012). A critical review of Excellence Theory in an era of digital communication. Available at https://wadds.co.uk/blog/2018/7/18/a-critical-review-of-excellence-theory-in-an-era-of-digital-communication [Accessed 31 March 2021]

3   Ethics

Chapter Contents

3.1 Learning Outcomes

On finishing this chapter, the reader should be able to:

- Understand the ethical issues and theories at play in public relations (PR).
- Understand the responsibilities that PR professionals have to the enivornment and society.
- Apply ethical theory to the practice of PR.

3.2 Introduction

In her book on Ethics in Public Relations, Prof Patricia J Parsons defines ethics in the context of PR as '*the application of knowledge, understanding and reasoning to questions of right or wrong behaviour in the professional practice of public relations*'. Parsons states that it is very much at the discretion of the professional to decide what is right or what is wrong (Parsons, 2016). Parsons identifies the five following pillars of Public Relations PR ethics to guide PR professionals in their actions: Veracity (to tell the truth), Non-maleficence (to do no harm), Beneficence (to do good), Confidentiality (to respect privacy), Fairness (to be fair and socially responsible). These principles, Parsons states, should be thought of as

DOI: 10.4324/9781003253815-3

the *'pillars that carry the weight of ethical decision-making in public relations practice'* (Parsons, 2016, p. 18).

In 2017, Bell Pottinger, the London-based PR firm, was expelled from the Public Relations Consultants Association (PRCA) in the UK for unethical practice. The expulsion occurred as a result of Bell Pottinger's £100K a month contract with the Gupta Family, a wealthy and controversial Indian business family in South Africa who were closely linked with President Zuma.

The Bell Pottinger firm was hired by the Guptas to improve their reputation. The Guptas specifically hired Bell Pottinger to initiate a *'grass-roots political activism'* campaign that was reported to be intended to *'help poor black people'* (Segal, 2018). However, what ensued was a deliberately deceptive and misleading campaign that succeeded in stirring up racial tension and resulted in one of the highest profile ethical issues to tarnish the PR industry to this day.

Bell Pottinger created a campaign using the inflammatory narrative of *'white monopoly capital'*. The premise of the campaign was that white people in South Africa were controlling the wealth while depriving black people of education and jobs. Fake Twitter accounts and controversial hashtags were created to retweet content from other disreputable accounts. Websites were created and mainstream media outlets owned by the Guptas were engaged. As the campaign evolved, groups such as the ANC became involved and it emerged, received media training and funding from the Guptas through their company, Oakbay (Segal, 2018). As a result of the campaign, racial tensions were reported to have risen to levels in South Africa, which had not been felt since apartheid.

An investigation into Bell Pottinger's work for the Guptas resulted in the expulsion of Bell Pottinger from the PRCA. The Director General of the PRCA at the time is reported to have said: *'In my years of running the P.R.C.A., I have never seen anything worse, never seen anything equal to it'* (Segal, 2018).

The PRCA in its report on Bell Pottinger stated that the consultancy had breached both its professional charter and its public affairs and lobbying code of conduct in this work (Burne, 2017). The company was found to have knowingly engaged in a dishonest campaign that set out to achieve its goals through deception. The campaign was particularly divisive as it caused harm to people by stirring up racial tension in what was an already volatile environment.

The only other agency to have been expelled from the PRCA is reported to be a company called Fuel PR who was responsible for the 'Sweaty-gate' scandal (Griggs, 2015). The agency was expelled after it was found to have breached the PRCA's professional charter for misrepresenting an employee of the firm as a 'real life' user of the product it was endorsing. The PRCA decided it was in breach of professional standards and the *'gravity of the reputational damage to the industry was so great that termination of membership was the only option'* (Griggs, 2015).

This scandal wasn't the first time Bell Pottinger had been involved in controversy. Mr Bell had once claimed that *'morality is a job for priests. Not P.R. men'* (Segal, 2018). For approximately 30 years prior to this particular incident, Bell Pottinger had built up an extensive and controversial client list that included the Belarus president and dictator, Alexander Lukashenko, Chile's president, Augusto Pinochet and the South African Olympian, Oscar Pistorius, following his charge for the murder of his girlfriend.

Contrary to Mr Bell's reported opinion, morals are extremely important in PR. They determine if the powerful persuasive communicator uses their skills for good or bad persuasive communication has been in existence since the beginning of time and can be used for both good and bad purposes. In the past, we have seen how the work practices of some of the famous PR professionals, including Ivy Lee, Edward Bernays and the Bell Pottinger agency as described here have tainted the image of the PR profession. Without ethics, the PR profession cannot succeed in challenging this perception of the industry. In today's society in particular where consumers are calling for their brands to have a purpose and to act responsibly, ethics have never been more important.

Ethical theory forms the basis of the national and international codes of conduct to which public relations practitioners world wide adhere to. To follow is an explanation of the key ethical theories that impact on PR and a discussion on the ethical standards set by various public relations professional bodies.

3.3 Ethical Theories

PR professionals are bound by international codes of ethics that have been developed by the industry based on the theories of ethics. According to Theaker (2016), in the context of PR, ethical theory can be divided into two groups: Utilitarianism and Deontology.

3.3.1 Utilitarianism

Utilitarianism is based on the teachings of the English philosophers, Jeremy Bentham (1748–1832) and John Stuart Mill (1806–1873). Utilitarianists believe that an action can be judged as right or wrong based on the perceived consequences or outcomes. Utilitarianists would judge if an action was right or wrong after analysing its potential effect on society. The most morally correct action is deemed to be the action that results in the most 'good'. In essence, Utilitarianists believe that it doesn't matter how you get there, even if through lies and manipulation, if most people benefit in the end.

An example of Utilitarianism could be the decision by governments during the pandemic to advocate for mandatory mask wearing in the Western world. Although not a popular communication initially due to the perceived constraints that mask wearing put on social interaction, the intentioned outcome was a reduction in the transmission of COVID-19 and therefore a happier and healthier population. Another example of this could be in the case of a press conference involving a missing person. Often messages are conveyed in such a press conference or information is held back in order to influence the perpetrator. This principle however depends on the communicator's interpretation of the 'greater good' and comes undone when the judgement of the Utilitarianist is questionable.

If the principle of Utilitarianism is applied to the Bell Pottinger case, it could be said that there was a clear rationale for the organisation to take on the Guptas controversial campaign. It could be argued that the campaign they wished to run in South Africa was intended to bring maximum benefit to people. However, this was proven to be a dishonest rationale and as the report from the PRCA stated, Bell Pottinger understood the real rationale for this campaign when they took on the client. The PRCA report stated that *'by any reasonable standard of judgement'* the campaign was *'likely to inflame racial discord in South Africa'* (Burne, 2017).

3.3.2 Deontology

Deontology comes from the Greek word for duty (deon). The theory of Deontology is based on the teachings of the philosopher Immanuel Kant (1724–1804), one of the foremost theorists in ethics. Deontologists proffer that it is motivation rather than consequences that determine whether an action is right or wrong. Deontologists would believe that there are universally re-cognised rules about what is right and what is wrong and this is what guides people (and businesses) in ethical decision-making. For example, rules such as don't steal or don't lie.

In PR practice, a Deontologist would inevitably always tell the truth even if that truth resulted in unwanted consequences for the business the practitioner is representing. A Utilitarianist on the other hand may find himself or herself telling a white lie in order to protect the reputation of an organisation against an unwanted consequence.

Most PR professionals operating in today's world face the dilemma of managing that delicate moral balance between Utilitarianism and Deontology. Does the end justify the means or is it a matter of duty to act in a certain way? Deontology in practice is evident, for example, in the case of a potential client who may approach a firm in which there is a conflict. Often an agency might refuse to do business with a controversial political figure or an organisation such as in the Bell Pottinger case because the individuals involved in the company fundamentally disagree with the morals of the client.

When devising PR campaigns, Deontology and Utilitarianism will com-monly both play a part. The PR professional will undoubtedly analyse the potential outcomes of a campaign and they will decide on a strategy based on this and based on what they believe to be right and wrong. It could be argued that controversies, such as in the case of the Bell Pottinger campaign in South Africa, occur when Utilitarianism and questionable personal judgement and morals collide.

3.4 Professional Codes of Conduct

PR professionals are bound by the Code of Lisbon, the European Code of Professional Practice, and/or the Code of Athens, which is the International Code of Ethics. The codes outline the various duties that PR professionals have to themselves, to their employers and to the societies in which they operate. The codes have been adapted by national professional PR bodies and tailored to the practice of PR in individual countries.

The website of the Public Relations Institute of Ireland (PRII) offers an example of these codes of conduct as they relate to Ireland. These codes are outlined in the figures as follows (PRII, n.d):

3.4.1 The Code of Lisbon

The following are the criteria and standards of professional qualification set out for practitioners bound by this Code. Every member of the PRII duly admitted as such in accordance with the rules of the Institute is deemed for the purpose of this Code to be a PR practitioner and to be bound by the Code.

General Professional Obligations

In the practice of his/her profession, the PR practitioner undertakes to respect the principles set forth in the Universal Declaration of Human Rights and, in particular, freedom of expression and freedom of the press which affect the right of the individual to receive information. He/she likewise undertakes to act in accordance with the public interest and not to harm the dignity or integrity of the individual.

In his/her professional conduct, the PR practitioner must show honesty, intellectual integrity and loyalty. In particular, he/she undertakes not to make use of comment or information that, to his/her knowledge or belief, is false or misleading. In the same spirit, he/she must be careful to avoid the use, even by accident, of practices or methods incompatible with this Code.

---

1 PR activities must be carried out openly: They must be readily identifiable, bear a clear indication of their origin, and must not tend to mislead third parties.

2 In his/her relations with other professions and with other branches of social communications, the PR practitioner must respect the rules and practices appropriate to those professions or occupations, so far as these are compatible with the ethics of his/her own profession. A PR practitioner must respect the national Code of Professional Conduct and the laws in force in any country in which he/she practices his/her profession and must exercise restraint in seeking personal publicity.

Specific professional obligations

A. Towards Clients or Employers

3 A PR practitioner shall not represent conflicting or competing interests without the express consent of the clients or employers concerned.

4 In the practice of his/her profession, a PR practitioner must observe complete discretion. He/she must scrupulously respect professional confidence, and in particular must not reveal any confidential information received from his/her clients or employers – past, present or potential – or make use of such information, without express authorisation. A PR practitioner who has an interest that may conflict with that of his/her client or employer must disclose it as soon as possible.

5 A PR practitioner must not recommend to his/her client or employer the services of any business or organisation in which he has a financial, commercial or other interest without first disclosing that interest.

A PR practitioner shall not enter into a contract with his client or employer under which the practitioner guarantees quantified results.

A PR practitioner may accept remuneration for his/her services only in the form of salary or fees. On no account may he accept payment or other material rewards contingent upon quantifiable professional results.

A PR practitioner shall not accept as a reward for his/her services to a client or an employer any remuneration from a third party, such as discounts, commissions or payments in kind, except with the agreement of the client or employer.

When the execution of a PR assignment would be likely to entail serious professional misconduct and imply behaviour contrary to the principles of this Code, the PR practitioner must take steps to notify his/her client or employer immediately and do everything possible to see that the latter respects the requirements of the Code. If the client or employer persists in his/her intentions, the practitioner must nevertheless observe the Code irrespective of the consequences to him/her.

B. *Towards Public Opinion and the Information Media*

6   The spirit of this Code and the rules contained in preceding clauses, notably clauses 2, 3, 4 and 5, imply a constant concern on the part of the PR practitioner with the right to information and, moreover, the duty to provide information, within the limits of professional confidence. They imply also a respect for the rights and independence of the information media.

7   Any attempt to deceive public opinion or its representatives is forbidden. News must be provided without charge or hidden reward for its use or publication. If it should seem necessary to maintain the initiative in and the control of the distribution of information within the principles of this Code, the PR practitioner may buy space or broadcasting time in conformity with the rules, practices and usages in that field.

C. *Towards Fellow Practitioners*

8   The PR practitioner must refrain from unfair competition with fellow practitioners. He/she must neither act nor speak in a way which would tend to deprecate the reputation or business of a fellow practitioner, subject always to his/her duty under clause 10b of this Code.

D. *Towards the Profession*

9   The PR practitioner must refrain from any conduct which may prejudice the reputation of his profession. In particular, he/she must not cause harm to the PRII, its efficient working or its good name by malicious attacks or by any breach of its constitution or rules.

10   The reputation of the profession is the responsibility of each of its members. The PR practitioner has a duty not only to respect this Code personally but also to:

a   Assist in making the Code more widely and better known and understood.

b   Report to the competent disciplinary authorities any breach or suspected breach of the Code which comes to his notice.

c   Take any action in his power to ensure that rulings on its application by such authorities are observed and sanctions made effective.

3.4.2 The Code of Athens

CONSIDERING that all member countries of the United Nations Organisation have agreed to abide by its Charter which reaffirms 'its faith in fundamental human rights, in the dignity and worth of the human person' and that having regard to the very nature of their profession, PR practitioners in these countries should undertake to ascertain and observe the principles set out in this Charter.

CONSIDERING that, apart from 'rights', human beings not only have physical or material needs but also intellectual, moral and social needs, and that their rights are of real benefit to them only insofar as these needs are essentially met.

CONSIDERING that, in the course of their professional duties and depending on how these duties are performed, PR practitioners can substantially help to meet these intellectual, moral and social needs.

And lastly, CONSIDERING that the use of techniques enabling them to come simultaneously into contact with millions of people gives PR practitioners a power that has to be restrained by the observance of a strict moral code.

On all these grounds, the PRII hereby declares that it accepts as its moral charter the principles of the following Code of Ethics and that if, in the light of evidence submitted to the Council, a member of the Institute should be found to have infringed this Code in the course of his professional duties, he will be deemed to be guilty of serious misconduct calling for an appropriate penalty.

Accordingly, each member of the PRII:

Shall endeavour

- To contribute to the achievement of the moral and cultural conditions enabling human beings to reach their full stature and enjoy the indefeasible rights to which they are entitled under the Universal Declaration of Human Rights.
- To establish communication patterns and channels which, by fostering the free flow of essential information, will make each member of the group feel that he/she is being kept informed and also give him/her an awareness of his/her own personal involvement and responsibility and of his/her solidarity with other members.
- To conduct himself always and in all circumstances in such a manner as to deserve and secure the confidence of those with whom he/she comes into contact.
- To bear in mind that because of the relationship between his/her profession and the public, his/her conduct – even in private – will

have an impact on the way in which the profession as a whole is appraised.

Shall undertake

- To observe, in the course of his/her professional duties, the moral principles and rules of the Universal Declaration of Human Rights.
- To pay due regard to, and uphold, human dignity, and to recognise the right of each individual to judge for himself/herself.
- To establish the moral, psychological and intellectual conditions for dialogue in its true sense and to recognise the fight of the parties involved to state their case and express their views.
- To act, in all circumstances, in such a manner as to take account of the respective interests of the parties involved: Both the interests of the organisation which he/she serves and the interests of the publics concerned.
- To carry out his/her undertaking and commitments, which shall always be so worded as to avoid any misunderstanding, and to show loyalty and integrity in all circumstances so as to keep the confidence of his/her clients or employers, past or present, and of all the publics that are affected by his/her action.

Shall refrain from

- Subordinating the truth to other requirements.
- Circulating information which is not based on established and ascertainable facts.
- Taking part in any venture or undertaking which is unethical or dishonest or capable of impairing human dignity and integrity.
- Using any manipulative methods or techniques designed to create sub-conscious motivations which the individual cannot control of his own free will and so cannot be held accountable for the action taken on them.

3.4.3 Code of Professional Practice for Public Affairs & Lobbying

In addition to these codes of conduct, the PRII outlines an additional Code of Professional Practice for Public Affairs & Lobbying which states as follows.

Professional public affairs practice and lobbying are proper, legitimate and important activities that are essential within any democratic system. Those activities ensure an open two-way communication between national and local government (including the Oireachtas, the entire public service, as well as other bodies funded wholly or mainly from public funds), the institutions of the European Union (EU) and bodies whose activities and interests are governed, regulated, impacted or otherwise influenced by such institutions.

PR practitioners will, from time to time, make representations to public representatives of all types, whether elected, co-opted, appointed, public servants, those employed in the public service, or those appointed to public bodies (for the purposes of this Code all such people will henceforth be referred to as public officials).

In order to ensure that the activities of its members are conducted to the highest possible standards of practice and ethics, the PRII adopted this Code of Professional Practice in 2003, which is a condition of membership of the Institute. In light of the Regulation of Lobbying Act 2015, it was amended in 2016.

The code directs PRII members to the acceptable and appropriate standards of behaviour in public affairs activity. It reflects the requirement of the Regulation of Lobbying Act and complements the obligations of public officials under the Ethics in Public Office Acts, Local Government Acts, Electoral Acts and standard terms of employment and other rules which also govern the activities of such officials. However, it goes beyond the basic legal minimum requirements and speaks to the high professional standards demanded by and of PRII members.

For the purposes of this Code of Professional Practice, public affairs practice is defined as:

All activity associated with representing the interests of a client or employer in relation to any matter of public policy, including:

- The provision of professional advice to clients/employers on matters relevant to public policy or law; or procurement, selection, nomination or appointment for public contract or office.
- Lawful and ethical actions intended to promote a change of public policy, law or the expenditure of public funds.
- The making of representations, or the advocacy of a point of view, to any persons or institutions, including the provision of information and advice.

Code of Professional Practice

All members of the PRII:

A. Conduct Towards the Public

1 Shall at all times be familiar with and observe all relevant EU, local, national and international law in force, with particular regard to the Regulation of Lobbying Act 2015; shall have due regard for the public interest and shall not seek to improperly influence the decision-making processes of government, whether local or national, or the EU Institutions.

2 Shall take reasonable steps to ensure that all information supplied, and representations made by them to third parties are factually accurate and honest.

3 Will actively disclose, at the earliest possible opportunity, the identity of clients on whose behalf they are making representations on matters of public policy or decision-making, current or proposed legislation, or in respect of the business of the Oireachtas, Northern Ireland Assembly, local authorities, the European Parliament or any other parliament or legislative assembly.

4 Shall ensure that any financial relationships involved in their professional dealings are legal and ethical. Members shall not act in such a way as to place public officials in a real or potential conflict of interest, or to make any offer, inducement or reward (direct or indirect) that would result in the public official being in apparent breach of his/her obligations under ethics legislation or statutory codes of conduct.

5 Shall act at all times in a professional, ethical and reasonable manner and shall not bring unreasonable or undue pressure or influence to bear in their activities as public affairs practitioners. All public officials should, at all times, be treated with courtesy and respect.

6 Where he/she is a member of a local authority or is appointed by the government to any state or semi-state body, or is engaged by such organisations on a consultancy basis, shall not offer public affairs consultancy services to third parties in respect of the business or related activities of that authority, body or organisation as well as to related, linked or subsidiary organisations.

7 Shall not offer public affairs consultancy services and simultaneously be a member of the Oireachtas, Northern Ireland Assembly, United Kingdom Parliament, European Parliament or other parliaments or legislative assemblies.

8 Shall not offer public affairs consultancy services for financial reward or other inducements and simultaneously be employed in the public service or engaged as a full-time adviser to government.

9 Shall, while attending any parliamentary or other representative assembly, national or local government building, observe the rules and procedures of that institution.

B. *Conduct Towards Clients/Employers*

10 Recognise their duty of professional care to their clients and/or employers.

11 Shall make their clients/employers aware of their obligations under the Regulation of Lobbying Act 2015 if relevant.

12 Shall take all necessary steps to ensure that they are properly informed of their clients' or employers' relevant concerns and interests and shall at all times properly and honestly represent these interests.

13 Shall properly inform clients about any potential conflicts of interest or of any competing interests arising from their professional practice or other business, family or social associations. If it should emerge that an actual conflict of interest exists and it cannot be resolved, the member must cease to act for that client. A member may represent such competing interests only:

   a Where he/she has obtained the explicit and informed consent of all the parties involved.
   b Where the member is enabled to act for each of the parties with an equal professionalism and duty of care.

14 Shall, in all cases where any conflict of interest or potential conflict arises between their professional duties and their personal activities, give precedence to their professional responsibilities and where necessary either cease the relevant personal activity or withdraw from their professional duty.

15 Have a positive duty in all their professional dealings to maintain full and proper client confidentiality.

16 Where he/she forms the opinion that the objectives or activities of his or her client/employer may be unethical, illegal or contrary to good professional practice, including this code of conduct, are required to so advise the client/employer. In circumstances where this advice is not acted upon in the appropriate manner, the member shall forthwith cease to act on behalf of the client/employer in such matters.

17 Shall not make improper claims regarding their access to, or influence over any institution of the EU, national or local government, public official or member of the media.

18 Shall not knowingly guarantee the achievement of results nor undertake assignments which are beyond the member's capabilities.

C. Conduct Towards the Profession

19 Reaffirm their commitment to the European Code of Professional Practice (Code of Lisbon) and the International Code of Ethics (Code of Athens) and their successors.

20 Shall not bring professional public affairs and PR practice into disrepute.

> **Breaches of the Code**
>
> Breaches of this code of conduct shall be treated as breaches of the Disciplinary Code of the PRII and shall be subject to such procedures and sanctions as provided for in the Disciplinary Code.

Ethical guidelines exist in every industry to try and ensure that its practitioners act transparently and with integrity. These codes of conduct as outlined by the Irish PR institute, demonstrate how the profession has interpreted ethical theory and applied it to the modern practice of public relations to ensure its practitioners act morally.

However, businesses are run by humans with their own individual moral standards and it is unrealistic to expect that all practitioners will adhere to the codes of conduct and act in an ethical manner. There are plenty of examples of PR practitioners throughout the years who have brought the profession into disrepute. For example, Ivy Lee's work for the Nazi party brought the profession into the centre of the Nuremberg Trials. Edwards Bernays was accused of influencing the Nazi party in Germany with propaganda and using manipulation to achieve his goals. In more recent examples, we have already discussed the expulsion of Bell Pottinger from the PR industry in the UK. Another example comes from the US, during the Gulf War period. In the 1990s, an international PR consultancy represented the *'Citizens for a Free Kuwait'* and created a false testimony that was delivered to the Congressional Human Rights Caucus. It later emerged that the Kuwaiti government had sponsored this group to influence the United States in its Gulf War strategy (Bowen, 2007).

As we have referenced in Chapter 1 (History of PR), the profession is regularly referred to as 'spin' or 'propaganda' as a result of some of these unethical highly publicised practices. In a more globalised Postmodern world where access to technology is increasing and people are empowered to challenge authrotiy the signs are that people are seeking more empathetic leaders and requiring businesses to have a purpose other than solely profit. This could be leading to an ever increasing role for PR in counteracting disinformation. It could also lead to an increasing place for activism, in addition to PR's traditional role of corporate communications. This may in turn lead to a growth in Environmental and Social Governance (ESG) as businesses become more responsible and act in a more ethical manner. Now, and into the future, PR could demonstrate its real value in upholding the truth, championing causes and evoking trust amongst the public in the business, media and political sectors.

3.5 For Discussion

Research and read about the Bell Pottinger PR consultancy and its expulsion from the PRCA.

- Do you think the organisation acted unethically?
- If so, why? What ethical codes did they breach?
- Which ethical theory relates most to the Bell Pottinger case?
- How do you think the crisis could have been averted? What could they have done differently?

References

Bowen, S. (2007). https://instituteforpr.org/ethics-and-public-relations/

Burne, S. J. L. (2017). https://www.prweek.com/article/1443592/bell-pottinger-thrown-prca-bringing-industry-disrepute

Griggs, I. (2015). https://www.prweek.com/article/1368002/sweaty-gate-agency-fuel-pr-expelled-prca

Parsons, J. P. (2016). *Ethics in Public Relations: A Guide to Best Practice.* 3rd Ed.

PRII (n.d). https://www.prii.ie/about/codes-of-practice/code-of-lisbon.html

Segal, D. (2018). https://www.nytimes.com/2018/02/04/business/bell-pottinger-guptas-zuma-south-africa.html?searchResultPosition=2

Theaker, A. (2016). *The Public Relations Handbook.* Routledge: London and New York.

4 Public Relations and Related Disciplines

Chapter Contents

4.1 Learning Outcomes

On completion of this chapter, the reader should be able to:

- Demonstrate an understanding of the communications mix and how public relations (PR) interacts with the other disciplines of marketing and advertising.
- Identify advertisements, news articles and features generated through PR, in the media and understand the differences between these three types of media features.
- Further understand the close relationship between media and PR and how these industries have evolved and work together.

DOI: 10.4324/9781003253815-4

4.2 Introduction

Between 2009 and 2013, a European medical brand (who we will refer to as Brand X) entered the Irish market. The brand specialised in radiology and specifically aimed to open access to medical scans to all Irish patients, both public and private. At the time, Waiting lists for medical scans (CT, MRI, X-rays, etc.) were excessively long and it was difficult for general practitioners to refer their patients for such scans in order to make a diagnosis.

'Brand X' was an international company that made significant investment in the Irish market. A spend of approximately 2–10% of sales was made on marketing at the outset to ensure the brand had a strong consistent presence across the country and it was ideally positioned to capture market share and generate revenue.

Firstly the organisation conducted focus groups in order to determine attitudes, values and beliefs of the public. A strapline and messaging for the organisation specific to the Irish market were designed around this.

Next, brochures were designed to distribute to potential suppliers and cutomers. A website was developed with content and imagery relevant to the market and the website was optimised to ensure prospective customers or patients could find it easily on search engines. Social media sites were designed and developed and a content campaign was initiated.

Print and online ads were designed using the new branding created. Ad space was selected and purchased and ads were placed in targeted local print media and online to reach a wide national audience. Radio ads were scripted and recorded for local radio to promote new clinic openings. A tagline was developed for these ads that resonated with the general public and encouraged them to take action.

'Brand X' was now on track to promote itself and potentially generate revenue in the Irish market. However, there was an issue. The brand was relatively unknown in the Irish market. Research demonstrated that trust and word of mouth were extremely important in such circumstances, particularly when it comes to healthcare but not many people aware of Brand X and it needed to generate awareness and trust.

A strategic PR campaign was devised and implemented to communicate the key messages and attributes of the brand with its publics (patients in this case) and stakeholders (doctors and medical professionals). For each new clinic opening, lists of public representatives and key opinion leaders in each area were compiled and meetings took place between them and representatives from 'Brand X'. Local launch events were organised to officially open the clinics to which local politicians, public representatives, business leaders, medical professionals and journalists from local and national media outlets were invited.

At a national level, interviews were pitched into and published in national print, online and broadcast on radio, with the CEO and other relevant representatives of the Irish operation. Photographs of the key representatives were taken and press releases, outlining the brand's objectives, strategy in Ireland and details of clinic openings were written and issued to media. The purpose of this was to present the public with information, to demonstrate the human face behind the brand and evoke trust amongst stakeholders and public.

Over a period of time, the public and particularly stakeholders began to become familiar with the story behind the brand. The PR activity enabled them to understand who the brand was and what it represented. It helped them to develop trust in and to develop a relationship with the brand. This activity supported the advertising and marketing and motivated consumers to purchase or in this case to avail of the service.

This situation common for many large brands that engage in a full 360-degree marketing strategy and illustrates the various components involved in marketing, advertising and PR. Often new students of PR can find the differences between these three disciplines difficult to grasp. This chapter sets out to explain these differences with the aim of encouraging a more in-depth understanding of the discipline of PR and its purpose in business. The chapter aims in particular to support students in understanding the differences between advertising, news stories and PR stories in the media.

4.3 What is Marketing?

Many people new to or unfamiliar with PR will often assume that PR is a function of marketing. However, according to many experts and as outlined in The Excellence Theory, PR is very much independent from marketing and should form part of the strategic management structure of an organisation with the PR professional reporting directly to the head of the company and not to a marketing manager.

The reality is that PR and marketing have the same priority – to assist a business in generating revenue and achieving its long-term goals. However, PR is ultimately concerned with the role the long-term reputation of the organisation has in achieving this aim and marketing is concerned with the immediate sales of an organisation's products and/or services to assist the business in achieving this aim. Unfortunately, a clear lack of understanding within certain areas as to what PR is often results in PR being sublimated into a marketing department and therefore not fulfilling its true potential.

Figure 4.1 illustrates the Marketing Mix and outlines where PR and advertising sit within this mix. PR Theory states that PR performs best when it is independent of marketing and not sublimated into the marketing department. PR, therefore, sits outside the Marketing Mix in this figure. The issue that causes confusion most often is when PR is used to encourage the sale of products. This is termed 'Product PR' or 'Consumer PR'. This type of PR is very often confused with advertising and that is why communications is slightly linked to advertising in this figure.

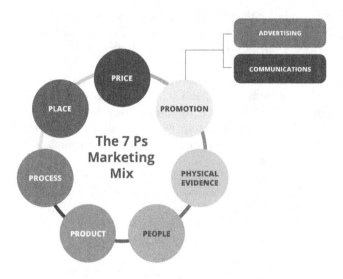

Figure 4.1 The Marketing Mix.

4.3.1 The 7 Ps of Marketing

In the sixties, McCarthy and Perreault (1984) developed an innovative structure called the *'4 Ps'* that became world renowned and used by organisations and teachers all over the world in their marketing practises and teaching. The *'4 Ps'* at the time referred to Product, Price, Promotion and Place and these were recommended as essential components to be considered in an organisation's marketing strategy. The *'4 Ps'* have evolved with time and have been joined by three more *Ps*: Process, People and Physical Evidence.

The 7 Ps of Marketing

1	**Product:**	The characteristics of the product/service – e.g. a new smartphone.
2	**Price:**	The cost of the product/service.
3	**Promotion:**	How the product/service will be promoted – e.g. through advertising online or on TV, through PR or through email marketing, newsletters, etc.
4	**Place:**	Where will the product be on sale? Where can the service be availed of?
5	**Process:**	What is the process for purchasing? What's the purchasing journey for the customer?
6	**People:**	Who are the people involved in the purchase? E.g. shop assistants, customer service representatives, health workers, etc.
7	**Physical Evidence:**	What does the customer receive when purchase has been made? For example, a ticket for a concert, a 'receipt of order' email from an online purchase.

4.4 What is Advertising?

Many people can recall Christmas television ads for big brands such as Coca Cola or John Lewis. Ads for new cars, a new film release or even Easter eggs are visible on billboards adorning motorways throughout the world. Advertising is a hugely powerful and influential means of motivating a wide audience to make a purchase or take a course of action.

Jeremy Bullmmore stated in 1975 that advertising was 'any paid-for communication intended to inform and/or influence one or more people.' He later revised this definition to state that advertising could be explained as 'any communication, usually paid-for, specifically intended. to inform and/or influence one or more people' (Bullmore, n.d.).

Accoring to Bullmore, advertising's origins can be traced back to the industrial revolution as mass production led to increased competition for goods and services. He states that *'advertising came into existence because of the needs of trade. But once established it has been found to be of value, among a huge variety of roles, in the recruitment of staff, in fundraising for charities and in the dissemination of government information. Its value in the building of brands has been well-documented. More recently, it's become increasingly clear how advertising does not just help build brands but helps sustain them'* (Bullmore, n.d.).

Like PR, the advertising industry has grown in tandem with the evolution of mass media. The industry is now worth X m in the United States for example. The main difference between it and PR is that advertising media in print, broadcast or online media is paid for by an organisation or a media buyer on its behalf. PR on the other hand, is considered to be earned based on the merit of its newsworthiness. The confusion arises often when it is difficult to identify if the media coverage has been paid for. This is something that many PR students find difficult to understand. This topic is discussed in more detail in section 4.6 in this Chapter.

4.5 What is PR?

Chapters I and II in this book aim to lay the foundations for a deeper understanding of what PR is. To further elaborate on this topic in the context of the overall marketing mix, it is useful to look at the various definitions of the discipline from professional bodies throughout the world.

Harold Burson, the esteeemed communicator and founder of international public relations agency, Burson Marsteller, is reported to have described PR as: *'a process that impacts public opinion. Its objective is to motivate individuals or groups to take a specific action. Like buying a certain brand of toothpaste or automobile; voting for a specific candidate; supporting one side or the other of a political issue or signing up with one cable provider over another. As such, PR is an applied social science that draws on several social sciences, among them, psychology, cultural anthropology, sociology, political science, economics, geography. Actually, one could more accurately describe public relations as a maturing applied social science. It is all too slowly developing theories and a body of knowledge, mainly case histories, that can bring about greater descipline, uniformity and predictability in delivering our services' (Ovait, n.d.).*

This definition of PR is quite comprehensive and recognises the important role that behavioural science plays in successful communications. Further definitions of PR follow:

In the United States of America, the Public Relations Society of America (PRSA) describes PR as:

'a strategic communication process that builds mutually beneficial relationships between organizations and their publics'

(PRSA, n.d.).

In Canada, the Canadian Public Relations Society quotes Flynn et al. (2008) in its definition of PR on its website. It states that:

'public relations is the strategic management of relationships between an organisation and its diverse publics, through the use of communication to achieve mutual understanding, realise organisational goals and serve the public interest'

(CPRS, n.d.).

In the UK, the Chartered Institute of Public Relations defines PR as:

'the discipline which looks after reputation, with the aim of earning understanding and support and influencing opinion and behaviour. It is the planned and sustained effort to establish and maintain goodwill and mutual understanding between an organisation and its publics'

(CIPR, n.d.).

In Nigeria, the founding father of PR, Bob Ogbuagu, is cited by Olisa (2021) as defining PR as *'the art of building bridges of rapport between an organisation and its publics'.*

Across the various definitions, certain themes or key words appear frequently: organisations and their publics, two-way communication and reputation.

In 1978, world leaders in PR made an attempt to standardise the profession when they came together in Mexico and drafted what is the most commonly referred to definition of PR in the Western world, The Mexico Definition. This definition states the following:

> '*Public Relations is the art and social science of analysing trends, predicting their consequences, counselling organisation leaders and implementing planned programmes of action which will serve both the organisation's and the public interest*'.

The Mexico Definition describes PR as both an art and a social science and recognises the wide-ranging strategic role that PR plays in helping organisations to understand trends and markets. It emphasises the importance of two-way communications (between organisations and their publics) that represent both the persuadee's and the persuader's interests.

Also to consider for future definitions is a reference to media relations which is missing from the existing Mexico Definition and from many of the local definitions. In PR, the majority of the persuasive communication is done through the media. PR as a profession, as we have seen in Chapter I is believed by many to have evolved as a profession in tandem with the evolution of mass media in the early 20th Century. As the western world moved out of war, businesses began to to employ wartime communications tactics in the corporate sector. At the same time, industry was beginning to boom throughout Europe and the United States, media was evolving and becoming more accessible and psychology was becoing recognised as a science. All these factors palyed a part in the evenutal evolution of PR into the structured and highly valued 'art and social science' that the Mexico Definition has identified.

The world however has changed significantly since the Mexico Definition was drafted. Further research on the roles and functions of PR in a Postmodern era may yield a more wide reaching and inclusive definition of PR.

4.5.1 *Publics and Stakeholders*

An understanding of human behaviour plays a huge role in successful communications. If public relations professionals are to communicate with and persuade people to change behaviours and attitudes, then they need to understand the public and what motivates them.

To understand PR, it is important to understand the distinction between publics and stakeholders. Informed PR professionals are positioned to provide counsel to organisation leaders and to implement strategies that are capable of communicating with the organisation's public. The word 'publics' is used interchangeably in PR with other words such as audiences and stakeholders.

Publics can be identified in the context of PR as a group of people who are affected by an issue.

In today's world, much of the information on an organisation's public is derived from algorithms which help organisations to analyse trends by informing them as to how their customers are behaving online and what motivates them.

In the 1960s, PR's foremost theorist, James Grunig, undertook a study of publics and the role they play in communications. He found that when companies sought to engage with an audience, communications activity was sometimes unsuccessful because organisations engaged ineffectively with their publics and developed policies and programmes that did not resonate with their target audiences as a result (Grunig et al., 2002). This study eventually evolved into the four models of PR and, subsequently, the Theory of Excellence as discussed in Chapter 2.

The example used at the beginning of this chapter can demonstrate the difference between publics and stakeholders. 'Brand X' had just entered the Irish market and was required to communicate its services, first and foremost with medics who were operating private businesses and may have been potentially interested in selling their businesses to 'Brand X'. Next, the brand was required to raise awareness of its services amongst general practitioners as these were the group who were responsible for referring in patients to the clinics. Finally, the brand was needed to raise awareness amongst patients of the existence of the brand to enable them to take control of their own health and avail of its services. These groups are all **publics** in this particular example.

'Stakeholders' can be defined as those who are invested in the organisation but may not be directly affected or impacted by direct sales activity. In this case for example, it would be businesses who worked as suppliers to Brand X, local politicians and patient groups. Using the same example, stakeholders in this instance would be any other audience who could be affected or impacted by 'Brand X's' activity. These would include, local business owners, leaders of patient bodies or groups, health minister and local politicians. These groups are all impacted indirectly by the business of the company and therefore become a secondary audience for who the brand needs to communicate with. Often in PR, the term audience is used to include both stakeholders and publics. An audience is defined by (Butterick, 2011) as anyone with whom the organisation could potentially communicate to.

To understand the difference between PR and the other areas of marketing, it is important to understand the three main categories of PR: corporate, consumer and public affairs. A brief explanation of each of these is provided in Figure 4.2. A more detailed explanation is offered in Chapters 8 (PR for Business) and 9 (Public Affairs and Political Communications).

4.5.2 Categories of PR

Figure 4.2 illustrates the three main categories of PR: Corporate, consumer and public affairs.

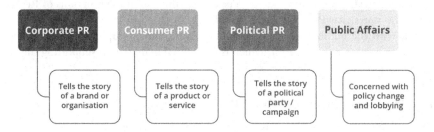

Figure 4.2 Categories of PR.

PR works to build the reputation of an organisation by creating a narrative around the brand, its products and its services. According to Reptrak, the reputation data and insights company, reputation is an *'intangible value that defines up to 84% of the market value for a company'* and can yield 2.5 times better stock performance for companies when compared to the overall market (Reptrak, 2021). This is the reason that many brands engage in PR activity, to protect and enhance their reputation, which in turn generates revenue. They do this through the use of what is termed as 'Corporate PR'. In the example used at the beginning of the chapter, 'Brand X' used Corporate PR to raise awareness of its services and to generate trust amongst the public in order to motivate them to avail of its services.

Consumer PR works to tell the story of the product or service. This is sometimes where the lines between PR and advertising can become blurred. In the example we used at the outset of this chapter, consumer PR in this instance would have been used in the publication of a story about a member of the public perhaps having a condition such as or another condition for which a medical scan would be used to produce a diagnosis. This humanises a product or a service enabling the general public to understand and relate to the . In the story, the subject may have availed of a scan in 'Brand X's' clinic to assist in the diagnosis. This is in fact consumer PR as it is using editorial to promote a product or service. Another example of this type of PR can be seen at Christmas time in the numerous 'Gift Lists' that appear across media channels. These lists are usually compiled as a result of press releases and imagery issued to relevant journalists by PR professionals working on behalf of the products. Often students or those unfamiliar with how PR works will misinterpret these lists as advertising.

Political PR aims to tell the story of the political party or campaign. Often political PR executives are working as press officers for political representatives or parties. Public affairs is concerned predominantly with lobbying and trying to effect policy change. Public affairs is very different from corporate and consumer PR as it tends to be more reliant on stakeholder as opposed to media relations to achieve its aims. In corporate and consumer PR, the ultimate goal is often a longer term one, to increase revenues. In politcal PR it is about votes. We will come back to this in the later chapter on political PR and public affairs.

Alison Theaker (2016) provides a very clear definition of the functions of PR when she states that PR operates at two levels: A strategic level which is concerned with the building of reputation and relationships (Corporate PR) and a consumer level (Consumer PR), which is concerned mainly with supporting the sale of products or services.

4.6   The Use of Media – News, PR and Advertising

Earlier chapters in this book aim to give the reader an overview as to how PR has evolved as a profession. The history of PR demonstrates the close links between PR practitioners and journalists with many journalists transitioning to roles as public relations practitioners as the profession became more established. This is a channel that is well traveled to this day by many journalists throughout the world and contributes to the close relationship between both industries as they often share professionals. As businesses began to pro-actively target the media to tell positive stories about themselves to their public, journalists found themselves ideally placed to be able to do this, knowing the media well and understanding how to create a narrative that would help an organisation to achieve its media goals.

The next reason why media and PR are so closely related is because both industries are dependent on each other. Eventhough many journalists would be slow to admit it, the reality is that a large proportion of what is in the headlines in many news outlets, has been generated by a PR practitioner. This doesn't mean the story is not true or 'fake', it just means it has required assistance to be heard or seen by the public. This assistance usually takes the form of a PR professional who can communicate a business story in an interesting way. Journalists and media outlets need PR therefore to provide content, particularly for business and lifestyle media. For example how would you hear about a hotel's plan for expansion or an airline's plans to launch a new route? A journalist or content manager more than likely doesn't turn up at work one day and decide that they'd like to write about a particular hotel, bank or restaurant. A film critic doesn't just decide that they are going to write about a particular film they saw or plan to see. They reality is that these people have been contacted by a PR representing a business, an actor or a film company to tell them about the latest developments in order to raise awareness that will improve their reputation and ultimately their revenues.

On the other side, PR people need journalists and media outlets too. They depend on media coverage to justify their salaries and their fees to clients. For years the industry measured this coverage, compared it to the cost of advertisingand used this to evaluate the success of PR programmes. However evaluation methods as discussed in a later chapter on measurement are now gradually evolving beyond these basic means.

Media is hugely important to PR practitioners and in many cases it is the contacts within the media that the PR firm or practitioner has that wins them a contract. In the old days, PR practitioners would have tried to nurture these contacts through gifts and expensive outlings for journalists. However, in recent times with the advent of online media in particular, these relationships are more commoly developed and nurtured through the provision of good quality content. If the PR can regularly turn around high grade content capable of generating 'click-throughs' and audience reach, relationships may flourish between the journalist and practitioner.

To really understand PR, it is important to understand media relations and the results of its work. Students of PR should be able to identify content that they view, read or hear online, in print or in broadcast media and identify the probable source of the story. Has the story been self generated, generated by PR or is it an ad? This is often one ofthe most difficult concepts for new students of PR to understand.

The first thing to think about is where on the news site the story is positioned. Stories on the home page, for example, would most likely be a general news story that is being featured of its own accord. Often stories, for in the business section of a news website, may be generated by PR. Secondly, think about how they sourced the story. Are they writing about a general election in the United States, for example, or the latest outbreak of a disease or a plane crash? If so, then these items are most likely topical news stories that the journaist sought out. However, if they are discussing positive news from a company that will impact on its reputation, such as the hiring of new staff, the launch of a new product or service or its annual financial results, then these are most likely stories generated by PR and would most likely have come to the attention of the journalist through the company itself or a PR representative acting on its behalf.

Advertising on the most part should be easier to identify in the media. An ad will commonly mention the company name and/or logo and will have a specific position on a page, a webpage, an online video, a radio or TV programme. There will usually be a 'call to action' included such as 'buy now', 'call us today', 'donate now', 'vote for us', etc. The objective with advertising is to elicit an immediate direct response from the recipient of the message and this is how it differs from PR. PR aims to inform and persuade. Advertising has one priority – to sell.

The confusion between advertising and PR however occurs when ads are designed to look like editorial. In print format again, although slightly trickier, these woud be easier to identify than online. For example if a motor brand is launching a new model, they might take ads out on various popular websites encouraging people to click through to book a test drive.

The motor company may also decide to engage the services of a celebrity to be a brand ambassador, which means the celebrity is gifted one of the new cars and asked to commit to making a certain number of posts. In this case the brand ambassador becomes an opinion leader where the association between them and the car resonates with their followers and in the long term will encourage sales of the model amongst its target demographic. Although a fee will be agreed to pay the brand ambassador, this is actually PR as the coverage generated by the influencers is not controlled by the brand. This deems the coverage more credible than advertising and the idea is that it will further the reputation of the brand and the new product and eventually motivate people to make a purchase. A motoring journalist may also receive a gift of the new car for limited period in return for a review in the motoring pages. Again, this is PR as the content of the media is not controlled by the brand.

The news media would come in to play, if for example the new model had to be recalled. A journalist may get a 'tip off' about this and break the story in the media leading to a news feature and a crisis for the brand.

4.7 Conclusion

The ultimate aim of this chapter is to provide the reader with an overview of the communications landscape and help them to understand where PR fits in and the role that it plays. A key objective of the chapter is to encourage the reader to think about the source of the media coverage that they consume and identify if it is an ad, editorial or media coverage that has been generated through PR. The disciplines of marketing and advertising are defined and the reader is given a further insight into the close working relationship between PR and Journalism. After reading chapters I and II in this book, the reader should have a feel for how the PR industry has evolved in tandem with the media sector and the interchangeable roles that PR professionals and journalists often take. This chapter delves into this further by helping the reader to understand how media articles or features are generated and the specific role that PR plays in media relations. This will be further explored in subsequent chapters.

4.7.1 Discussion

1 **Identify difference between PR, advertising and news:**

- Find three examples of each of the following from an online news channel in your country.

  - Advertisement.
  - News story.
  - Story generated by PR.

- In the case of each, think about why you believe it to be an ad, a news story or a PR generated story.
- If it is an ad, is there a logo or a call to action included?
- In the case of a news story, who sourced the story? How did it come to the attention of the journalist?
- In the case of a story generated by PR:

  - How did this come to the attention of the journalist?
  - Is there a photograph?
  - Is there a logo included?
  - Is the company mentioned?

- Is the story good or bad for the organisation's reputation?
- If it's bad for the organisation's reputation, is the organisation defending its reputation?
- Is a representative from the organisation quoted in the article?

References

CIPR (n.d.). https://www.cipr.co.uk/CIPR/About_Us/About_PR.aspx

Flynn et al. (2008). as cited on the CPRS. Available at: https://www.cprsns.com

Garnet, J. (n.d.). Digital marketing study notes: Percentage of sales. Available at https://digitalmarketinginstitute.com/resources/lessons/budget-and-resourcing_budget-process_94mt

McCarthy, J. E. , & Perreault, W. D. (1984). Basic Marketing, A managerial approach. 8th Edn. Irwin.

Olisa, S. (2021). Why PR in Nigeria Needs PR. Available at https://govandbusinessjournal.ng/why-pr-in-nigeria-needs-pr/

Reptrak (July 2020). https://reptrak.com/blog/what-companies-can-learn-from-facebooks-latest-reputation-challenge/

Theaker, A.(2016). *The Public Relations Handbook*. 5th Edn. Routledge: New York.

5 Corporate Communications by Mark Campbell

Chapter Contents

DOI: 10.4324/9781003253815-5

5.1 Learning Outcomes

On completion of this chapter, the reader will be able to:

- Know what is meant by the term 'corporate communications'.
- Have an understanding of corporate legal forms and structures and the need for communicators to be involved in investor relations (IR) and corporate governance (CG).
- Understand how press and media relations are affected by the corporate status of the organisation.
- Have knowledge of the context in which public relations (PR) and communications are managed in any organisation.
- Appreciate the growth and accessibility of information on corporates and their public affairs.
- Understand the value of stakeholder relations including IR and financial PR.
- Apply corporate communications theory to professional practice.

5.2 Introduction to Corporates, Corporate Structures and Corporate Communications

5.2.1 Corporates – Unique Organisations

A prerequisite to successfully managing corporate communications is a full understanding of what a 'corporate' or 'company' is; why it is a unique form of entity; and why the nature of this unique organisation type affects how communications are managed, both internally and externally.

Most (certainly smaller) businesses are not corporates. They are sole traders or partnerships which are owner-run or owner-managed, i.e. there is no separation between those who own and those who operate the business. An increasing number (particularly of medium-sized and larger businesses), however, move from being sole traders and partnerships to become corporations as they grow. The corporation – or company or corporate as it is more commonly known – is the dominant legal form of economic organisation found today.

The company exists as a structure to enable the business to startup and/or grow through attracting capital from investors. Only organisation as a company allows the raising of capital from larger numbers of diverse and widely dispersed shareholders, who exist independent of the managers and workers of the firm. It is a legal structure that is permanent and gives protection. Arising from this, there is a requirement for the company to communicate with its shareholders (and other stakeholders) through corporate communications and PR.

Unlike other organisations, which may have significant overlap between ownership, management and operations, corporates are entities that (at least legally) separate ownership (represented by directors) from operations (represented by managers and conducted by operatives). Companies can enter into contracts, own property, make use of tax advantages and other things that are normally the preserve of individual human beings. Like humans, companies need to communicate identity, style and personality.

Communications practitioners need to be aware that their organisation's communications and PR content and style occur within this context of corporate form and structure. For a newly appointed communications or PR practitioner appointed to a company it is important to ask: who owns this company? who directs it? who manages it? who operationalises its strategy? who are its various publics or audiences and how and why do corporate identity and personality – expressed through such things as logos, brands, advertising, annual reports, and social media presence – help deliver its overall aims and objectives?

In an organisation, responsibility for communications is not usually the function of communications and PR specialists in a marketing department nor is it solely a function of the finance department. Rather, it is a component in every director's, manager's and worker's role and function. The aim of the corporate communicator is to orchestrate key messages from a wide range of internal actors to various audiences through the organisation of words, images, and other aesthetic elements, regardless of who in the organisation communicates them.

5.2.2 Corporate Structures

Balmer (2008) states that an understanding of the legal theory and practice of the corporation is a necessary prerequisite to comprehending how corporate communications works. While the laws, regulations and rules for corporates vary from country to country, depending on the prevailing political, legal and economic conditions, in general, we can distinguish between the following:

- Public Limited Companies (PLCs): Companies which raise capital by offering shares on a public market, such as the stock exchange. Typically a PLC will have thousands of owners who will meet annually (at an AGM – Annual General Meeting) to elect a board of directors. The board of directors have oversight and drive strategy through the activities of the company. The directors employ managers (who in turn employ others) to operationalise the strategy. Historically, such companies were set up to raise substantial amounts of capital to attract investment for costly infrastructure projects such as building canals, ports, railways and roads and often made a return for investors by successfully managing the related operations (rail transport services). Over time, PLCs became involved in a much wider range of activities. Today, in most countries, the top 100–500 companies will be PLCs. Ownership of these companies remains in the independent hands of shareholders, whose shares can be bought and sold on a public market. Shareholders are the primary and most visible, but not the only, audience for corporate communications.

- Private Limited Companies: Companies which raise capital by offering shares to a private group of individuals, usually by invitation. In reality, these individuals often comprise family, close business associates, friends and others who are 'known' to the management team. The buying and selling of shares is more tightly controlled by the board of directors. The investors' debt is limited to the amount they invest in the company.
- Family-owned Limited Companies: Companies for which there is, in many cases, overlap between owners/shareholders, the board of directors and the managers/employees of the firm. Private companies and the organisation is said to be 'tightly controlled'. Similarly, the direction and strategy of the company and the operations of the organisation are closely integrated.
- Unlimited Companies: Unlimited companies can be sole operators, partnerships or cooperatives for example. Such businesses are typically less formally structured and do not have the same level of legal protection as limited companies. If an unlimited company (whether public or private) were to become insolvent, the shareholders' liability to those to whom money is owed would be limited to the value of the shares; in an unlimited organisation, those owed money could pursue the entire assets of the owners – including all their business and personal assets such as their home. Unlimited companies tend to be found in sectors that are regulated, e.g. professional accounting firms.

The majority of the World's largest companies – the so-called, Trillion-Dollar Club – are publicly traded companies. They have managed to achieve $1 trillion or more in market capitalisation. According to Companies Market Cap (2021) – which tracks over 5,000 of the World's largest publicly traded stocks – only 6 businesses have achieved a 13-digit market capitalisation. As of 2021, the six companies were Apple, Microsoft, Saudi Aramco (all with a $2T+ market capitalisation) followed by Alphabet (Google), Amazon and Tesla. Meta/Facebook had reached the $1T barrier but dipped below it in 2021. All of the companies are considered to be US headquartered, with the exception of the World's largest oil and gas giant – Saudi Aramco. There are few PLCs with a market capitalisation above $500 billion who might join the club. Among them are Facebook, Berkshire Hathaway, TSMC, Tencent and Visa.

The World's Largest Private Company

A company that some have probably never heard of – Cargill – is the most valuable private company in the world. Only a dozen or so PLCs (see above) earn more revenue than Cargill which operates in 70 nations, employs 155,000 people and imports almost one-quarter of all the beef that enters the United States. Its interests range widely from phosphate production to energy trading. Revenue totals $113 billion annually. The understandably secretive Cargill family owns 90% of the conglomerate (Investopedia, 2021).

Two Family Companies

While Cargill is a family-owned company, it is an outlier. Most private companies are family owned and range in size from very large to small-medium in size. A good example is Schmitz Cargobull which was founded in 1892 and produces, markets and distributes vehicle trailers – from box body trucks for temperature-controlled transport to swap systems. The company has remained in the hands of the family throughout its 130-year history and continues to grow by providing innovative solutions that support daily transport operations. The company has annual revenue of circa $2.5 billion (Family Capital, 2021).

A Company That Has Encompassed All Forms (P&G)

Procter & Gamble Company was originally formed when two sole traders – William Procter, a British candlemaker, and James Gamble, an Irish soap maker – merged their businesses in Cincinnati (the two met when they became in-laws). They realised the main ingredient for both their business' products was animal fat, which was readily available in the hog-butchering centre of Cincinnati, and their father-in-law persuaded them both to go into partnership in 1837. They later formed a company which went public in 1890.

5.2.3 Corporate Communications

Balmer (2008) suggested that corporate communicators must understand the unique legal form of their company. This sets out the role of shareholders, directors, managers and employees and the legal basis for the organisation (expressed through legal documents known as the memorandum and articles of association). He outlines three other key considerations that should be taken into account.

- Efficacy, taking into account the needs, wants and desires of broader stakeholders such as politicians, customers, etc.
- Ethicality, the explicit ethical/corporate social responsibility (CSR) remit of the organisation.
- Temporality, consideration given to key stakeholders of the past (the founders who may have established and financed the entity), current managers and employees (who meaningfully contribute to its success) and prospective future stakeholders (whose perspective may, for example, influence concepts such as sustainability).

It is useful to think of corporate communications as evolving over five generations (see Table 5.1).

- In its initial generation (up to early-1900s), its role was mainly one of 'IR' which aimed to ensure good 'CG', i.e. communicate that the activities of the directors and managers of the organisation were conducted correctly on behalf of the owners – the shareholders.
- During the second generation (mid-1900s), investor and PR typically merged. Key IR and PR activities combined into an amalgamation of IR, CG, PR and communications to create the type of corporate communications that is found in most corporations up to the present time.
- The third generation of corporate communications (late-1900s) saw further evolution of the function to reflect the involvement of an increasing number of stakeholder groups in a company, giving rise to CSR.
- Adding further complexity, in the fourth generation (early-2000s), corporate communications has evolved into what has been referred to as total communications – the complete management of all communications in the company in one department.
- Where next? The fifth generation (early-mid 2000s) that we are facing into over the next few decades reflects the fast-changing reality of socio-technological change. This will increasingly require companies to respond to developments such as stronger stakeholder advocacy, the requirement for companies to have more sustainable practices and the power of social media.
- By the third generation, corporate communications could be viewed as a scaffolding or 'framework in which all communications specialists (marketing, organisational and management communications) integrate[d] the totality of the organisational message, thereby helping to define corporate image as a means to improving corporate performance' (Van Riel, 1995). External profile was perceived as the key benefit of corporate identity, while the

benefits of internal communication were viewed as varying widely (Schmidt, 1997). Since it moved into the fourth generation, corporate communications and PR have increasingly involved wider target audiences, especially customers, other individuals and groups in the value chain and the general public (Schmidt, 1997). At the same time, more complex messages are being delivered through a wider range of broadcast, narrowcast and social media. Increasingly, companies depend on relationships with a wide range of other groups – internal and external – to conduct and grow their businesses. It has converged around fundamental business processes of several, traditionally separate, functions, such as IR, PR, employee communications, human resources management, marketing and quality management. It has amalgamated communications roles from these functions into a single, core organisation and management resource. Balmer (2017) suggests that the fourth generation can be considered as comprising a 'Total Corporate Communications' approach which differs from standard corporate communications in that it is a panoptic approach which recognises the importance of:

- 'Controlled' (integrated)/primary (latent) communications which influence an organisation's corporate identity traits, e.g. directors' behaviours, and secondary (overt, planned and managed) communications, e.g. advertising.
- And 'uncontrolled' tertiary (tangential) communications, e.g. third-party communications independent of, but linked to the firm, e.g. comments on social media.

- For Communications Directors and managers, managing, coordinating and controlling activities related to the identity and corporate personality of the organisation, among a wide variety of stakeholders, in multiple media, is core to achieving the overall aims of the organisation. In the fifth generation, which is still at the early stage of development, the volume of information is continuously increasing, due to growth in social media and virtual networks. Organisations need to learn more about information management in corporate communications (Cacciatore et al., 2017) and adopt a more dynamic approach in which they can continuously react to and anticipate changing requirements in communications.

Corporate communications' historic importance is highlighted by Wright's 1997 survey among managers outside the communications field, which saw them rank external communication activities as considerably more important than internal ones. The year previously, when launching the journal – *Corporate Communications*, the editors surmised that there was 'increased awareness that an organisation's communications are part of the whole organisation, and that the relationship an organisation has with its external public requires careful management' (1996).

Table 5.1 Five Generations in the Development of Corporate Communications

Generation	Name	Main Audience(s)	Media Focus	Characterised by	Examples
1 Up to early-1900s	IR	Owner investors Stockbrokers Investment intermediaries	Direct written communications	One-way communication and legal requirements	CG. Investor letters. Annual reports. General Meetings.
2 Mid-1900s	Corporate Communications	External, e.g. members of the organisation's value chain Internal, e.g. employees	Communications using multiple broadcast, narrowcast and direct media	Two-way communication and customer service	Advertising. PR. Corporate Video. Conferences. Exhibitions.
3 Late-1900s	CSR	Wider stakeholders in society who are affected directly or indirectly by its actions	Multi-layered communications using a wider range of media than above	Two-way communication and social concerns	Sustainability reports. Ethical communications.
4 Early-2000s	Total Communications	360-degree stakeholders	Multi-layered and multi-directional communications using all media available	Two-way communications driven by needs of all stakeholders	Digital marketing. Social media.
5 Early to mid-2000s	Dynamic Communications	All past, current and potential stakeholders, whether affected directly or indirectly by its actions	All the above and including social and interactive media, and developing media such as ubiquitous hardware/software, super/quantum computing andartificial intelligence.	Multiple levels and lenses used for real time, interactive communication, both with people and machines	Media stewardship. Digital nudging. Interactive digital comms. AI interaction.

*Time frames for generations are approximate as different regions and countries of the world, varied in their adaptation of each.

- In its first generation, the theoretical foundations for corporate communications drew initially on the concepts of the legal form of the corporation, IR and CG.
- By the second generation, a wider interpretation of communications and PR theory began to drive considerations (Kitchen, 1997).

Earl and Waddington (2018), authors of *#BrandVandals,* summarise the current state of corporate communications well: 'The omnipresence of the internet, and of smartphone use for recording and sharing so many aspects of our daily lives means that it has never been easier to capture and share wrongdoing, make a prominent point or wreak havoc through direct action and pull on the power chord of the online crowd'.

5.2.3.1 The Role of the Corporate Communicator

For a person who is appointed as a corporate communicator, it is vital that they understand the history and legacy of these five generations and the combined legality, efficacy, ethicality and temporality of communications. These factors underpin the nature of the role to which they are appointed. Roles within corporate communications can comprise any and all those outlined to follow.

5.2.3.2 Corporate Communications Hierarchy

The titles of roles in corporate communications and PR outlined in Table 5.2 are examples. In practice, a wide range of titles, responsibilities and skills/formal qualifications are found, and depending on the size and nature of the organisation, there can be a single or multiple positions. A Head of Marketing and Communications or a Communications and PR Director can, confusingly, refer to someone who is on the board of directors, with all its related directorial responsibilities, or to a senior manager role with no director responsibility but who directs the corporate communications functions and orchestrates PR activities on behalf of the company.

It is worthwhile noting that for many smaller businesses, including companies, the practice of corporate communication is less structured and planned. In such cases, responsibility for corporate communications may be incorporated in another functional role, e.g. a marketing manager may assume responsibility for PR or a company secretary takes charge of IR. A study by Oliver and Reilly (1996) concluded that corporate communications in smaller businesses is characterised by a lack of understanding both of what corporate communication is and how it can be of benefit to the business. Corporate communications can be as formal, planned and managed as directors and managers choose it to be.

Table 5.2 Roles and Responsibilities in Communication

Typical Title	Role and Responsibilities	Knowledge, Skills and Abilities Required
Communications Committee	The board of directors may appoint a committee to oversee relations with investors and other publics	No specific knowledge, skills or abilities but those appointed are likely to be experienced communicators and/or directors with investor-facing roles
Company Secretary	Responsible for ensuring legally required documentation and CG regulations are adhered to	A formal qualification as a Company Secretary is the norm. Secretarial role usually requires a full-time position in a PLC but duties may be fulfilled by others, e.g. Finance Director or even an external professional
Head of Marketing and Communications	Senior manager who directs all corporate communications and PR activities for the firm (responsibility is delegated to the holder from the board)	10+ years of management experience. A bachelors and masters level degree such as an MBA, MSc in Marketing, Digital Communications or PR. Fellow or Senior Membership of appropriate professional institution(s)
PR Manager	Development of the communications and PR strategy and plan for the organisation and its implementation	5+ years of experience in marketing, communications and/or PR, often promoted from an Assistant Manager role. Bachelor and preferable masters level qualified and Member of a suitable professional body
Assistant Marketing/ PR Manager	Assisting in the development of a marketing and communications strategy and operationalising planned activities	3+ years of experience in marketing and communications. Bachelors degree in marketing, communications or general business degree and perhaps a postgraduate diploma in a specialised area such as PR
Communications Executive	Operationalising communications or a specific element, e.g. digital communications	0–2 years of experience in communications and/or a specific component. Recent graduate or studying of a degree or professional qualification on a part-time basis

5.3 Corporate Governance

In the early generations of companies, communications were often focused on IR and CG, the name given to 'the system of rules, practices and processes by which a company is directed and controlled' (Chartered Governance

Institute, 2021). This element of corporate communications has grown in importance and coverage over the past 150–200 years.

All companies should have a CG system (although not all do, and some pay lip service to the idea). Governance is necessary at a basic level because it identifies who has ownership, power and accountability and who makes decisions within the company. Traditionally, its role was to enable the board and management to ensure that the organisation had appropriate decision-making processes and controls in place so that the interests of all shareholders were balanced. Often, their progress was reported on in an 'Annual Report' – verbal and/or written – to the shareholders. The traditional cornerstone of successful IR is the provision of all available pertinent information to current and potential investors. Modern governance extends that audience to include a much wider range of internal stakeholders – managers and employees – and external stakeholders – such as suppliers, customers and advocacy groups.

Governance comprises 'the processes through which a company's objectives are set and pursued in the context of the social, regulatory and market environment' (Chartered Governance Institute, 2021). From a communications perspective, the aim is to convey corporate and PR messaging that confirms the company is run in such a way that it achieves its aims and objectives, while ensuring that all stakeholders have confidence that their trust in that company is well founded. This can be a two-way process, as a related role is to ensure there is infrastructure in place to listen to all stakeholders and collect data and information from them to continue in order to continuously improve the quality of the decisions made; ensure ethical decision-making; build a sustainable business; and enable the creation of long-term financial and other value.

Historically, governance was conducted on behalf of the shareholders (owners) of the business through the board of directors, often nominated and elected by the shareholders. The board, typically comprising 2–12 persons, was responsible and accountable for 'directing' the strategy and plans of the organisation and ensuring governance – both the formal, legal conformance of the firm, and the informal, managerial performance of the company. As Gaved (1997) pointed out, however, the reality was that the ownership of publicly listed companies is concentrated and the ten largest investors control around one-third of the company's shares. These shareholders are also those most likely to vote and their greatest influence on companies is through their direct relationships and private meetings with key members of the board. Gaved called, at the time, for directors and investors to balance the 'apparent efficiency of these relationships' with their impact on corporate performance and accountability if long-term shareholder value was to be maximised.

Desmond (2000) argued that most companies' annual reports do not actually communicate with stakeholders, choosing instead to present basic information as required by law. They suggest that companies can produce leaner annual reports that are timely, encourage dialogue, more inclusive and less burdensome, as well as creating a common language for business success.

Example of Traditional CG

Despite the existence of corporate law and CG since the inception of corporates, there have been high-profile cases where directors ignored their responsibilities, either consciously or unconsciously. These led to some of the largest corporates failing, leading to shareholder losses running to billions of dollars and large-scale redundancies (Enron, Mirror Group and the collapse of one of the World's largest auditing firms (Arthur Andersen)). In response, international trade groups and governments have developed new laws, regulations, policies and financial reporting standards.

CG is not limited to large, public companies. Private companies, whether limited or unlimited, also need it as the specialisation, professionalisation and globalisation of capital markets/private IR have led to all stakeholders becoming more systematic in their approach to capital allocation. Larger and more powerful. Investors no longer shy away from engaging executives and questioning their stewardship of the company. Journalists are emboldened to ask the PR Executive questions about ethics. Customers query the sustainability practices. In a smaller private limited company, for example, a significant investor might insist on receiving quarterly financial, performance and other communications, while other stakeholders such as employees may be entitled to the same or similar information. Camilleri (2018) has tracked how both public and private companies are increasingly disclosing material information on both financial and non-financial capitals in integrated reports in order to improve their legitimacy with institutions and stakeholders, in response to an expectation that they communicate on all aspects of their value-creating activities, business models and strategic priorities. All of these activities fall within the remit of CG and the corporate communications and PR professional.

In the fourth and fifth generations of corporate communications, governance has become associated with the wider concepts of 'governance and corporate social responsibility' (GCSR). What differentiates GCSR from normal CG is that it is aimed at a much wider group of stakeholders – not only shareholders but potential investors and other lenders; managers and employees; suppliers and distributors; end-sellers and customers; journalists and the wider public – anyone who may have a business or social interest in the organisation and what it does. Communications from the organisation must have sufficient reach or coverage – the percentage of stakeholders in the target group who have an opportunity to see or hear the communication (Bridgewater, 1987). It also has a wider remit, which can include areas of political, legal, economic, environmental, social and other areas, but its key aim remains the same – the maintenance of balance.

Frankental (2001) warns that paradoxes inherent in GCSR include procedures of CG, the market's view of organisations' ethical stances, the lack of clear definition, acceptance or denial, the lack of formal mechanisms for taking responsibility and the placing and priority that most organisations give to social responsibility; thus GCSR can legitimately be branded an invention of PR rather than a true attempt at good, social relations.

5.4 Corporate Purpose, Vision, Aims, Mission and Objectives

Wright's (1997) study of corporate communications found that few executives at that time thought corporate communication or PR people need to be involved in strategic planning or organisational decision-making. Over the intervening quarter-century that view has changed significantly. One way in which GCSR can provide good governance, as well deliver other corporate achievements, is through establishing and setting out the overall strategic aims for the organisation.

5.4.1 Purpose

At the heart of any corporation is its overall purpose – what it aims to do, or achieve, within a specified period of time. This purpose drives everything that the organisation does. From a legal perspective, the shareholder-appointed directors have primary responsibility for setting these high-level goals, but in practice, the purpose is determined equally by the directors, the management team and sometimes other employees and is influenced by the other stakeholders mentioned previously. Typically, there is a two-way flow of information about purpose, from all stakeholders to the directors/management/employee team and from the latter to the former.

5.4.2 Vision

At the core of this activity is often the foundational leader of the company or a senior team of 'strategists' who set out the purpose of an organisation in the form of a vision – a visual, verbal and aural picture of the direction in which the company should head. It is typically espoused by the Chair of the Board, or by proxy the Chief Executive Officer of the company through a variety of internal and external media managed by the Head of Communications. A study by Conte et al. (2017) suggests that CEOs are more likely to act as the corporate face and spokesperson, engage in communication concerning the dissemination and sharing of institutional values and corporate vision and play a leading role in communication activities of strategic value. CEOs tend to not delegate to communication managers but will use professionals as advisors and operators of communication. For example, the CEO may create key messages and the communications team set these out in the form of a visionary article in an in-house newsletter or a speech at a staff meeting.

5.4.3 Aims

Subsidiary, but closely related to the overall purpose, are the communications aims of the organisation as they relate to the external audiences covered by GCSR. These should, in most cases, be the same or very similar to those communicated internally, but require finessing and customisation for the audiences they are aimed at. Thus, an interview with the Chair in the business pages of a newspaper or a radio interview with the CEO would probably focus on sharing the high-level goals of the organisation with a broad audience. Advertising campaigns for the organisation and its products and services may incorporate such a vision. Oft-cited is the well-known leisure clothing company: 'Patagonia: We're in business to save our home planet' and 'TED: Spread ideas'. Visions do not always work in reverse, i.e. if it is quoted on its own, the organisation name or brand is not always obvious, e.g. which organisation has the vision: 'To accelerate the world's transition to sustainable energy'? Almost any organisation could claim that vision today (it is usually associated with Tesla). Rumelt (2011) warns against using 'fluff': Leaders often use gibberish and what he claims are 'Sunday' words to describe their vision, e.g. 'building a technology-ready platform through customer-centric inter-mediation in order to launch market-facing experience initiatives' – this creates an impression of high-level foresight and thinking, but is weak on actual strategic concepts and arguments.

5.4.4 Mission

Accompanying the vision may be a mission or mission statement – verbal or written copy that sets out the scope of what the company does now and plans to do in future. A mission statement is usually communicated in written form, but can be translated into many other message styles, ranging from posters pinned to the walls of premises such as offices or customer centres, through visual media such as television advertisements, visual materials on channels such as YouTube and website pages on the Internet (as well as intranets) to oral communications such as the Chairman's speech at the Annual General Meetings, Management Strategy Days, Staff Conferences, radio interviews, etc. All these media and channels serve to spread and share the purpose, vision, aims and the mission.

Often, the target of such communications is to get the various stakeholder groups 'on board', sharing perhaps in the construction and development of the company's purpose and thus creating loyalty. More often, the board of directors take the lead. A content-analysis study by Clarke (1997) indicated that there are both similarities and differences between investment company chairmen's statements based on their financial results and their mission objectives. For example, Chairperson statements from firms with negative results try to divert attention away from the company and its directors by referring to the environment, target markets and emotive words, rather than company action and performance indicators. Risk and security were the pre-occupation of chairmen's communications with their shareholders in companies whose mission objectives were either capital income or both. Clarke recommended that if corporates intend to attract individual shareholder through the annual report, consideration of the communications content and its interpretation is likely to improve this medium of information exchange.

5.4.5 Objectives

Objectives, by comparison, are the specific, measurable, time-bound goals and related measures that are used to plan and control the direction of the organisation. While these might be shared, at a high level with the shareholders, directors and managers, they are often simplified or summarised when communicated to other stakeholder groups (internal groups such as staff; external groups such as intermediaries).

There is often an element of secrecy surrounding objectives as to an extent they may help competitors and others to discern the strategy of the organisation. Some communications experts suggest that objectives can be viewed in terms of the desired communications outcomes for the organisation and that the achievement of them can be seen as a measure of success and acknowledgement – expressing thanks for contributions to delivering and achieving the vision and mission.

5.5 Organisational Structure, Culture and Management Systems

5.5.1 Structure

While companies legally differentiate between owners and operators this distinction is mostly found in public and larger private companies. Small and medium-sized enterprises and some larger organisations often have overlaps between the two – with significant shareholders acting as both directors and managers in the company. This is where the integration of structure and culture becomes important.

An organisational structure is a system that outlines how activities are directed in order to achieve the vision, mission and objectives of an organisation. These activities can include rules and responsibilities that enable individuals to differentiate between their ownership and management roles, while also remaining efficient and focused. Put simply, the organisation's design and structure enable work flows through an organisation and allows individuals and groups to work together within their functions to manage tasks.

Traditionally organisational structures were formalised, typically with employees grouped by function (such as finance or operations), region or product line. Less traditional structures have emerged over time and tend to be more loosely woven. Modern organisation structures are flexible and agile, possessing the ability to respond quickly to changing business environments; and often virtual, allowing the company to embody a fluid, free-forming and entrepreneurial approach among all members.

5.5.2 Culture

Supporting the legal and organisational structure is an organisation's corporate culture which Capriotti (1999, pp. 24–25) defined as 'the set of beliefs, values and behaviour patterns, shared and unwritten, by which the members of an organisation are governed, and that is reflected in their behaviours'. Each stakeholder assigns a meaning to the institution according to his or her experience and gives makes it relevant to his or her own daily life. Shared beliefs are described as 'invisible structures, unconscious and assumed as pre-established'. Values are the principles of the members 'in their daily relationship within it' and have a 'higher degree of visibility … but are not clear or obvious'. Behaviours are visible and observable in a wide group of members of the organisation and 'express its beliefs and values'.

Examples of how culture, with its beliefs, values and behaviours, and corporate communications can interplay can be found in the areas of 'stewardship' and 'sustainability' within GCSR. Directors and senior managers have both a legal and a leadership role and responsibility in ensuring their organisation's is socially responsible: This goes beyond green-washing statements of intent (stated beliefs) to ensure that the organisation's roots, founder's and owners wishes and long-term obligations for stakeholders (values) of the future are aligned with its strategy and corporate marketing approach (behaviours).

Organisational culture can come in conflict with other cultures and this has particular resonance for corporate communications. If, for example, a company that is headquartered in a European Union country such as Germany, and traditionally serves markets and countries within the EU, makes a move into another region, such as Africa and country such as Ethiopia, it will need to manage the cultural transition carefully. Its corporate culture, honed on traditional European beliefs, values and behaviours, will come into contact with sets of social, religious, technical and other dimensions which are very different. In such cases, employment of 'local' communications professionals already embedded in Ethiopian culture would prove useful when 'translating' communications messaging for that country's audiences.

5.5.3 Management Systems

Management systems, in the context of corporate communications, are the policies and procedures that are built onto the structure and culture and which enable the implementation feasible and valid activities that reflect them. These are usually 'operational' processes that help directors and managers to translate organisational design and culture into meaningful communication for the company's various audiences.

5.6 Corporate Identities and Brands

5.6.1 Corporate Identities

The mix of governance, mission, purpose, objectives, structure, culture and management systems means that corporates can be seen as having a tangible essence and distinctiveness that are expressed in a combination of corporate characteristics/traits. Balmer (2017) suggests that in establishing and managing corporate identity managers need to be able address questions of considerable consequence including – but not limited to – the following: 'What is the entity legally allowed or obliged to do, or how is it constrained in what it can do?'; 'For whom – and for whose benefit – is the organisation primarily acting in legal, realistic and pragmatic terms?' 'What is the organisation's purpose?'; 'What is the firm's business?'; 'What are the institution's distinguishing and differentiating traits?'; 'What value does the organisation accord to customers and other key stakeholders?'; 'What is the nature of the mutual profitability of the company –customer/stakeholder relationship?'; 'What is our corporate image and reputation among customers, employees, shareholders and other key stakeholder groups?'; 'What do we communicate and to whom apropos corporate communications?'; 'What changes in the competitive and business environment should the organisation be mindful of?' Balmer points out that corporate identities are never entirely 'fixed'. They are in a constant state of internal or external flux that changes their identity traits and corporate marketing activities.

5.6.2 Organisations, Their Publics and Their Stakeholders

Earlier, when discussing the unique nature of the corporate organisation and CG, we focused primarily on the core of the business – that part fixed within the organisation's boundary and including owners, directors and managerial/operative employees. Koch et al. (2019) state that involvement of employees in a company's GCSR programme is one of the key factors for its success, provided the management team is aware of their expected benefits. This core group of people does not work in isolation, and as GCSR has gained in popularity corporations have become cognisant of the need to better communicate with other participants in the organisation's value chain. These usually include inter-alia, suppliers, inbound and outbound intermediaries such as transport companies, customers, advisers, etc. They may be extended to other interested parties, including potential joint-venture partners and even competitors. Each and all of these represent 'publics' or groups of people the company will wish to communicate with (sometimes one-way, other times both ways).

It can be useful to categorise communications and internal audiences in a number of ways.

- Internal versus external, e.g. who are the members, managers and employees of the organisation over whom there is direct management and control versus other stakeholders whom we can, at best, influence from a distance.
- Downward versus upward versus diagonal, e.g. which members (or wider stakeholders) hold positions, roles and responsibilities at the top of the organisation (directors and managers, for example) and who desire to communicate in a downwards direction versus those whose positions, roles and responsibilities are lower in the organisation and who desire to communicate in an upwards direction versus who desires to communicate across the organisation (there can be considerable overlap between them all).
- Formal versus informal, e.g. formal communications such as emails, reports, etc., versus informal communications such as the grapevine, the water cooler, gossip, etc.
- Structured versus networked, i.e. the extent and direction of communications.

From an external perspective, communications and PR activities include 'publicity, corporate advertising, seminars, publications, lobbying and charitable donations' (Jobber & Fahy, 2009, p. 232). These often involve a mix of the factors mentioned above and contribute to what is called corporate identity.

5.6.3 Brand Values, Branding and Rebranding

For each of a corporate's audiences, the company may be presented in a different way and perceived through a different perspective. Shareholders, for example, will view the firm as a legal and financial entity; customers and clients will view it through a series of products and services; while other stakeholders will view it primarily through their brand or brands. 'Branding is the process by which companies distinguish their product [and other] offerings from competition' (Jobber & Fahy, 2009, p. 135). As the commonalities between legal entities and products/services become less differentiable, brands permit corporates to distinguish those entities and products by developing associations that affect audiences' perceptions and ease the communications between the organisation and members of those groups.

The World's Largest Brands

One of the World's largest companies – part of the so-called Trillion-Dollar Club – is Alphabet. This company is better known by its main brand (Google). Research group Kantar BrandZ ranks companies based on their 'brand value', each year. This differs from market capitalisation and is based on the brand's total financial value (contribution it brings to its parent company), the brands proportional impact on its parent company's sales and quantitative survey data, sourced from over 170,000 global consumers. The end result of Kantar's study is a holistic review of a company's brand equity, reputation and ability to generate value.

Many companies with high market capitalisation also have high brand values. One notable exception to this general rule, amongst the top group, is Saudi Aramco – despite being one of the world's largest corporates – it does not appear on Kantar BrandZ's top 100 as it mainly sells its product to other energy companies (Exxon, Shell, Texaco, etc.) who have retail brands. Another is Tesla, which was ranked 6th by market capitalisation in 2021, is ranked 47th by brand value as in branding terms it is a relatively 'new' brand.

Among the trends noted in Kantar BrandZ's (2021) report are that the biggest brands keep outgrowing the smaller ones, and companies which invest in marketing and research and development are also among those with the highest values and growth rates (Kantar Brand, 2021).

Creating a distinct corporate identity, brand and corporate personality has potential benefits. It can:

- Fix the company (or its products/services) in a location in the consumer's mind (some have been so successful that the brand name has capitulated the generic word, e.g. Biro).
- Communicate or develop the organisation's heritage (e.g. a well-known Champagne house).
- Add value to the company and its products (representing core beliefs or characteristics).
- Add financial value (strong brands drive higher growth rates, product values, share prices and acquisition values).
- Have positive effects on customer perceptions, preferences and purchasing habits.

- Function as a barrier to competition.
- Support advertising through below-the-line promotion of the entity.
- Build communities of customers, potential customers and other interested parties.

Its importance can be seen among corporates which have been involved in mergers and acquisitions – where there have traditionally been high failure rates, in part attributable to the undue attention that is given to short-term financial and legal issues to the detriment of long-term identity and communication issues, inadequate recognition of the impact of leadership issues on identity and communication and failure to secure the goodwill of a wide range of stakeholder groups common to both companies (Balmer & Dinnie, 1999).

Corporate branding can be seen as a process by which companies distinguish their product and service offerings from competitors. It permits customers to develop a short-cut association between the values of the organisation (e.g. quality versus economy) and the products or services they consume (purchase, own and/or use). This is not just a case of communicating the values alongside the product/service, but of building a distinct perception of the company and all its related assets which can be used to position the company, what it does and what it makes in its marketplaces. This perception is often based on the heritage of the company or brand – its history, legacy, background, context and culture, e.g. Ferrari sports cars. Indeed, brands with strong heritage can give rise to sub-brands or brand extensions, e.g. Dove Soap and Deodorant. The brand's perception can equally be built around other elements, e.g. its:

- Core meaning, e.g. the brand LEGO is derived from 'play-well' in the company's home country.
- Traditional place in the market (the brand domain), e.g. Audi is perceived as more upmarket than other brands manufactured by the same company, VAG (which includes other brands such as Volkswagen, SEAT, Skoda). This can be referred to a physical place, e.g. the use of nation in the word 'British' in British Airways.
- Characteristics or descriptions, e.g. The Body Shop or Vodafone Mobile.
- Value associations, i.e. the core characteristics of the brand such as upmarket or economical, e.g. Rolls Royce versus Hyundai.
- Personality, i.e. its similarity to other things that share similar characteristics, e.g. Tony the Tiger for Kellogg's Frosties. The personality can be achieved through celebrity endorsement or sponsorship, e.g. sports clothing and leading Premiership footballers. Some products reflect the identity of the customers who buy and use them.
- Complimentary assets, i.e. the presence or absence of other, like assets or brands, e.g. the Apple suite of products.

Corporates have options about the extent and depth to which they pursue a brand strategy:

- For larger companies, a family or umbrella brand strategy is usually pursued, whereby the same brand is used for all products and services, e.g. Ford, Google and Heinz. Often a shortened version of the company's legal name is used – one that is easy to pronounce and memorable such as Shell. This strategy is particularly suited to companies that have a large product portfolio. The goodwill attached to the company is extended as brand equity to its tangible products and intangible services and continuously enhanced through positive, supportive communication – above-the-line advertising and sponsorship. The main benefit, from a communications perspective, is coherence, but that is also its potentially biggest risk – if a specific product or service receives unfavourable publicity, the whole family of products and services, and the organisation itself, will be tarnished. Most of the world's most valuable brands share their name with their corporate owners, e.g. Microsoft and Coca-Cola.
- A strategy of applying individual brand names to a specific product or group of products is used where it is believed that each needs a unique and different identity, often completely separable from the company itself, e.g. Procter & Gamble uses its corporate name minimally and for IR/governance, and promotes unique identities for its Pampers and Head & Shoulder brands. A positive with this approach is that individual and distinctive brands can be independently promoted and effectively have their own, mini-corporate identity and marketing/communications strategy. Such an identity is often associated with the key benefits of the product or service, e.g. Right Guard deodorant.
- A mix of family and individual branding (so-called combination branding) can be used, e.g. Kellogg's Frosties. This makes use of the positives of both company and product/service brand name, but can be confusing to customers.
- Some companies prefer or are compelled by their place in the value chain, to allow their company or brand name give precedence to other, stronger or more customer-facing organisations or brands in the value chain. This is most acutely seen in food marketing, where manufacturers may produce branded products but also manufacture own-label brands for a distributor or retailer (own-label brands) such as Aldi or Lidl. In most developed economies, growth in own-label brands outstrips growth in manufacturer brands.
- Brand stretching is less used as a strategy but can be very valuable and is used where a company with strong brand equity extends the brand name to unrelated products or markets, e.g. Virgin which was originally a music producer but now runs everything from trains to space tourism.

- Co-branding combines two brands, either physically or in terms of communications. The former is where two brands are physically combined into a new, single product or service, e.g. Guinness used as an ingredient in a sauce product.
- Rebranding involves the replacement of one or several, brands with a new brand.

Rebranding

Another of the World's largest companies – previously best known as Facebook but including other organisational brands such as WhatsApp – combined in 2021 to form Meta. This rebranding reflects the culmination of ownership, organisational structure and cultural changes internally and a response to what the company claims is 'a change in the metaverse – the next evolution of social connection – [the] company's vision is to help bring the metaverse to life' (Meta, 2021) as well as reputational damage affecting the company in the years prior to this. The rebranding covered what the company considered to be what it is, what it builds, what its actions are, who its community is and its resources. Initially, the rebranding was superficial, adding a new visual logo to the existing product and service representations of the company, but the rebrand is also part of a more extensive reconfiguration of all aspects of the brand.

5.6.4 Corporate Logos, Straplines and Messaging

A brand name is not, in and of itself, of value. To make it whole and attribute value to it, the brand must be capable of being captured by all the senses through the continuous projection of a corporate identity. Bridgewater (1987) described corporate identity as the 'house-style' – 'elements of design by which a company ... establishes a consistent and recognisable identity through communication, promotion and distribution material'.

- In a visual sense, an organisation or a brand can be distinguished by the way in which the brand name is written (design, composition, format, typeface, size, colour, etc.), a visual image (an outline shape of the organisation's main product, for example) or a symbolic logo (a stylised shape or form of word(s) or letter(s) such as Exxon's tiger or the Dulux dog, etc.). Visual branding can extend to images such as photographs, sketches, cartoons, advertising copy, etc. – anything that can provide a focal point that represents the organisation. Graphic design is based on two- and three-dimensional processes such as illustration, typology, photography and printing/video production, collect-ively aimed at creating and distributing suitable images to support the vision.

- The organisation and brand must also be identifiable in an oral and aural sense, e.g. by the way in which the organisation or brand name is pro-nounced (e.g. the company and brand names of IKEA and Lidl are said differently in distinct locations) or through a recognisable sound (e.g. the unique sounds your laptop computer or smartphone makes on startup). For oral/aural audiences, 'slogans' can highlight an important feature of the organisation's image or product (e.g. Nike's 'Just Do It' or BMW's 'The Ultimate Driving Machine'). Often, a slogan is accompanied by singing and/or music, making a 'jingle' – a catchy tune that acts as a reminder of the words. 'Gags' (short lines of company information that accompany visuals), 'Anecdotes' and 'Vignettes' in the form of written or spoken advertising copy can deepen and broaden the messages around slogans. If imagery can be viewed as the visual content that supports the vision as a whole, then the combined oral and aural content can be heard as messaging that supports the mission.
- For some brands, the messaging extends beyond sight and sound to other senses. Touch adds the third dimension to graphic design (think about how a specific brand of smartphone feels in the hand when compared to another). Touch can be communicated through elements such as embossing, engraving or etching of a logo on a product, quality and bulk of paper or packaging used to protect and promote the product, die-cutting of product and packaging shapes, quality of binding of key publications such as the annual report or service manual, etc. Think of your favourite perfume or after-shave and how it is presented to you. These elements support the overall identity.
- For completeness, we have to include taste and smell. Does a McDonalds burger taste different to Burger Kings? Do certain retail outlets have a particular smell that you associate with them? All of these sensual cues can be applied to the tangible assets of the organisation (its buildings, vehicles, products, etc.) and in some cases its intangible ones (symbols, images, relationships, etc.). Taken collectively they can represent the 'personality' of the organisation.

5.7 For Discussion – Topics for Learners to Consider

- Think about the organisation where you work or one for which you are a customer.
- What is its legal format, e.g. is it a public or private limited company?
- What is its overall aim or purpose?
- What communications objectives does it have?
- How is the aim or purpose communicated to its various publics?
- Is the aim or purpose of the organisation communicated clearly?

- What role does a brand or brands have in achieving the communications aims of the company?
- How does the growth in the quantity of information, driven by the growth in social media and virtual networks, need to be managed?

Case Study & Exercise

Fuego Heat Pumps Ltd.

Fuego Pumps is a Spanish, private limited company which is 55% owned by members of the Alvarez family. The company traditionally manufactured gas boilers for use in residential, central heating systems. Since it was established in the early 1990s, the company grew from selling its products in its home market to marketing its products across 16 European Union countries. The company had an annual turnover of circa €40 million and net profits of €1.7 million last year. Revenue comes mainly from the manufacture, marketing and distribution of approximately 80,000 gas boilers per annum. The company has three products, the Fuego I, Fuego II and Fuego III.

New CEO

The company's board of directors, chaired by Carlos Alvarez, recently appointed its first, non-family member as its new Chief Executive Officer. Since joining the CEO, Marta Moreno has pushed the management team in the company to share their action plans for how their business models should support a net-zero economy by 2050. This year the Design and Production departments joined forces to develop a prototype heat pump – with the project title of 'Fuego IV' – which is aimed at being the company's first sustainable product.

The Fuego IV

The Fuego IV offers an energy-efficient alternative to gas boilers, furnaces and air conditioners for all the company's markets. Like a refrigerator, heat pumps use electricity to transfer heat from a cool space to a warm space, making an already cool space cooler, or an already warm space warmer. During the heating season, the Fuego IV moves relative heat from the outdoors into a warm house, and in the cooling season, heat pumps move heat from a house into the outdoors. Because they transfer heat rather than generate it, heat pumps can efficiently provide comfortable temperatures for your home. The Fuego IV is a Ducted Air-Source Heat Pump that uses a new technology patented by the company and utilises new materials for manufacturing. Combining these into the new product will enable customers to reduce their electricity use for heating by approximately 65% compared to a sector average for heat pumps of 50%. While the Fuego IV has a unique selling point, the cost of developing the product from prototype to production stage will involve an investment of €8.2 million. The company plans to fund its development through the issue of additional share capital to existing shareholders.

Corporate Communications

As the Head of Corporate Communications, the new CEO has tasked you to develop a suitable communications and PR strategy for the new product.

Exercise

- Identify the key target audiences for communications and PR for Fuego Pumps Ltd.
- Develop an outline, three-year, plan for IR/CG.
- Decide on a suitable identity (brand name, logo, etc.) for the new product.
- Suggest how the company can use social media to portray the beginning of its move to manufacturing and distributing more sustainable products over the next three years.

References

Balmer, John M.T. (2008). Identity based views of the corporation. *European Journal of Marketing*, 42, 879–906. 10.1108/03090560810891055

Balmer, J. M. T. (2017). The corporate identity, total corporate communications, stakeholders' attributed identities, identifications and behaviours continuum. *European Journal of Marketing; Bradford* 51, no. 9/10, 1472–1502.

Balmer, J. M. T. and Dinnie, K. (1999). Corporate identity and corporate communications: The antidote to merger madness. *Corporate Communications; Bradford* 4, no. 4, 182–192.

Bridgewater, P. (1987). *An Introduction to Graphic Design*. Quintet Publishing Limited.

Cacciatore, M. A., Meng, J., & Berger, B. K. (2017). Information flow and communication practice challenges. *Corporate Communications: An International Journal*, 22, 292–307. 10.1108/ccij-09-2016-0063

Camilleri, M. A. (2018). Theoretical insights on integrated reporting: The inclusion of non-financial capitals in corporate disclosures, Camilleri, Mark Anthony. *Corporate Communications; Bradford* 23, no. 4, 567–581.

Capriotti, P. (1999). "Comunicación corporativa: Una estrategia de éxito a corto plazo", in Reporte C&D–Capacitación y Desarrollo, 13, in Apolo, D., Báez, V,

Pauker, L, and Pasquel G (2017): "Corporate communication management: Considerations for the approach to its study and practice". *Revista Latina de Comunicación Social*, 72: 521–539.

Chartered Governance Institute. (2021). What is corporate governance? [online]. Available at https://www.cgi.org.uk/about-us/policy/what-is-corporate-governance. Accessed 21-09-2021.

Clarke, G. (1997). Messages from CEOs: A content analysis approach. *Corporate Communications; Bradford* 2, no. 1, 31–39.

Companies Market Cap. (2021). Largest companies by market cap [online]. available at https://companiesmarketcap.com/. Accessed 26-10-2021.

Conte, F., Siano, A., and Vollero, A. (2017). CEO communication: Engagement, longevity and founder centrality. *Corporate Communications; Bradford* 22, no. 3, 273–291.

Corporate Communications; Bradford Vol. 1, Iss. 1, (1996).

Desmond, P. (2000). Reputation builds success – tomorrow's annual report. *Corporate Communications; Bradford* 5, no. 3, 168–173.

Earl, S. and Waddington, S. (2018). 'Who'll win in the twenty-first century: The corporations or the brand vandals' in Langham, T. (2018), Reputation management: The future of corporate communications and public relations. *Emerald Publishing Ltd./ProQuest Ebook Central*, 234.

Family Capital. (2021). The World's top 750 biggest family businesses. [online] available at https://www.famcap.com/the-worlds-750-biggest-family-businesses/. Accessed 26-10-2021.

Frankental, P. (2001). Corporate social responsibility – a PR invention? *Corporate Communications; Bradford* 6, no. 1, 18–23.

Gaved, M. (1997). Corporate governance: The challenge for communications practitioners. *Corporate Communications; Bradford* 2, no. 2, 87–91.

Investopedia. (2021). The World's most valuate private companies. [online] Available at: https://www.investopedia.com/financial-edge/1112/the-worlds-most-valuable-private-companies.aspx. Accessed 26-10-2021.

Jobber, D. and Fahy, J. (2009). *Foundations of Marketing*, 3rd Ed. McGraw Hill Higher Education.

Kantar Brand, Z. (2021). Top 100 most valuable global brands. [online] Available at: https://www.kantar.com/campaigns/brandz/global. Accessed 27-10-2021.

Kitchen, P. J. (1997). Was public relations a prelude to corporate communications? *Corporate Communications; Bradford* 2, no. 1, 22–30.

Koch, C., Bekmeier-Feuerhahn, S., Bögel, P. M., and Adam, U. (2019). Employees' perceived benefits from participating in CSR activities and implications for increasing employees engagement in CSR. *Corporate Communications; Bradford* 24, no. 2, 303–317.

Meta. (2021). Connection is evolving and so are we. [Online] Available at https://about.facebook.com/. Accessed 28 October 2021.

Oliver, S. and Riley, D. (1996). Perceptions and practice of corporate communication in small businesses. *Corporate Communications; Bradford* 1, no. 2, 12–18.

Rumelt, R. (2011). *Good Strategy, Bad Strategy – The difference, and Why It Matters*. Profile Books: London.

Schmidt, K. (1997). Corporate identity: An evolving discipline. *Corporate Communications; Bradford* 2, no. 1, 40–45.

Van Riel, C. B. M. (1995). *Principles of Corporate Communications*. Prentice-Hall International: Englewood Cliffs, NJ.

Wright, Donald K. (1997). Perceptions of corporate communication as public relations. *Corporate Communications: An International Journal*, 2, 143–154. 10.1108/eb046545

6   Sustainable Public Relations

Chapter Contents

6.1 Learning Outcomes

On finishing this chapter, the reader should have an understanding of:

- The evolution of Corporate Social Responsibility (CSR).
- The theory of CSR.
- The role of CSR in modern busines and how it works together with PR.

DOI: 10.4324/9781003253815-6

6.2 Introduction – What Is Corporate Social Responsibility?

The European Commission defines corporate social responsibility (CSR) as *'the responsibility of enterprises for their impacts on society'*. CSR can be explained simply as the responsibility that businesses have for the environment and communities in which they operate. Over the years, there has been much debate about this role and if businesses in fact have any responsibility other than to increase revenues. For example, in 1970, Friedman stated that *'the social responsibility of business is to increase profits'*. Supporters of Friedman's theory may argue that if a business is making money, they are contributing to society through the creation of jobs and the contribution to taxes. However, this argument has grown weaker in modern times as world events have caused distrust and the climate crisis has caused consumers to demand that companies take responsibility for the environment and the societies in which they function.

In most countries throughout the world, CSR is not mandatory and the approach to and the reasons for engaging in CSR vary greatly between the developed and the developing worlds.

In the developed world, CSR can play more of a strategic role to mitigate against the impact the business has on communities, workforce and the environment. In Nigeria for example, large corporations in the extractive industries, such as Shell have wreaked considerable damage on the environment through their operations. These CSR programmes support education and the local economies and can bring great economic benefit and reduce poverty as a result. Like many countries however in Nigeria, CSR is not mandatory. In recent years, a proposed CSR Commission stated that it should be made mandatory for companies operating in Nigeria in order *to provide reliefs to host communities for the physical, material, environmental or other forms of degradation suffered as a result of the activities of companies and organisations operating in these communities'* (Mordia, Chima).

By contrast, companies operating in India are required to spend 2% of net profit on CSR. However, there have been concerns raised about this approach by some, including Azim Premji who stated: *'My worry is the stipulation should not become a tax at a later stage … Spending 2% on CSR is a lot, especially for companies that are trying to scale up in these difficult times. It must not be imposed'* (The Guardian).

In Europe, CSR is also not mandatory for companies. However, the European Commission stipulates that enterprises *'should have in place a process to integrate social, environmental, ethical, human rights and consumer concerns into their business operations and core strategy in close collaboration with their stakeholders, with the aim of maximising the creation of shared value for their owners/shareholders, other stakeholders and society at large, and identifying, preventing and mitigating their possible adverse impacts'* (European Commission, n.d.).

In areas such as Africa, Latin America and Asia, corruption and lack of regulation from governments enables businesses often to set their own rules and effectively self-govern. CSR programmes can therefore be disengaged with local communities and fail to deliver the social and environmental benefits promised.

For CSR to be truly effective, regulation is required to ensure the CSR activity meets the societal and environmental demands and that local communities fairly benefit from the economic benefits. However, as identified by Hilson (2012), *'the drive to regulate and enforce regulations is lacking'*.

In a recent Nielsen report on global sustainable shopping, it found that 81% of global respondents feel strongly that companies should help improve the environment (Nielsen, 2018, p. 5). In countries where the effects of climate change are being felt more strongly than others, its consumers are placing greater demands on its businesses to be more environmentally responsible. Businesses are responding to these demands by implementing sustainable strategies for example to reduce waste, to eliminate plastic or to diversify their product ranges and these new strategies need to be communicated to generate sales and improve reputations through marketing and public relations (PR).

The good news is that businesses are communicating to a receptive audience. In 2022, the Edelman Trust Barometer revealed that businesses were the most trusted institutions in the world, with 61% of global respondents citing businesses as their most trusted institution, ahead of media, NGOs and governments. In the Report, it found that fake news and disinformation had contributed to a default felling of distrust in society. The Report concludes that there is an onus on companies to act responsibly and to present clear, consistent and fact-based information to break the cycle of mistrust in the world (Edelman, 2022).

CSR addresses the ethical requirement of businesses to act responsibly and to demonstrate good corporate citizenship and therefore enables them to build trust and improve their reputations. It also helps the business to make a profit as it is meeting the needs of its consumers. One of PR's core objectives is to protect and develop the reputation of the company. The development of the CSR programme for an organisation therefore should be a core function of the PR department's. The PR department is also responsible for the communication of the CSR activity and its results to the organistion's publics.

In tandem with the consumer and investment demand for businesses to act responsibly, at a governance level, there is an obligation on businesses to work in partnership with governments throughout the world to drive sustainable practices that will reduce inequality and protect the environment. In 2015, all member states of the United Nations adopted the 2030 Agenda for Sustainable Development. The Agenda sets out 17 Sustainable Development Goals (SDGs) to *'improve health and education, reduce inequality and spur economic growth – all while tackling climate change and working to preserve our oceans and forests'* (UN, n.d.).

The requirement therefore for businesses to act ethically and responsibly is two-fold. To make a profit or increase revenues and to demonstrate values that will appeal to investors and consumers. Secondly, to protect and improve their reputations, organisations should have a CSR strategy that they can communicate widely to the public who demand it, through their marketing and PR channels.

6.3 Theory of CSR

Corporate Social Responsibility or CSR has risen steadily in prominence amongst the world's corporations since the 1980s. In recent years, it has become a necessity rather than a luxury for organisations to proactively and visibly engage in CSR programmes due to the critical acute threat posed to the environment.

The debate around CSR is focused on the responsibilities of businesses and what they actually are. Is a business accountable to the society in which it operates or is it merely responsible for its profits and shareholders?

In 1979 Milton Friedman argued that the only responsibility that companies had was to deliver a profit to their shareholders (Friedman, 1979). Other theorists have identified the functions of CSR as assisting a company in its objectives to manage its reputation, protect human capital assets, respond to consumer demands and avoid regulation. However, it has been argued that these are standard functions of a business and CSR could therefore be more cynically classed as merely PR activity that supports the business in achieving its objectives (Hilson, 2012).

Utting would appear to support this view and uses the term 'greenwashing' to describe the practice of using CSR as a public-facing tool to project a certain image of the company rather than real practical and tangible activity that initiates change. Utting stated: *'CSR allows ample scope for "free-riding" (whereby economic agents benefit from a particular initiative without bearing the costs) and "greenwash" i.e. the ability of companies, through PR and minimal adjustments to policy and practice, to project an image of reform while changing little, if anything, in terms of actual corporate performance. The capacity of big business to modify its discourse is often considerably greater than its capacity to improve its social and environmental impacts. Many instances have been documented of companies saying one thing and doing another, or adopting but not effectively implementing environmental policies or codes of conduct. Hence corporate responsibility policy and practice is often characterized by piecemeal and fragmented reforms and window dressing'* (Utting, 2005).

One of the best-known and widely used models for creating CSR programmes is Carroll's CSR Pyramid, which was originally published in 1979.

In Carroll's model, he identifies four categories of responsibilities that businesses have to society with the most important, as perceived by the business executives who participated in the study, at the bottom of the pyramid. The four categories of responsibilities in order of importance and as depicted in the figure are economic, legal, ethical and philanthropic.

6.3.1 Economic Responsibilities

Carroll argues that businesses have a basic requirement to sustain themselves by being able to operate effectively, to make a profit and to inspire confidence from investors and shareholders. This is a responsibility to society because society requires businesses to produce and sell the products and services it requires. Businesses also create employment making a valuable contribution to the economies in the communities in which they operate.

6.3.2 Legal Responsibilities

There is an expectation on businesses to operate in a particular way and comply with a set of laws and regulations. Carroll states that these regulations ensure that businesses perform in a *'manner consistent with expectations of government and law'*, that they comply with *'various federal, state and local regulations'*, that they *'conduct themselves as law-abiding corporate citizens'*, that they fulfil *'all their legal obligations to societal stakeholders'* and *'provide goods and services that at least meet minimal legal requirements'*.

6.3.3 Ethical Responsibilities

Businesses are required to act in an ethical manner. This means that in addition to the legal requirements that they will adhere to certain standards and norms that are expected by society, such as integrity, acting in a fair and objective manner and respecting the spirit of the laws and regulations and not just the laws themselves. Ethical responsibilities come down to morals and are based on the principles of moral philosophy: Deontology, Utilitarianism, Contractarianism and Aristotelianism. Deontologists believe that there are universally recognised rules about what is right and what is wrong and it is these values that guide businesses in their behaviour. Utilitarianists believe that actions are governed by perceived consequences.

6.3.4 Philanthropic Responsibilities

Philanthropic responsibility refers to the businesses own aims to improve the society and environment in which it operates. Businesses will often donate to not-for-profit organisations that are in synergy with their own business or to a completely unrelated charity altogether. Often, organisations will create their own charitable organisation or foundation.

6.4 Types of CSR

Carroll's theory forms the basis for most modern CSR models used by businesses. CSR generally comes in one or all of the following four categories: environmental, philanthopic, ethical and economic (Stobierski, 2021).

6.4.1 Environmental CSR

Environmental CSR strategies ensure that the company behaves in an environmentally friendly way, such as reducing harmful practices, regulating energy consumption or offsetting a negative environmental impact. For exampe, a restuarant chain could be committed to reducing the use of single use plastics in its eateries (reducing harmful practices); a large organisation responsible for data centres could make an effort to power these centres using renewable energy (regulating energy consumption) or a large multi-national fossil fuel organisation could invest in local infrastructure and education in the community it opperaties to offset the damage it is doing to the environment (offsetting a negative environmental impact).

6.4.2 Ethical CSR

Ethical CSR is concerned with ensuring that the organisation acts in an ethical way as is outlined in Chapter 3 in this book (Ethics). Organisations practicing ethical responsibility aim to ensure that all groups involved in the organisation are treated fairly, for example, employees, customers, suppliers and investors. Businesses concerned with ethical responsiblity might for example place a strong emphasis on the work-life balance of employees or maybe offer particular benefits for minority groups. For example, in 2022, the Bank of Ireland announced paid 'menopause leave' for female employees experiencing menopause symptoms. On its website, the bank stated: '*as an employer we are committed to building a more supportive and inclusive culture within the Bank. We want to help our colleagues at all stages of their lives including the menopause. This new policy and training have been introduced as important supports for our colleagues who are going through the menopause. This will help us continue to build a work environment in which everyone is treated with fairness, dignity and respect. "The menopause supports policy is one of a series of progressive policy improvements we are implementing at Bank of Ireland. It follows the recent launch of our enhanced paternity leave policy, the domestic abuse support policy as well as fertility leave and supports. We will continue to explore ways that we can improve at the experience and wellbeing for all of our Bank of Ireland colleagues."* Bank of Ireland colleagues in need of support can contact people managers directly on a confidential basis, and can also avail of the support provided by Here for You 24/7, the Bank of Ireland Group's Employee Assistance Programme (Bank of Ireland, 2022).

6.4.3 Philanthropic CSR

Businesses concentrated on philanthropic CSR are concerned with making the world a better place. Often this means that they might donate to a not-for-profit or a charity of some description. In some cases they may even set up their own foundation. For example, the Vodafone Foundation stipulates on its website, that 'by investing in the betterment of communities in which Vodafone operates, focusing on the challenges where we believe Vodafone's technology can make a difference, we aim to improve 480 million lives by 2025.' (Vodafone, n.d.)

The United Bank of Africa (UBA) also set up a foundation that supported students in education in Africa. Both of these are forms of philanthropic CSR.

6.4.4 *Economic CSR*

Economic responsibility means that business will invest in areas that will assist it in achieving its CSR goals. It will ensure that its finances impact positively on the environment, its employees and the society in which it operates.

6.5 From CSR to ESG

In recent times, with climate concerns being at the forefront of consumers' minds and motivations, businesses have had to respond appropriately to keep their shareholders and consumers happy and meet their ethical and legal obligations.

UN member states have committed to the achievement of the United Nations' Sustainable Development Goals and require the assistance of businesses, institutions and organisations to achieve these objectives. This commitment from businesses has been incorporated into new business terminology – Environmental Social Governance (ESG). ESG can be defined as a set of standards which determine an organisation's ethical behaviour.

An ESG strategy has become an important requirement for individuals seeking to invest in an organisation. Reptrak, the global reputations organisation has recognised this in its annual listing of companies based on their reputation. On its website, Reptrak states *'ESG has a lasting impact on reputation and business outcomes'* (Reptrak, n.d.). As we have seen, consumers are actively seeking out empathetic brands and brands that have an environmental conscience. Investors are looking for brands with a strong ESG strategy to invest in.

6.6 Conclusion

CSR plays a significant role in modern day organisations with environmental CSR in particular being high on consumers' agendas. From a communications and PR point of view, CSR has many benefits for an organisation. First and foremost, a company's CSR activity contributes to its reputation, which helps to retain and attract staff and keep customers, shareholders and all stakeholders happy. The PR function serves to both help develop a CSR strategy and communicate the activity to the organisation's publics. The ultimate result of CSR activity is a positive impact on reputation and revenues.

6.7 For Discussion

- Explain the CSR strategy of a company you are familiar with.
- What type of CSR do they engage in?
- Do you think this is genuine CSR or greenwashing?
- What impact do you think the activity has on the organisation's reputation?
- What value does this activity bring to the organisation?

References

Bank of Ireland, 2022. http://www.bankofireland.com/about-bank-of-ireland/press-releases/2022/bank-of-ireland-introduces-paid-menopause-leave/

Edelman. https://www.edelman.com/trust/2022-trust-barometer

European Commission. https://ec.europa.eu/commission/presscorner/detail/en/MEMO_11_730

Friedman, M. (1979). The social responsibility is to increase its profits. New York Times.

Hilson, G. (2012). *Corporate Social Responsibility in the Extractive Industries: Experiences from Developing Countries*. Resources Policy.

Nielsen. https://www.nielsen.com/wp-content/uploads/sites/3/2019/04/global-sustainable-shoppers-report-2018.pdf

Reptrak. https://www.reptrak.com/serving-up-sustainability-acqua-minerale-san-benedetto/

United Nations. https://sdgs.un.org/

Utting, P. (2005). Corporate responsibility and the movement of business. *Development in Practice* 15, no. 3–4, 375–388.

7 Crisis Communications

Chapter Contents

7.1 Learning Outcomes

This chapter sets out to introduce crisis communications and explain the difference between the terms crisis management and crisis communications. The chapter offers an analysis of the theory that underpins crisis communications and a discussion on the types of crises that organisations worldwide experience. A formula for devising a crisis communications plan is provided along with

DOI: 10.4324/9781003253815-7

examples of crisis communications in action. Discussion points for further research and reading are offered at the end of the chapter and a Situational Judgement Test relating to crisis communications is included.

On completion of this chapter, the reader should be able to:

- Demonstrate a critical understanding of crisis communications theory and practice.
- Critically assess the types of crisis that affect organisations and identify the common mistakes that organisations can make when communicating in a crisis.
- Demonstrate an in-depth understanding of the stages involved in crisis communications planning.
- Formulate a strategic and practical crisis communications plan.
- Develop a competency in critical thinking through the analysis of crisis responses and the Situational Judgement Tests associated with this chapter.

7.2 Introduction

A dictionary definition describes the word *'crisis'* as *'a time of great danger, difficulty, or confusion when problems must be solved, or important decisions must be made'* (Oxford Learners Dictionaries). Fink (2000) sums up a communications crisis as occurring *'when an event increases in intensity, falls under close scrutiny of the news, media or government, interferes with normal business opportunities, devalues a positive public image, and has an adverse effect on a business's bottom line'*.

All over the world, crises are happening to people, businesses and governments every day on both large and small scales. Irrespective of size, a crisis could be defined as a serious incident for an organisation or a person that has the potential to affect the reputation of the organisation and ultimately impact on its bottom line. For example, the Coronavirus Pandemic was a global crisis that threatened both the health and the economies of the worldwide population. It presented multiple crises, for businesses, for governments and for healthcare providers worldwide and presented huge challenges in crisis management and communications in terms of changing behaviours and attitudes. There are numerous other crises that have occurred however that might not be as instantly memorable but important for the organisations involved nonetheless. For example, in 2018, the fast food chain, Kentucky Fried Chicken (KFC) experienced a crisis in the UK when it ran out of its core product – chicken! The company was forced into a crisis communications strategy as a result, which it handled very well. Goya Foods, the Latino food producer, had a crisis in 2020 when its Chief Executive, Robert Unanue, lavished praise on the then US President, Donald Trump, at an event in the White House. The Latino community in the States expressed their outrage on social media stating that Trump's policies were responsible for numerous injustices against the Latin American community. As these issues gain attention on social media initially, they have the potential to spread and get worse for the company, its reputation and ultimately its bottom line, very quickly unless a well-executed crisis communications programme is immediately actioned.

When analysing a crisis from a communications perspective, it is important to make a distinction between crisis management and crisis communications. These terms are commonly used interchangeably and erroneously. Fink (2013) attempts to explain the difference when he states that 'crisis management' is *'the management of the realities'* and crisis communications is *'the management of the perception of the crisis'*. Crisis management is a process an organisation will hopefully have engaged in long before a crisis hits. It involves a risk assessment of potential crises that could affect an organisation and scenario-based simulation training around such crises. For example, an oil company may look at an accident on an oil rig as a potential crisis situation and plan with and train its staff to respond to such a disaster. A technology company might look at a potential breach of data as a risk to the organisation's business and might train its management team in responding to such a crisis. The crisis management process should include a detailed analysis of best practice in managing such crises looking at precedent within the organisation and amongst similar organisations and the development of a plan of action in the eventuality of such a crisis occurring in the future. Topics of concern for an organisation involved in crisis management planning would include: Deciding on the members of the crisis team, identifying the departments of the business that could be affected, human resources issues particularly if the crisis could result in redundancies or lay-offs and legal issues, especially in some large crises where customers may be entitled to compensation. These are all operational crisis management issues and ones that take place under the remit of crisis management.

Crisis communications on the other hand becomes active after a crisis has materialised but should also form part of the management planning process. The main concern of crisis communications is the public response of the organisation to the crisis. The crisis communications has the ability to protect and in some cases even enhance an organisation's reputation. This is important because reputation is recognised by companies as hugely important to their value. For example, an article in the Harvard Business Review states that markets believe that organisations with good reputations *'deliver sustained earnings and future growth'* (Eccles et al., 2007). This is further substantiated in a study from global market research company, IPSOS. In its 2019 report on the value of reputation, it found that 87% of consumers around the world say that they take the reputation of the company into account when purchasing a product or service (IPSOS, 2019). Unfortunately, however, in many cases, despite the unlimited finances and resources that organisations have at their disposal, many organisations cannot build or maintain a good reputation. As Warren Buffett famously said: *'It takes twenty years to build a reputation and five minutes to ruin it'* (Snyder, 2017). Starting with a good crisis communications plan is the first step in ensuring that your company is best placed to protect its reputation if and when a crisis hits. At the very least, the organisation should not make the crisis worse through poor communication. An example of a company that did just this is British Petroleum (BP).

There is no chapter or article on crisis communications that can be written without mentioning the communications of BP and in particular the performance of its CEO in the aftermath of the largest oil spill in US history and one of the worst environmental disasters of all time. In 2010, there was an accident at the BP oil rig in the Gulf of Mexico that reportedly resulted in the leakage of more than 300 Olympic-sized swimming pools of oil into the sea, destroying marine life and polluting the waters and beaches throughout the Gulf of Mexico (Borrunda, 2020). A total of 11 people died in the incident and the local fishing industry was decimated as a result. The Chief Executive of BP at the time was Tony Hayward and he was dispatched to front the crisis communications campaign to try and protect BP's reputation. However, to the untrained eye, it would seem that BP's communications activity was designed to do exactly the opposite. From the outset, the company was accused of covering up the real story. It gave vastly underestimated figures of how much oil was leaking into the sea to the public, was unable to give a timeline as to when the leaking might stop and was obstructive in allowing media access to the areas affected. In a television interview a month or so after the disaster, Hayward stated that *'the environmental impact of this disaster is likely to be very modest'* and he famously told one journalist in an interview that there was no one who wanted the crisis to be over more than him as he wanted to have his life back! BP's strategy and Tony Hayward's performance were shocking for an organisation that was in the midst of a reputational crisis to the extent that it would leave experts wondering how they got the crisis communications so wrong. Clearly a company this large had trained for such an event? The answer would seem that the company was completely out of touch and out of its depth in terms of the scale of this disaster and was unable to pivot its communications strategy to one of transparency and truth, which was what was required. A demonstration of empathy was also sorely lacking in the personal interactions from Tony Hayward. Empathy is a key component of crisis communications and we will look at this in more detail in the *'Crisis Communications Checklist'* later in this chapter. The crisis cost BP billions and Tony Hayward was eventually replaced in his position by Bob Dudley who said in a television interview shortly after his appointment in 2010: *'We will earn back trust in BP and begin to restore the company's battered reputation'* (Madslien, 2010). Dudley then set about a post-crisis communications programme in which the company attempted to provide up to date information as to the stage the attempts to fix the leaks were at and the steps BP was putting in place to ensure this wouldn't happen again. The extent of the damage caused by this disaster is still being uncovered to this day over ten years later.

Whereas crisis management's focus is to prepare an organisation for the logistics of managing a crisis, crisis communications is about protecting the reputation of an organisation in the event of a crisis occurring. Crisis communications planning will help an organisation to develop explanations for its stakeholders, to communicate key points on what the organisation is doing to mitigate, give clear facts and dates to the public as to the stage of the problem and explain how the organisation plans to prevent similar crises happening in the future. In a well-managed communications-savvy organisation, the communications aspect of the crisis will have formed part of the crisis planning strategy and a well thought out public response will have been anticipated and developed. The ultimate goal of a crisis communications plan should be to communicate the details of the crisis clearly and not to further damage the reputation and revenues of the organisation involved. In some cases, the crisis communications can even improve the reputation of an organisation. For example, in the KFC crisis, the company responded immediately through a clever social media campaign which became a positive reputational campaign in itself. When it became public knowledge on social media that the company's outlets were closed as it had run out of chicken, it took to social media to immediately apologise to its customers and explain that there had been an issue with its new courier company that had resulted in the failure of the chicken to be delivered. The courier company then verified KFC's claim and KFC succeeded in projecting an image that was proactive and one that had good relationships with its contractors – all key attributes of a good reputation. Next, the company set up a webpage and developed a humorous campaign on social media entitled #wheresmychicken. This was an immediate, transparent and humorous response that worked well for this company. It is important to note that this type of response would not be suitable in a more serious situation in which the crisis involved a loss of life, for example, or a major environmental disaster as such that had occurred with BP. However, no matter the magnitude of the crisis, immediacy and transparency in all situations are key to the successful execution of a crisis communications strategy.

To look at the origins of crisis communications we can go back to the early 20th century when Ivy Lee, one of the first public relations practitioners drafted what is thought to be he first known example of a press release. The press release was composed in response to the Pennsylvania Railroad train crash in the US in 1906 in which approximately 50 people lost their lives. At the time of the crash, transparent communication from organisations to their stakeholders was not common practice. On the contrary, businesses were fearful or sceptical about the media and would commonly opt to hide information and avoid communicating with their stakeholders until such a time as the media came looking for answers. However, Lee's response to this crisis changed this practice. He drafted a statement updating the public as to what had happened and what the company was doing in response and he invited media to the crash site to report on the incident. His press release was published by news media, including in the New York Times and Lee then went on to publish his 'Declaration of Principles' which laid out the foundations for future public relations professionals and organisations as to how they could communicate in an informative and transparent way with the public through the news media.

Although the types of crisis and processes of crisis communications have evolved with the time that has elapsed since the Pennsylvanian Train Crash, the basic principles of the communications response as laid out by Lee, including transparency and honesty have remained the same. Probably the most significant factor that has influenced crisis communications since the time of Ivy Lee and particularly in the last 15 years is the emergence of new technologies and new media channels through which news is consumed and which has resulted in increased and immediate access to news. Both bad and good news now enters the public domain immediately through social media and that has placed an increased onus on companies to be prepared and to respond quickly. To illustrate this point, imagine the Pennsylvanian Train Crash had happened in 2020. Almost as soon as it had happened, either a passenger involved in or a spectator to the crash would have posted about the crash on Twitter and the news of the crash would have instantly become public knowledge. In this instance, Ivy Lee would not have had the luxury of drafting a press release for the next day's newspapers. Rather, a journalist would most likely have been on the phone to Lee within a few minutes looking for a comment. In a further illustration of this need for immediate communication in a crisis, in 2015, the American railroad company, Amtrak was ridiculed for its response to a train crash in which eight people died and numerous others were injured. The company was heavily criticised for its uncoordinated response and its failure to engage quickly and responsibly through the media, including social media, in the immediate aftermath of the accident. This led the author of an article on the crash in PR Week to pose the question *'when are companies and organizations going to learn that effective and immediate communications are a must-have in a crisis, not a nice-to-have?'* (Barrett, 2015). The importance of being prepared and the immediacy of response are key factors for organisations and public relations professionals to consider in their crisis communications planning.

Companies both large and small should engage in a crisis management strategy and incorporate communications into this strategy. The larger the organisation and the more risk the organisation takes, the greater the need for a crisis plan. A clear communications strategy is required to address each of the potential crisis situations identified and a spokesperson is required to be trained in media relations prior to the crisis event taking place. This will ensure that the company is best placed to respond to a crisis and ensure that at the very least it can protect and maintain the organisation's reputation in a time of crisis and avoid making the crisis worse through poor communications. An analysis of previous crisis events combined with crisis communications theory will inform a crisis communications programme ensuring it is grounded in best practice and research.

7.3 Crisis Communications Theory

Public relations and crisis communications borrow theories from the fields of communications, rhetoric and the social sciences. An analysis of these theories offers public relations practitioners an explanation as to how communications activity has worked for organisations and impacted on its stakeholders and society in the past and how communications can be used in the future. These theories are outlined in more detail in Chapter 2 of this book. For the purposes of this chapter, we will look at the theories that specifically impact on the practice of crisis communications.

When discussing crisis communications and rhetoric, it is worth referencing Aristotle's 'Five Canons of Rhetoric', which is a practical model used by communicators to this day. The Five Canons proposes that there are five stages involved in rhetoric: Invention, arrangement, style, delivery and memory. Invention is where the idea is devised, proof is found and arguments are developed. Arrangement involves the structuring of content into an introduction, a middle and a conclusion, for example. Style relates to the style of the rhetor or communicator. For example, does the speaker stop often to let ideas sink in? Does s/he use repetition to make a point? Style can also relate to the style of communications that is communicated visually through powerpoint, video or images, for example. Delivery relates to non-verbal communication which plays a huge role in how communicators are perceived by their audience. Albert Mehrabian's often-quoted research is a demonstration of the power of delivery from modern times. Mehrabian's research was centred around the likability of a speaker and found that an audience will make the decision to like a communicator using the following criteria: 55% on non-verbal communications, 38% on tone of voice and only 7% on what you actually say (Mehrabian & Ferris, 1967). The final canon of rhetoric was identified by Aristotle as memory in terms of what the speaker says and how the audience recalls the speech.

Communications campaigns that have the luxury of time to develop and research would naturally take into account all five canons of rhetoric. In crisis communications, when there is often little time to develop a plan from the start the hope would be that the organisation in crisis would have spent time developing a crisis communications strategy with consideration to the rhetoric that will be used and that can be initiated immediately and effectively in the event of the crisis. If we look at Tony Hayward's response to the BP crisis in 2010, we can see how important rhetoric was. Tony Hayward, may have had empathy for the people who had lost loved ones or those who had lost livelihoods but he did not communicate this in his rhetoric. Comments such as *'I would like my life-back'* served to communicate an out of touch elite businessman who was lacking in empathy for those affected. Rhetoric is hugely important in crisis communications and in the immediate response, the style and delivery of the rhetoric have the ability to make the communications worse as Tony Hayward demonstrated.

Fearn-Banks (2017) looks at responses in crisis communications and how rhetoric theory and theories of the social sciences can help plan for and respond to a crisis. Fearn-Banks identifies four theories of note in this respect: The Apologia Theory, the Image Restoration Theory, Decision Theory and Diffusion Theory. The Apologia Theory and Image Restoration Theory are concerned with the response stage of the crisis, whereas the Decision and Diffusion Theories are relevant to the planning stage.

7.3.1 The Apologia Theory

The Apologia Theory states that when an accusation is made against an organisation, it has the option of denying the accusation, dissociating itself from the crisis, explaining what happened and making an attempt to redefine the message or finally apologising for the crisis. Apologia Theory does not suggest that organisations should always apologise for a crisis. The question of whether or not to apologise largely depends on the crisis involved and the context of the crisis, which we will discuss later in this chapter.

7.3.2 Image Restoration Theory

The Image Restoration Theory builds on the Apologia Theory and brings us back to the point of reputation. In this theory, the organisation is required to have researched the potential risks to the organisation and what has the potential to threaten its reputation, a process which we have identified as occurring in the crisis management stage. The organisation in this theory also needs to have a good understanding of public sentiment and how to communicate with its various publics. This theory proffers that this knowledge will help the organisation to identify a response strategy. For example, in some instances 'no comment' might be preferred and in others, it might be preferable for an organisation to control the message and communicate the bad news first.

7.3.3 Decision Theory

Decision Theory is commonly used by psychologists in studying behaviour and by mathematicians, statisticians, philosophers and politicians. It involves analysing outcomes from various decisions in order to decide on the course of action that is most advantageous for the organisation. This activity would again take place during the crisis management stage. An example of the Decision Theory in practice in real life can be seen in the modelling activity that various health bodies would have engaged in during the COVID-19 pandemic. These public health bodies would have created various models taking into account the scientific information on the virus and combining it with behavioural psychology to predict outcomes.

Governments would then make decisions based on these models. Fearn-Banks notes that often organisations may not decide on the outcome that has the maximum benefit but rather on the decision that will satisfy the minimum requirements, a process that is referred to as 'satisficing'. This is often, she states, as organisations do not have data at hand to take the ultimate decision.

7.3.4 Diffusion Theory

The Diffusion Theory is concerned with how ideas spread amongst a population or a public. Diffusion is explained as the process by which new ideas are adapted over time. The theory identifies five steps in the adaptation process.

1 Awareness – the organisation is exposed to the idea.
2 Interest – the organisation becomes interested in the idea.
3 Evaluation – potential benefits of adapting the idea are analysed.
4 Trial – the idea is trialled for a temporary period.
5 Adaption – the idea is adapted or not.

Adaptation of new ideas, products, services or ideas according to this theory depends on what has happened in the past, who the decision makers are and the idea itself and the level of change a public has to make in order to adapt the idea.

In reality, an organisation responding to a crisis will most likely incorporate elements from each of these theories into its crisis communications strategy, combined with knowledge of communications and rhetorical theory and the Theory of Excellence. These theories should form the foundations for all communications campaigns and position an organisation to be prepared for a crisis.

7.4 Crises Categories

There is no universally referenced classification system for categorising crises, and this may be because crises come in very many forms. For example, a company expanding or going out of business is a very common crisis that businesses around the world experience regularly. For example, Jet Airways, one of India's largest airlines went out of business in 2019 after 26 years in operation. As the company began to run out of money, it was forced to ground planes and lay off hundreds of staff, including its management and communications professionals. Another example of a crisis took place in 2015 when following an investigation by the Environmental Protection Agency (EPA) in the US, Volkswagen admitted to cheating emissions tests in order to sell its diesel cars. The company was found to have used special software in some of its cars that enabled it to perform well in emissions tests. The software was discovered by the EPA and Volkswagen was forced to recall millions of its cars worldwide. The product recall cost the company billions. Another example of a modern crisis situation is a breach of data, which can cause a serious problem for an organisation today. In 2018, Facebook was found to have used personal information harvested from more than 50 million Facebook profiles without users' permission. It emerged subsequently that Facebook had known about the data breach for three years previously and had even received several warnings about its data security policies. Billions of dollars were wiped off Facebook's stock market valuation as news of the crisis broke and a #delete-facebook campaign ran across social media threatening the organisation's reputation. Crises come in all shapes and sizes, from the seemingly minor as in the case of KFC's missing chicken crisis to the major crisis that can costs companies vast sums of money as in the case of Facebook's or Volkswagen's issues or BP's environmental disaster in the Gulf of Mexico.

Although there is no universally used classification system for crises, many authors have made an attempt to provide some clarity. Coombs (2019), for example, identifies crises as either disasters or organisational. Disasters according to Coombs are large-scale crises that require responses from *'multiple governmental units'*. An example of such a crisis would be BP's oil spill or another example is Boeing's 737 crisis. In 2019, a Boeing *'737 Max 8'* aircraft, operated by Ethiopian Airlines, crashed in Ethiopia killing all 157 people on board. The crash followed an earlier incident in October 2018 when the same make of aircraft, this time operated by Lion Air, crashed in Indonesia, killing all 189 people on board. It emerged following the accidents that there had been concern expressed prior to the incidents for the safety of the aircrafts involved. Following the accidents, there was no immediate worldwide directive from Boeing to ground the aircraft with the result that airline regulators took the decision to ground the planes into their own hands. Eventually, air accident investigators found that a series of faults with the plane design was linked to both crashes. Following this report, Boeing said that it was *'taking actions to enhance the safety of the 737 Max to prevent the flight control conditions that occurred in this accident from ever happening again'* (BBC, 2019). In the end, Boeing's Chief Executive of Commercial Airplanes, Kevin McAllister was fired, followed later by Chief Executive, Dennis Muilenburg and the company's profits decreased in the immediate aftermath of the crisis. This crisis could be termed a disaster as it was an incident of worldwide interest that resulted in the deaths of hundreds of people. At a company level, it also represents an organisational crisis for Boeing.

An organisational crisis is probably the most common type of crisis that the majority of communications professionals could expect to face. Coombs describes this type of crisis as: *'the perceived violation of salience stakeholder expectations that can create negative outcomes for stakeholders and/or the organisation'*. Examples of organisational crises are prevalent. The Facebook issue described earlier in this chapter was an organisational crisis for Facebook, for example. Another interesting example of a crisis that impacted on both the reputation of the person and the organisation was Prince Andrew's television interview in the UK. The ill-fated interview resulted in a crisis for both the Prince and for the organisation that is the British Royal Family. In 2019, Prince Andrew decided to voluntarily take part in a national television interview with esteemed journalist Emily Maitlis on the BBC's flagship television current affairs show, Newsnight. The Prince intended to take part in the interview presumably to clear his and his family's good name in the light of the allegations made against him regarding his connection with convicted paedophile, Jeffrey Epstein. The interview was an unmitigated disaster for the Prince and for the Royal Family. The Prince performed extremely poorly in the interview and he was ridiculed across social media immediately as the interview aired and in the news media thereafter. Most importantly in terms of crisis communications, the Prince did not apologise or show any empathy for the victims involved in the case. Prince Andrew's reputation suffered as a result and he lost his role in the Royal Family.

Another example of an organisational crisis is Astra Zeneca's response to the COVID-19 pandemic. As pharmaceutical organisations worldwide started to roll out vaccines, Astra Zeneca suffered reputational damage as it appeared to renege on its contractual arrangements with the European Union. Its vaccine then also received negative media coverage as to its efficacy and reported side effects. These are serious crises for the organisation that has the potential to impact on its reputation, share price and revenues into the future.

Doug Newsom offers a useful guide in the classification of crises. She proffers a three-category classification model to identify types of crises as an act of nature, an intentional crisis or an unintentional crisis (Newsom, 1992). An act of nature is similar in concept to Coombs' 'Disaster'. It is a crisis, the fault for which cannot be attributed to any individual or organisation. Examples of an act of nature include an earthquake, a tsunami or the COVID-19 pandemic. The Coronavirus Pandemic represents a significant global crisis that offers extensive learning opportunities from a communications perspective. At a macro level, this pandemic created a worldwide international public health and economical crisis for governments. At a micro level, individual businesses worldwide suffered their own crises as a result of the actions that were taken to try and control the pandemic, with economies closed and businesses prevented from trading. Many businesses were immediately plunged into organisational crises of their own where they had to make immediate plans to facilitate staff to work remotely, lay off staff either temporarily or permanently and process issues with many businesses in the retail trade pivoting to online sales. An intentional crisis according to this topology is a crisis that occurs as a result of the deliberate actions of others. For example, the terrorist attacks of 9/11 in the United States could be classed as an intentional crisis as the terrorists deliberately attacked the Twin Towers and caused destruction, loss of life and an immediate crisis for the American Government as well as governments and businesses throughout the world. An unintentional crisis is an issue that occurs as a result of an organisation's normal day-to-day activity but one which wasn't intended. This is differentiated by an Act of Nature as it can be commonly caused by some form of human error. The BP Oil Spill in the Gulf of Mexico, for example, or the Chernobyl Nuclear disaster in the 1980s are good examples of this type of crisis.

An analysis of crisis topology demonstrates the very different forms that crises present in. If the crisis is large in scale and has caused or has the potential to cause loss of life, it is a very serious crisis that could be classified as a Disaster according to Coombs or maybe as a result of an 'Act of Nature' according to Newsom. If, however, the crisis affects an organisation's or a person's reputation and/or revenues, it is likely to be an organisational crisis and one that could be intentional or unintentional. Although crises occur in different forms and have different catalysts, the tools and tactics for planning and responding to all types of crises are the same and can be tailored to an individual crisis as it occurs.

7.5 Crisis Communications Planning (The 3As)

As we have identified, there are two distinctive elements involved in a crisis, crisis management and crisis communications. This chapter is mainly concerned with the communications phase which aims to manage public perception of the crisis, to protect the reputation of the organisation and to ensure the crisis is not made worse through the company's or person's response to the crisis. As we have discovered, crises happen quickly, and news of a crisis can travel fast, particularly in the modern era with widespread use of social media. It is vital therefore for organisations to be prepared for a crisis and to ensure they have the processes and systems in place to respond immediately. To follow is a three-stage crisis communications model (see Figure 7.1) that demonstrates how this can be done effectively to give organisations the best chance in minimising further damage to their reputations through their crisis communications. This model identifies the three stages or actions involved in crisis communications planning as: Anticipate, Act and Appraise.

7.5.1 *Anticipate*

This stage should be completed during the crisis management phase. During the 'Anticipate' phase it is helpful to consult the Decision and Diffusion theories

Figure 7.1 'The 3As' of Crisis Communications Planning.

explained earlier in this chapter. During this stage, the management team at the organisation will conduct research and a risk analysis to identify the issues that could potentially occur and how best to manage them. One of the most effective ways of training for a potential crisis is the use of scenario-based simulation. In a study in the US, Wang (2017) found that crisis simulation can significantly increase students' crisis management competencies. During the *'Anticipate'* stage, the management of the organisation should conduct a risk assessment and assemble a crisis response team. The team should then be trained using scenario-based simulations that analyse various outcomes and decide on how best to manage and respond in each crisis scenario. Precedent should be considered, both in terms of the organisation's history and best practice in the sector in general. It is preferable for organisations to include their communications executive on the crisis management team at this point. However, this is not always what happens, particularly with smaller organisations who may not have an internal communications representative. At some point, however, a communications professional will need to take charge of the communications planning element of the crisis plan and if this expertise is not available within the organisation or *'in-house'*, the skills can be sourced from a trusted outside consultant. In the *'Anticipate'* stage, the communications team will lead the communications response to the various scenarios that could potentially face the company. The following activity should take place during the *'Anticipate'* phase.

7.5.1.1 Identification of Stakeholders

Stakeholders are classed as any group who are invested in the company. These can be both internal (employees, shareholders, board members, suppliers, contractors) and external (customers/clients – existing and potential, referrers, regulators, governments). For example, in Boeing's case, its internal stakeholders are its staff, pilots, air stewards, engineers, administrators, organisations that provide contract staff and suppliers of catering services, cleaning and so on. External stakeholders include airlines who buy and use the planes and their passengers worldwide as well as the individual airline regulators within various countries. As identified in the Excellence Theory and the Four Models of PR, stakeholders should be segmented into their various groups and communications plans and relevant communications messages can then be designed and tailored to each of the stakeholder groups.

7.5.1.2 Identification of the Spokesperson

Every organisation requires a spokesperson, a person dedicated to managing the public interactions of the company with the media. This spokesperson should be clearly identified during the *'Anticipate'* stage of the crisis communications planning. The spokesperson's suitability should be assessed in terms of their ability to communicate clearly, competently and consistently and to show empathy, which is extremely important in a time of crisis as we have seen in the case of Tony Hayward's response in the BP Oil spill. As part of the scenario-based crisis simulation exercise mentioned above, the designated spokesperson should receive media training to ensure that s/he is comfortable with conducting media interviews that may arise in response to this crisis. Media training involves taking the scenarios that are likely to affect the organisation and conducting a simulation of the media interviews that may take place in response. Spokespeople are trained on how best to present their organisation and to deliver bad news and most importantly in answering difficult questions.

7.5.1.3 Media Audit

An analysis of past media coverage and online commentary that has affected the organisation and its competitors should take place as part of the '*Anticipate*' stage. This coverage should be examined to ascertain how similar stories have been interpreted in the media and to identify potential pitfalls that could occur. A list of target media should be compiled, and it is important for the organisation to be familiar with these channels and publications as well as with the journalists who write or broadcast in their sector. This will become extremely important during the next stage.

7.5.2 Act

The 'Act' stage may sometimes be referred to as the response stage. The aim would be that with good communications planning, the organisation's spokes-person would be transitioning into this phase armed with all the information and training required to ensure that the communications protects the reputation of the organisation and does not make the crisis worse. At this stage, the crisis has happened, and the public and news journalists are looking for answers. The organisation's spokesperson at this point is required to manage and control how this message is communicated through the media. To do this, the following factors should be taken into consideration.

7.5.2.1 The Media

As we know, a crisis will most likely hit social media first and this will generate almost immediate inquiries from journalists as a result. The company may be immediately required to give a 'holding statement' to media to acknowledge that the crisis is being addressed and that they will be in a position to communicate at a later point (preferably the same day). The level of the response initiated then really depends on the size of the crisis. For example, during the COVID-19 pandemic, once the virus had been confirmed as being present in communities, the department of health in each country was required to provide information to the public. An event of this magnitude generally would merit a press conference. Press conferences offer an opportunity to address a mass media audience at once and allow the media to ask questions, to avoid repetition and to get news out quickly. Another option at this stage, which may be more suitable for smaller events or crises, is to issue a statement and facilitate a smaller number of media interviews on a one-to-one basis. This is why it is important to be familiar with the various media and journalists. For example, in response to the Facebook Cambridge Analytica scandal, Mark Zuckerberg offered an exclusive 'sit-down' interview to CNN Business' Laurie Segall. Rather than giving a big press conference that would be harder to control, the interview was offered exclusively to CNN at the company's own headquarters in Menlo Park, California. This allowed Zuckerberg to have greater control over the setting and the message. Perhaps Prince Andrew had intended on the same strategy when he chose to give an exclusive interview to Emily Maitlis on the BBC's flagship current affairs programme, Newsnight. However, an analysis of Emily's previous interviews and investigative interviewing style should have indicated to Prince Andrew that this perhaps might be a dangerous strategy in terms of the rhetoric he intended on using, which was ultimately lacking in fact and empathy.

Social media is a hugely important channel to monitor especially during a crisis as it provides insight into 'word of mouth' or what the public or a section of the public is thinking or saying. It should be monitored consistently, and a clear strategy should be in place for responding to comments and posts promptly. It is important to note however that social media is not a news channel. It is a repository where organisations, brands, news outlets, journalists and the general public publish their views or communicate their opinions, stories, new products and services. Twitter in particular is a channel where many go to acquire instant news from journalists or to engage directly with brands and organisations. It could be described as the online equivalent of the corner shop in that everyone and anyone is there offering an opinion on topics on which they are sometimes not fully informed. It might be interesting, but not all of it is factual. It is important to be aware of the role that these social media channels and in particular that Twitter plays in the dissemination of misinformation in times of crisis. This issue became particularly prevalent during the COVID-19 pandemic when a huge amount of erroneous information and false stories were circulated through social channels. The perception of a crisis will ultimately be led by the informed media coverage in trusted news outlets by expert journalists in their field and a good communications strategy should strive to communicate through these channels first and foremost.

7.5.2.2 Journalists

In advance of a press conference or a media interview, it is important to know who is likely to attend and from what publication or channel. Knowing who they are and what their style of reporting is will help decide how to approach the press conference or media interview. Watching press conferences, for example, held by politicians will help to demonstrate this point. In a political press conference, the politicians will know exactly who is in the room and from what channel or publication they are from. They will pick and choose who to answer questions from and how much time to give to these questions. Best practice in terms of fairness and open communication is to give all journalists equal time and consideration.

7.5.2.3 The Topline

Many pre-recorded interviews can last for many minutes or more and yet when the interview is broadcast, only a one-minute snippet or a *'soundbite'* is aired. This can be due to an editing decision or simply because the spokesperson didn't address the question asked in his or her answer. It is important that the spokesperson therefore knows that this might happen and makes sure that they know what their *'Topline'* is and that they communicate this clearly at the outset of their interview. The *'Topline'* is the one thing that the spokesperson wants to say above all else and if they don't get time to say much more than one sentence. For example, in the case of Boeing and many other serious crises or disasters as identified by Coombs, the *'Topline'* would most likely be an apology or an expression of condolence for those affected by the crisis. Apologies aren't always required as we have studied and should only be used when relevant. The Apologia Theory referred to earlier in this chapter offers a guideline as to other options available in the organisation's communication response.

7.5.2.4 3 Key Messages

In preparation for a media interview, the interviewee should prepare three key messages. Similar to the idea behind the *'Topline'*, these are the three points that the spokesperson wants to make. The messages should be worked out with the crisis communications team in advance and worked into a clear messaging structure that can be clearly communicated without technical or confusing company jargon. The messages will also serve to anchor the interviewee and assist them in staying consistent and focussed throughout the media interview.

7.5.2.5 Questions and Answers

In advance of a media interview and particularly a crisis interview, the spokes-person should prepare and rehearse answers to potential questions. Particular attention should be given to the questions that the interviewee would like to avoid. For example, in the event of an air disaster in which the plane's engineering was found to have been at fault, an interviewer is likely to ask, *'how long did you know about the fault?'* or *'why didn't you take any action?'*. It should be taken as guaranteed that if there is a question that the company would like to avoid, the journalist will pose it, so it is important to have answers prepared. Key messages can also serve as crutches to fall back on at this point, but they need to be used and worked into the communications carefully to avoid irritating the interviewer.

Figure 7.2 provides a checklist for the act stage of the communications planning process.

Media - Who and How?

- What type of media response will you engage in - press conference, press release, statement, one-to-one interviews, exclusives?

- What type of media is it? Broadcast (Television, Radio, Podcast, Video), Print/Online (broadsheet, tabloid - daily or weekend).

- Social Media - Monitor and have a strategy for responding.

Journalists - Who and How?

- Who are the relevant journalists?

- Understand the journalist's style and medium.

Topline

- If you only had one thing to say, what would it be?

3 Key Messages

- Refer back to these in media interviews.

Questions & Answers

- Prepare and practice - especially to the difficult questions you don't want to be asked.

Figure 7.2 The Act Stage – Media Response Checklist.

7.5.3 Appraise

It is vital during a crisis to update the public regularly on how the situation is progressing. However, it is important also to remember that the crisis will not last forever and companies should not become consumed by the crisis to the detriment of its other business streams as we will discuss in the next section of this chapter. When the crisis ends, the public needs to be informed and updated on the next steps. At the end of the acute phase, a full review should take place of the communications response to the crisis. This review should inform the organisation and the company can then use this to communicate with its audience and to build a sustainable communications plan to help rebuild the organisation's reputation into the future. It is worthwhile for a company to consider its Corporate Social Responsibility (CSR) strategy in the aftermath of the crisis. For example, if the crisis in question involves an environmental disaster such as the BP Oil Spill in the Gulf of Mexico, the company could look at engaging in an environmental support strategy to commit funds and resources to environmental objectives. However, it is important that CSR is not perceived as a cynical attempt by an organisation to cover up bad behaviour. For example, in Nigeria, Shell Oil has been accused of inadvertently contributing to corruption, conflict and poverty in the country, a problem it could be perceived as trying to fix through its sustainability programme that includes many health, education and infrastructure projects.

7.6 The Crisis Communications Checklist (The 5Cs)

As we have seen, all crises whether large or small, a disaster or an organisational crisis, share common traits in their communications responses. To follow is a guideline for crisis communications planning which draws on the theory and the real examples discussed in this chapter. This guideline is called 'The 5Cs of Crisis Communications' elements of which can be applied to all crises.

7.6.1 Clarity

A crisis is a time for clear communication. It is not a time for spin or jargon. People at a time of crisis, particularly during a disaster that may have resulted in the loss of life, can be fearful and require honesty and transparency. One of the worst mistakes a company can make in time of crisis is to try and cover up. Covering up is nearly always discovered and leads immediately to mistrust amongst an intelligent public. The concealed information will more than likely be revealed, and the organisation involved will lose control of the message when it is disclosed by a third party in the media. In the case of the crises of Boeing and Prince Andrew, both the chief executive of Boeing and Prince Andrew lost their jobs as a result of their actions and also due to their non-transparent communications' responses.

7.6.2 *Competency*

In a time of crisis, the public look to brands, organisations and their leaders for reassurance. They need competent leaders to bring them through the crisis. They need to know that the people in charge know what they are doing and that they are capable and trustworthy of managing the crisis. Boeing's Chief Executive, in his response to the media, for example, would have appeared more competent if he had taken the immediate decision to ground the planes, particularly when the pilots, who would be perceived as trusted experts by the public, had voiced their opinions so publicly. Boeing's response, coupled with its delay in coming forward and taking responsibility, allowed the public to assume that the organisation was not competent in dealing with the crisis.

Competent leaders evoke trust. They communicate clearly and consistently. They don't try to conceal information, speculate or blame. US President Donald Trump's communications during the COVID-19 pandemic offers an example of the antithesis of competent crisis communications. At the initial stages of the outbreak, Trump described the virus as merely like a flu. Like his international counterparts, Trump then proceeded to hold regular press conferences. However, at these press conferences, instead of addressing the legitimate concerns of the public, Trump used them as opportunities for blame and speculation. He blamed the media for perpetuating '*fake news*' and the WHO and China for mismanaging the pandemic. As is common in his rhetoric, he used racist language throughout instilling hatred and racism in those who follow him. In one now infamous appearance, he used his press conference to speculate if there was any merit in people consuming household disinfectant to treat the virus. Immediately manufacturers of such products were active on social media cautioning the public against ingesting their products. A poll by Reuters/Ipsos quoted in Forbes in June 2020 reveals that 58% of American's disapproved of Trump's handling of the pandemic (Porterfield, 2020).

7.6.3 *Consistency*

It is important to know what the key messages are and to stick to them when communicating in a crisis. For example, in Prince Andrew's case, he was inconsistent in his explanations and appeared to deny, for example, that the authentic photographic evidence presented to him was real. KFC decided on a humorous self-deprecating response and stuck to it throughout its response. As the United Kingdom and Ireland Head of Brand Engagement at KFC, Jenny Packwood commented: '*We know who we are as a brand and what our tone is and we stuck to it, which is light-hearted, honest, authentic and a little bit irreverent*' (Hickman, 2018). In the UK, in the initial stages of the COVID-19 pandemic, the Government was reported to be following a 'herd immunity' strategy, the idea being that if enough people contracted the virus, immunity could be reached within the population. After much discussion in the media on the effects that this route would have on the NHS and the fatality rate in the UK, the messages became more empathetic and clear and consistent with the messages coming from the WHO and from other countries: *'Stay Safe, Protect the NHS'*. The WHO in its guidelines outlined communications priorities for countries which it stated if they acted on them *'coherently and consistently'* then they had a chance to 'turn the tide' on the virus' impact (World Health Organisation, 2020).

7.6.4 Control

Crisis communications is about shaping perceptions and this can only be achieved by an organisation if it controls the message. It is vitally important for the organisation at the centre of the crisis not to lose control of the message. An example of this is evident in the Boeing crisis. In this situation, rather than taking control and grounding flights, Boeing allowed the individual airlines to make the decision to ground its planes and in doing so, added further to the company's woes by creating a sense of mistrust in the organisation. If Boeing had taken the decision to ground its own fleet and communicated this clearly and consistently, then it may have avoided some of the reputational damage that ensued. Often organisations may lose control of the crisis by passing the blame to a third party. For example, in the BP Crisis, Tony Hayward initially tried to pass culpability to a contractor which only served to evoke further mistrust in him and his message. In the Facebook Cambridge Analytica crisis, initially, Facebook tried to blame Cambridge Analytica for using data of its users without consent. As Facebook discovered, this strategy rarely works and will only serve to create mistrust and confusion. By contrast, KFC involved a third party in its communications but the difference was that this third party had willingly claimed responsibility for its part. KFC retained control of the message and shaped the perception of the brand as a humorous, self-deprecating brand with good relationships with its contractors.

Although the organisation needs to control the message, it is vital that it does not become consumed by the crisis and allows the crisis to filter through from one brand to the entire organisation. For example, the Facebook crisis could have permeated through Facebook-owned apps and damaged the long-term reputation of What's App and Instagram, for example, but the company took control of it and prevented that from happening. It is vital to isolate the crisis therefore to a specific team, area and/or brand within the company and not to let it consume the entire organisation. A company that becomes consumed by a crisis runs the risk of allowing a fault or an issue with one brand, product or service within its portfolio to spread and damage the reputation of the entire organisation.

7.6.5 Compassion

Arguably, the most important trait to demonstrate in a crisis response is compassion. The larger the crisis or the more serious it is, the greater the need for compassion. In almost every crisis where there has been a communications issue, there is often a failure on behalf of the spokesperson to display empathy. Tony Hawyard's infamous blunder in the television interview when he stated that he wanted his life back is probably the most famous of such displays of a lack of empathy in crisis communications. Prince Andrew, in his media interview never once expressed condolences with the victims involved and this had disastrous results for him. Displaying empathy is extremely important in getting your audience on board and can understandably make or break a crisis response.

Empathy should not be confused with an apology however. As discussed in the Apologia Theory, an apology is one of a few responses available to a respondent in a crisis. The theory refers to an apology as 'conciliation' but states that it is not always the required approach and, depending on the context of the crisis, the organisation may choose to explain, deny or redefine the situation instead. The question frequently arises in crisis communications planning: When should a spokesperson apologise? Frequently, this will cause issues with lawyers representing the firm who will most likely answer: 'never'. Fearn Banks offers the 'Five Ws' as a guide when considering that question: **W**hy apologise? **W**hat constitutes an apology? **W**ho should apologise? **W**here do you apologise? **W**hen to make an apology? These are questions that should be considered in the event of a crisis and in particular if the organisation is at fault. An apology, if it is going to be made, should always be truthful and heartfelt or it will only serve to add to the crisis and make things worse.

7.7 Conclusion

This chapter has attempted to explain crisis management and crisis communications, provide an outline of relevant communications theories and explain how these theories can be applied to the practice of communications. Practical crisis planning models and tips are provided as tools for the reader. To follow are some discussion points to consider for further research and a Situational Judgement Test is provided to encourage critical thinking in crisis communications planning.

7.8 For Discussion

The following are some discussion points to consider for further learning. These topics can be considered on your own or discussed in a tutorial setting, with peers or with colleagues.

- Think of or research a recent crisis that has been in the news.
- What type of crisis is it and why? (disaster or organisational/act of nature, intentional, unintentional).
- Rate each aspect of the organisation's communications performance from 1 to 5 (1 being very poor and 5 being excellent). Rate the performance of the company against each of the items in the Crisis Communications Checklist.
- List three things that the company did badly and three things it did well in each of the stages of its crisis' communications (Anticipate, Act and Appraise).
- What could have been done better? (List up to three things maximum).

References

Barrett, S. (May 2015). *Amtrak Crash Response Was Just Not Good Enough*. PR Week: US. Available on https://www.prweek.com/article/1347422/amtrak-crash-response-just-not-good-enough [Accessed 13 April 2020]

BBC. (October 2019). *Boeing 737 Max Lion Air crash caused by series of failures*. Available at https://www.bbc.com/news/business-50177788 [Accessed 20 April 2020]

Borchers, T. and Hundley, H. (2018). *Rhetorical Theory: An Introduction*. Waveland Press Inc: US.

Borrunda, A. (April, 2020). We still don't know the full impacts of the BP oil spill, 10 years later. Available at https://www.nationalgeographic.com/science/article/bp-oil-spill-still-dont-know-effects-decade-later [Accessed 10 April 2021]

Coombs, T. (2019). *Ongoing Crisis Communication. Planning, Managing and Responding*. 5th Ed. Sage: US.

Eccles, R. G., Newquist, S. C., and Schatz, R. (2007). Reputation and its risks. Harvard Busines Review. Available at https://hbr.org/2007/02/reputation-and-its-risks [Accessed 15 April 2021]

Fearn-Banks, K. (2017). *Crisis Communicaitons. A Casebook Approach*. 5th Ed. Routledge: New York and London.

Fink, S. (2000). *Crisis Planning For the Inevitable*. iUniverse: US.

Fink, S. (2013). *Crisis Communications, The Definitive Guide to Managing the Message*. McGraw-Hill: US.

Grunig, J. E. and Grunig, L. A. (2008). Excellence theory in public relations: Past, present, and future. Available at DOI: 10.1007/978-3-531-90918-9_22

Hickman, A. (2018). The crisis comms lesson behind KFC's FCK bucket. Available at https://www.prweek.com/article/1498405/crisis-comms-lesson-behind-kfcs-fck-bucket. [Accessed 21 April 2020]

IPSOS. (2019). The IPSOS reputation council. Findings from the thirteenth sitting – exploring the latest thinking and practice in corporate reputation management across the world. Available at https://www.ipsos.com/sites/default/files/ct/publication/documents/2019-06/ipsos_reputation_council_2019.pdf [Accessed 15 April 2021]

Madslien, J. (2010). BP sets out to rebuild reputation. https://www.bbc.com/news/business-11620902 [Accessed 8 April 2021]

Mehrabian, A. and Ferris, S. R. (1967). Inference of attitudes from nonverbal communication in two channels. *Journal of Consulting Psychology* 31, no. 3: 248–252. 10.1037/h0024648

Newsom, D., Scott, A., & Turk, J. V. (1992). This is PR: The realities of public relations (5th ed.). Wadsworth: Belmont, CA.

Oxford Learners Dictionaries. Definition of Crisis. Available at https://www.oxfordlearnersdictionaries.com/definition/american_english/crisis [Accessed 22 April 2020]

Porterfield, C. (2020). Trump's Coronavirus rating sinks to new low as cases surge. Available at https://www.forbes.com/sites/carlieporterfield/2020/06/24/trumps-coronavirus-approval-rating-sinks-to-new-low-as-cases-surge/?sh=704a9ee668ef [Accessed 15 April 2020]

Snyder, B. (2017). 7 insights from legendary investor, Warren Buffett. Available at https://www.cnbc.com/2017/05/01/7-insights-from-legendary-investor-warren-buffett.html [Accessed 15 April 2021]

Wang, M. (2017). Using crisis simulation to enhance crisis management competencies: The role of presence. *Journal of Public Relations Education* 3, no. 2, 2017: 96–109. Available at https://aejmc.us/jpre/2017/12/29/using-crisis-simulation-to-enhance-crisis-management-competencies-the-role-of-presence/

World Health Organisation. (2020). Risk communication and community engagement (RCCE) action plan guidance. Covid-19 preparedness and response. World Health Organisation (WHO). Available at https://www.who.int/publications/i/item/risk-communication-and-community-engagement-(rcce)-action-plan-guidance [Accessed 15 April 2021]

8   PR for Business

Chapter Contents

8.1 Learning outcomes

On finishing this chapter, the reader should be able to:

- Understand the role public relations (PR) plays in businesses.
- Identify the categories of PR and the differences between each category.
- Measure PR activity and explain how it can provide value and return on investment to an organisation.

8.2 Introduction

In 2010, the environmental organisation, Greenpeace launched a campaign against Nestlé to protest against the unsustainable clearance of rain forests for palm oil. Greenpeace claimed that Nestlé and other brands were sourcing palm oil unethically for use in their confectionary products. The campaign involved the production of an ad using the Nestlé product, Kit Kat. For years, Kit Kat had become well known for using the slogan *'have a break, have a Kit Kat'* in its advertising campaigns, usually accompanied by a person breaking a piece of Kit Kat in half before eating it. The Greenpeace campaign used this concept to

DOI: 10.4324/9781003253815-8

develop an ad campaign and instead of using a piece of Kit Kat, the subject took a bite from the finger of an orangutang to infer that Nestlé was destroying its natural habitat. The orangutang is one of many animals whose natural habitat is threatened by the destruction of the rain forests for palm oil.

The ad campaign was broadcast on YouTube and went viral. The ad was quickly and briefly removed from YouTube following a request from Nestlé citing copyright issues. It was reposted across other social media channels. The Greenpeace ad campaign was detrimental to Nestlé's reputation forcing the brand to announce a change in its palm oil supplier and a commitment to join the Roundtable for Sustainable Palm Oil. On its website, Nestlé now states that it is *'working to increase the proportion of sustainable palm oil that we source'* (Nestlé, n.d.). The brand however is regularly criticised for its environmental strategies including its policy on plastic pollution as well as the continued palm oil controversy. In 2018, Nestlé was suspended from the Roundtable for Sustainable Palm Oil for reported breaches of conduct (Kilvert, 2018). However, Nestlé still features at number 85 in the 'Strong Reputation' category in GlobalReptrak's 2021 reputation rankings.

The example of Nestlé demonstrates the valuable role that reputation plays in business and how important it is to manage the reputation of an organisation in the media. In the UK, the CIPR states in its definition of PR that *'public relations is the discipline which looks after reputation, with the aim of earning understanding and support and influencing opinion and behaviour'* (CIPR, n.d). The management of reputation is one of the key roles that PR plays in organisations throughout the world.

8.3 PR and Reputation

Reputation is defined by Dowling (2000) as *'The evaluation (respect, esteem, estimation) in which an organisation's image is held by people'*.

Reputation is extremely valuable to organisations as it impacts on revenue. The value of reputation is recognised annually by Reptrak, the global organisation that montiors reputations of international brands. Each year the organisation releases its index of global brands based on their reputation. As of 2022, the top three companies on this list were Rolex, Ferrari and Lego (Reptrak, 2022).

In an article in the Harvard Business Review, it stated that markets believe that organisations with good reputations 'deliver sustained earnings and future growth' (Eccles et al., 2007). This is further substantiated in a study from global market research company, IPSOS. In its 2019 report on the value of reputation, it found that 87% of consumers around the world say that they take the reputation of the company into account when purchasing a product or service (IPSOS, 2019).

So how does a company develop a good reputation?

Alison Theaker (2016) developed what she called the 'Relationship Onion' to explain the role of reputation in organisations. In this model, Theaker likened organisations to onions that were made up of many layers or skins of relationships that needed to be functioning in order to protect the outer most layer of reputation. At the core of the onion are its employees, this is followed then by customers and then other publics and stakeholders. This model demonstrates how the reputation of the company starts with its staff and permeates its way through the organisation to its publics or customers. Therefore staff within a company should be treated by the organisation in a manner that reflects how the organisation wishes for it to be perceived in the world.

To do this, organisations need to make committments to certain factors that have the potential to enhance its reputation. In 2006, Weber Shandwick and the Reputation Institute conducted a survey on reputation and found that there were several factors that impacted an organisation's reputation. These are outlined as follows.

Factors impacting reputation within organisations:

1 **Responsibility:** Supporting worthy causes – demonstrating environmental responsibility and community/societal responsibility.
2 **Communications:** Marked by transparency, full disclosure and openness to dialogue.
3 **Products and services:** Offering high quality and innovation, as well as customer satisfaction.
4 **Talent:** Rewarding employees fairly, promoting diversity and demonstrating an ability to attract and retain staff.
5 **Financial metrics:** Outpacing competitors and demonstrating financial soundness and long-term investment value.
6 **Leadership:** Established by the CEO and senior team and showing good governance and ethical conduct.

– Weber Shandwick and the Reputation Institute, 2006.

This explains why each of the above factors are considered to be essential in a public relations strategy. Responsibility is communicated through development of a CSR plan, the results of which are then issued to media and communicated to the public. The manner in which the company communicates will determine if its communications are perceived to be transparent. Audiences can be made aware of products and services also through consumer PR as will be discussed shortly. The talent in the organisation is commiunicated through blogs, social media, opinion articles placed in media and appointment notices. Financial metrics are communicated through Corporate PR and leadershihp is communicated through profiling senior representatives of the organisation's in the media.

The protecting and enhancing of an organisation's reputation is the key objective of PR. It can tell the story of an organisation, a public representative or a political party or cause by communicating each of the factors outlined by Weber Shandwick and the Reputation Institute as vital to the enhancement of reputation. It does this predominantly in the business world using one or all of the three main categories of PR: Cotporate, consumer and public affairs/political PR. Corporate and consumer PR will be discussed in this chapter. Political PR and public affairs will be discussed in Chapter 9. A brief explanation of all three categories illustrated by examples now follows.

8.4 Public Affairs

Whereas the main tool of the corporate and consumer PR professional is generally media relations, in public affairs and political PR, the emphasis is often on stakeholder relations. This means most of the activity will take place behind closed doors, through meetings or the placement of media questions at political meetings. An example of this can be seen in the award winning campaign from Norwegian Air and Cork Chamber of Commerce in Ireland's Public Relations Consultants' Association's Awards (PRCA, 2016).

Between 2014 and 2016, Norwegian Air was seeking approval to commence direct flights from Cork in the South of Ireland to Boston, United States of America. Cork Chamber of Commerce initiated a public affairs campaign to lobby businesses, political representatives and communities in Ireland and in the United States in order to obtain approval of a permit to operate the route. The route had been in demand for some time by the Cork business community but there had been a significant delay in the granting of the permit.

Cork Chamber, Cork Airport and the Irish Aviation Authority rallied to target the US Department of Transportation. They launched an extensive campaign targeting businesses and key stakeholders and also targeted European Union (EU) institutions as well as the Irish Ambassador to the US. A group of over 50 United States political representatives gave their support to the campaign. Finally, mainstream and social media were used to garner public support.

As a result, at the annual St Patrick's Day meeting of Irish and United States presidents, the then US President, President Obama mentioned the issue at his media conference following the planting of a question from a journalist. Four weeks later, the US Department of Transportation initiated a four-week consultation period with a view to approving the flights on completion of the period. However, in the interim, the American airline and pilot lobby groups commenced a high-profile campaign targeting the US Senate and Department of Transportation to prevent final approval being granted. The opposition was supported by several high-profile political representatives. However, the strong lobbying campaign from the Cork Chamber succeeded and approval was granted in 2016.

This is a typical example of public affairs in action. The core emphasis of the strategy is on stakeholder communications. This mainly involved the lobbying of the various groups including the politicians and business communities in Ireland and the United States as well as EU representatives. The media campaign was secondary to this, with media being used to support, persuade and influence the opinion leaders.

8.5 Corporate PR

Corporate PR is described by Van Riel (1995) as *'an instrument of management by means of which all consciously used forms of internal and external communications are harmonised as effectively and efficiently as possible, so as to create a favourable basis for relationships with groups upon which the organisation is dependent'*.

PR aims to communicate the narrative of the organisation or of its products or services. Consumer PR is the name given to the type of PR that tells the story of the product or service and corporate PR is the name given to the type of PR that tells the wider story of the organisation and its reputation. Public affairs, as we have seen in the previous example, is concerned with lobbying and political campaigning and is very different to corporate and consumer PR as we will now demonstrate in an example from German supermarket chain Lidl.

Lidl had engaged a PR agency in Ireland to improve its reputation. Following its entry into the Irish market, It seeked to position itself as part of the Irish supermarket framework and as a significant contributor to the Irish economy.

Lidl had become one of the largest supermarket players in the Irish market since it opened its doors over 15 years prior to this campaign. However, many consumers still had misconceptions about the origin of the products at the stores with many believing that they were sourced outside Ireland. There was a general misconception that Lidl was not as 'Irish' as other supermarkets.

A PR consultancy was recruited to challenge the misconceptions and highlight Lidl's commitment to working with and supporting Irish suppliers as well as the economy. The agency developed a narrative for Lidl. Firstly, it set up interviews for the local suppliers of products to Lidl stores with national and local media. Media features were broadcast on television, radio, print and online media.

Next press announcements were drafted and issued to all media announcing Lidl's commitment to equality in pay for employees and announcing new jobs. A photocall took place to accompany the release with the Minister for Enterprise. Details of an economic report undertaken by the company were released to media outlining the economic impacts of its operations in Ireland.

Finally, stakeholders were communicated with and a relationship building programme was initiated with them.

As a result, Lidl improved its position on the Reptrak report and moved into fifth place ahead of all other Irish grocery retailers. It increased its market share by 5% and increased its website traffic. The campaign was a huge success for Lidl and the agency involved because it succeeded in achieving its objectives and overall in improving the reputation of the brand in Ireland.

8.6 Consumer PR

Consumer PR is concerned with products or services rather than the over-arching brand itself. Again in 2016, the Irish Food Board sought to grow the sales of eggs in Ireland. The brand's research had revealed that consumption of eggs was high amongst young families and retired people but low amongst people in what they termed the 'pre-family' demographic. Therefore, it seeked to grow the sales of eggs amongst this group and increase the sales amongst the existing groups also.

The PR agency who was recruited to develop the campaign for the Food Board focussed its campaign around influencers, social and mainstream media.

Firstly brand ambassadors were secured with the two champion Olympic rowers, the O'Donovan brothers. The two brothers had gregarious personalities and performed very well in media interviews. A campaign tagline was developed: 'Fuel for a busy life'.

Video content was developed and broadcast across YouTube and social media. Interviews with the brothers were set up on radio, TV, print and online media.

In the end, 28 million more eggs were sold, traffic to the webpage increased by over 800%, and the volume of egg consumption increased significantly in the target group.

This is a classic example of consumer PR. In this case, the organisation involved was the Irish Food Board who wasn't concerned about its own brand reputation but about increasing the sales of one of its products amongst a wide demographic. The campaign and media activity reflect this. Consumer media was used widely as were social media channels popular with the general public. The media content was fun, easily accessible and very user friendly.

All the examples in this section come from the PRCA (2016) annual awards winning entries. The three examples demonstrate the key attributes of each of the main categories of PR and also highlight the differences between them. The consumer example is clearly focussed on a product, the corporate example is concerned with the reputation of the brand and not the products it sells and finally, the public affairs example is focussed on lobbying and stakeholder communications with media relations playing a secondary role. Stakeholder relations also plays a part in the corporate example but it is very much a secondary objective to the media activity.

8.7 Other PR Categories

Often in PR agencies, other terms are used to describe the type of PR carried out. For example, Not for Profit PR or Healthcare PR. All types of PR are using the same tools and categories as explained in Chapter 12 of this book. However, slight variances occur between these areas that are very specific to the type of sector. For example, if working as a PR official for a pharmaceutical company in what is called Healthcare PR, you might find yourself using your corporate PR skills to promote the organisation or your consumer PR skills to promote a product such as a new medicine launch. However, the manner in which you might do that is governed by very strict codes of conduct as set out by pharmaceutical societies.

The Not for Profit Sector is a popular sector and one that interests many PR students and those who seek to use their PR knowledge and skills for good causes.

Not for Profit is an umbrella term that covers all organisations that don't work for profit, such as charities, NGOs, community groups, voluntary organisations and more.

The Not for Profit PR professional is required to be a well-rounded individual with many skills and a knowledge of corporate, consumer and public affairs PR. Often Not for Profit PR will involve advocacy. For example, if working for a Cancer Society or for a Heart Foundation, you might be required to lobby the Government for the rights of your members. If representing a sports group, you might be required to lobby for community funding. Therefore, the Not for Profit PR professional should have knowledge of and contacts in the political world.

Fundraising is a large part of what a Not for Profit does and in this regard, the PR professional often crosses roles with the fundraising department. Raising awareness of fundraising events and activities becomes the consumer PR part of the Not for Profit role. The PR practitioner may also take on the role of website content writer as well as press release writer, media relations and social media content creator and moderator. It can be quite a broad and challenging role with large targets attached in terms of funding goals set by the Not for Profit organisation.

All of this of course must be achieved in a Not for Profit organisation with very little budget and this is perhaps the biggest challenge of all for this sector. Financial resources are limited. Transparency is key and finances and people must be stretched to their limits. It is a tough and rewarding sector to work in, in equal measure as a result.

The advocacy side of the Not for Profit role very much aims to raise awareness of a particular cause or concern to achieve a specific aim. However, the objectives of organisations working within this sector are very much in line with business objectives with many of the charities working to very ambitious targets to secure funding to perform their roles.

8.8 Conclusion

PR is a varied discipline that in the business world is mainly concerned with improving and protecting the reputation of organisations. It does this by creating a narrative for a brand, an organisation, a product, a service or a political campaign and communicating this narrative with its publics and stakeholders. As we discuss in this book, there is a growing responsibility on businesses in the Postmodern era to act ethically, to engage in Corporate Social Responsbility or Environmental Social Governance and to be seen to be empathetic in their leadership. This paves the way for a broadening of the categories of PR in the future.

8.9 For Discussion

- Think of a brand that has suffered a reputational crisis in recent times.
- Why do you think the brand had this reputational crisis?
- Devise a plan for the organisation to improve its reputation using corporate PR.
- In relation to the products or services of this company, how would you use consumer PR to promote it?
- How could this organisation effectively use public affairs?

References

Dowling, G. (2000). *Creating Corporate Reputations: Identity, Image and Performance.* OUP: Oxford.

Eccles et al. (2007). Reputation and its risks. Available at: https://hbr.org/2007/02/reputation-and-its-risks

Enders, A. and Lonescu-Somers, A. (2012). How Nestlé dealt with a social media campaign. against it https://www.ft.com/content/90dbff8a-3aea-11e2-b3f0-00144feabdc0

IPSOS (2019). The IPSOS Reputation Council Report. Available at: https://www.ips os.com/sites/default/files/ct/publication/documents/2019-06/ipsos_reputation_council_2019.pdf

Kilvert, N. (2018). Nestlé suspended from sustainable palm oil group following conduct breaches. https://www.abc.net.au/news/science/2018-06-29/nestle-suspended-sustainable-palm-oil/9923238

PRCA. (2016). https://www.prca.ie/prca-awards/#

Reptrak. (2022). https://www.reptrak.com/rankings/

Theaker, A. (2016). *The Public Relations Handbook.* 5th Edn. Routledge: New York.

Van Riel, C.B.M. (1995). *Principles of Corporate Communications.* Prentice-Hall International: Englewood Cliffs, NJ.

9 Public Affairs and Political Communications by Dr Robbie Smyth

Chapter Contents

9.1 What Is Public Affairs and Political Communication?

At its core level, political communications is the strategic application of key public relations (PR) theories within the environment of politics. As is the case with business-orientated PR, the objective of a political communications professional is to effectively plan and purposely communicate in a deliberate way. In the public affairs arena, PR professionals must represent clients and manage their relationships with key audiences and stakeholders. The difference here between

DOI: 10.4324/9781003253815-9

political public affairs and its corporate counterpart is the level of intensity and engagement involved. Corporate communications involves often finite and time-limited engagements in the public sphere. In public affairs, the engagement is ongoing unceasing as long as the client is a political representative. The media engagement is at a higher paced and often more hostile environment than encountered in corporate PR.

Political PR specialists compose press releases and organise photo opportunities and events. They identify key publics and develop strategic plans for their clients. The key difference is the goals of those plans. Political PR is about getting candidates elected. It is about being returned to office and ultimately wielding political power. The key currencies of political communications are votes in elections or referenda and public sentiment as measured by opinion poll.

The key differences between the two PR practices are as follows:

 i Channels of communications available.
 ii Objectives of a political communications strategy where focus is on winning.
 iii Specialised nature of conducting PR in government and elected assemblies.
 iv Communications tools available to practitioners.
 v Audience behaviours.

9.1.1 Learning Outcomes

Upon completion of the chapter, readers will have an understanding of:

 i Core classical and contemporary theories in the political communications sphere.
 ii How to plan and implement a political campaign.
 iii The key tools of political communication including the role and uses of political advertising, image building and issues management.
 iv The key professional roles and responsibilities in a political communication environment including lobbying and public affairs.
 v Outsider and NGO PR in a political context.
 vi Potential resources for future independent study and research.

9.2 Political Campaigning

Organising and implementing a political campaign is the foundation task of a political communication specialist. A campaign is a time-limited strategic plan, the objective of which is to promote your candidate and party in the most optimal positive way possible, given the available resources and the external environment the campaign is being launched into.

It involves the creation of key messages distributed across a range of media and communication platforms. The messages, oral, written and visual, articulate and frame the key themes of your candidate's ideological platform. A campaign involves selecting the appropriate channels of communication at the optimal moment to present and distribute these messages. A key theory to help aid this strategic planning is to consider Harold Laswell's theory of communication, synopsised by him as 'Who, says what, to whom, in which channel, to what effect' (Laswell, 1948). The phrasing by Laswell is a key template for considering before taking any form of communications action.

At a practical level, this means distiling the broad message and strategy of the political actor into specific PR activities. These include creating and executing press releases, photo notices, organising events, press conferences, speech writing, designing leaflets, posters, banners, back drops, stage design maybe and finally commissioning and editorialising political advertisements that can be broadcast on radio or TV as well as social media channels. It means forging a look or an image. It means creating a brand or developing an existing one to suit the objectives of your political actor.

9.2.1 There Are No Accidental Images

A first step in contemplating the campaigning process is to consider how do we forge a look or build a political brand. Images are key, and the political communications specialist should set themselves the goal that there should be no accidental images when it comes to promoting their candidate or party. They should always be considering the context in which the political actors they represent appear in public. This includes who is accompanying them and who will be in any photographs taken as a candidate enters and leaves a vehicle, a building or a stage. Often it is the case that the candidate is alone in these instances. This helps them to be clearly identified as the core symbol of the brand you are building. It also simplifies the process of forging a look and creating a style around the candidate.

A common example would be when politicians speak at party conferences and they are alone on stage. This practice is found across the world when it comes to political candidates.

A way to conceptualise what is needed is to establish a set of guides, beginning with a commitment to no accidental images. Add to this the idea of repetition between images. This means ensuring a continuity of message. It could be something simple like ensuring the campaign slogan, candidate or party name is clearly visible in every image. Then there is repetition within the image. This could be repetition of type of people, repetition of colours or the brand of a party, candidate or slogan. Finally, there is the principle of symmetry within the image.

Take the example of the presidential campaigns of Hilary Clinton and Donald Trump in the 2016 US presidential elections. Though the two candidates had very different campaign platforms, they employed similar methods when it came to creating a look. Hilary had a logo designed specifically for the campaign, while Trump used his surname helped by more than 40 years in the public eye and his singular use of the name in all his businesses.

Trump's campaign slogan was 'Make America great again', while Clinton's core slogan was 'Fighting for us' and 'Ready for Hillary'. Trump's static poster had his name always appearing in upper case against a dark blue background with five stars in red and a red rectangular border. Clintons' poster stressed her first name with either 'I'm ready for Hilary' or headlining 'Hilary' along with 'for president' and a hillaryclinton.com strapline, both in a much smaller type. Her 2016 logo was a capital H with an arrow superimposed point right and was often carried alongside the 'Hilary for president' text. The poster colour was predominantly blue with the logo and 'Hilary for president' in white, and the website details in red.

In both campaigns, these were printed in hard cardboard or plastic and distributed to rally attendees so the images could always appear in the shot. Clinton's campaign stops often had participants carrying these poster cards while wearing campaign T-Shirts. In both cases, there is clear repetition within and between images as the campaign develops. A quick search of other campaigns will find this method repeated, whether in Ireland, Britain and Europe – anywhere there is strategy to engage voters.

Symmetry is achieved sometimes simply by having the candidate in the centre foreground. Often this is achieved by using a lectern adorned with the appropriate background. It is possible though to achieve symmetry in the background also with a party or candidate slogan centre background or it could be more subtle through use of other images, such as use of flags evenly distributed on either side of the candidate or people if the audience is being used as a background. Again this method is used across the political spectrum.

So across the world candidates forge a look. Take the example of Muhammadu Buhari elected president of Nigeria in 2015 and 2019. As he transitioned from military office, he forged a new look where he consistently wears the same style of hat along with a usually white kaftan tunic, very different from when he became a military head of state in Nigeria in 1983. Indian Prime Minister Narendra Modi has also created a consistent look in all his public appearances, usually wearing a white khadi kurta.

9.2.2 Building a Campaign Strategy

Constructing a successful campaign strategy involves a parallel process of political marketing and a logistical campaign that optimises the marketing decisions taken. Newman describes political marketing as 'the application of marketing principles and procedures in political campaigns' (Newman, 1999a). This includes 'the analysis, development, execution and management of strategic campaigns'.

This strategic approach 'seeks to drive public opinion, advance their own ideologies, win elections, and legislation and referenda' (Newman, 1999a).

Newman introduced a still valid and workable template for a PR practitioner to build a campaign around their candidate or party. He called it a 'predictive model of voter behaviour' (Newman, 1999b). The key to Newman's theory is that there are 'five distinct and separate cognitive domains that drive voter's behaviour' (Newman, 1999b, p. 20).

The domains are as follows: (1) Political issues, (2) Social imagery, (3) Candidate personality, (4) Situational contingency, and (5) Epistemic value (Newman & Perloff, 2004, p. 20). You can begin the process of constructing a viable campaign by your strategic answers to these questions.

This would include identifying the key political issues of the period your campaign is being contested in. There is usually a variety of accessible sources. These would include summarising what your opponents present as the issues or what the news media is highlighting. It could involve consulting reliable and relevant stakeholders. Alternatively, undertaking the simple act of systematically canvassing your potential constituents can reap a deeper understanding of the political environment. This last step can be built into building constituency credibility for your candidate. A vital element in this is what solutions and policies your party or candidate proposes on this. These answers tie into the issues of situational contingency and epistemic value discussed as follows.

Social imagery involves forging a consistent look for your candidate. It is not just about their personal presentation, it encompasses where and with whom the candidate is pictured. You cannot change a candidate's personality, but you can audit how it is perceived and advise on how best to present themselves on the hustings, on the campaign trail and in their media engagements.

The last two elements of the Newman and Perloff criteria are the most challenging. 'Situational contingency' involves understanding how the political actor reacts and is understood in the current political reality. Consider the case of 2022 of Ukrainian President Volodymyr Zelenskyy, he had been elected president in a wave of anti-corruption sentiment in 2019. His presidency was challenging, his popularity declining and the news media questioning of his capabilities. The crisis has shown another side of Zelensky, and his spirited approach to coordinating the defence of Ukraine has won plaudits and admiration across the political spectrum. Many politicians struggle to adapt to changing political conditions and unforeseen crises, and this is why political PR practitioners must spend some time considering what challenges await their party or candidate.

Finally the question of 'epistemic value'. This means how is the knowledge, and the perceived capability of a candidate or party valued by voters and the news media. For example, political parties who are new entrants into legislatures, or who are challenging to enter government are often faced with questioning about their readiness. Are they up to the challenge of government if they have never held office? In the United States, there are a number of candidates and political representatives who have military service, and this has an epistemic value. On the other hand, candidates with impressive college and university qualifications do not have the currency with voters that such credentials would have once had.

There are other views and advice on how to organise a campaign. Parks and Weiner (2022) also favour a checklist approach. Their campaign planning criteria include 'figuring out how many votes you need to win office, you will need finance, communications and volunteer managers, and they stress the power of door to door canvassing, especially for local office' (Parks & Weiner, 2022). A good resource to access here is the campaign workshop (www.campaignworkshop.com)

9.2.3 The Campaign Trail Logistics

At its basic level, a political campaign is a number of predetermined events. How many places will the candidate visit? How many days, how many stops per day? At one level, this is based on practicality of geography and access, but you still need to plan this aspect of the campaign based on which areas and which events will have the greatest influence on voters.

But the physical campaign is not wholly centred on the candidate. Across the voting, constituency activists should be leafletting, postering and organising micro events. These heighten the party/candidate's visibility in the constituency without their actual physical presence.

There is also the opportunity to build deeper connections and understanding among your campaign team and with potential supporters who might take a more active role in the work. An example of a micro event could be an open house meeting, where a local supporter opens their home to neighbours to discuss the campaign. The householder, aided by a competent campaign team member, hosts a meeting where the key platform messages of the party and candidate are introduced. The use of local constituents is an important conduit to more long-lasting links to voters.

There is also the question of campaign content. This will be in print, online and where allowed also in the form possibly of party political broadcasts. There will possibly be TV and radio interviews, and candidate debates. Your candidate will need a poster, a slogan that is derived from the strategic assessment of the conclusions of your campaign strategy. The literature and media interventions of the candidate must optimise the key issues and positive aspects of the candidate's personality. They must also translate into a positive situational contingency and epistemic value for the candidate.

Earlier I stated that there should be no accidental images of political actors, and there should also be no accidental written communications, which as ever returns us to the already mentioned 5W method from Laswell. Every media intervention whether it is in print, online or TV and radio should be carefully considered and planned beforehand.

For example, one simple strategy is to always allow a candidate time to prepare for a media interview. This could mean taking a few hours off the campaign trail, but the rewards for a well-conducted and presented interview outweigh the harm caused by ill-thought answers. A workable approach here is for the PR professional to do an interview run through with the candidate asking the testing questions that a media interviewer will put to the candidate.

Similarly, when it comes to using the growing range of social media platform, there should be a coordinated review process. It is common for candidates and their local party organisations to have separate social media presence. This is fine and can be advantageous. However, the output from both should be continually in sync. A communications manager should act as a clearing house for social media content, which should always be tied back to the strategic goals of the campaign. This links back into other aspects of this book where communication plans are discussed.

Finally, attention needs to be given to what material is being distributed on behalf of the candidate. It too must be aligned with the strategic goals of the campaign. It is quite common for a candidate to distribute at least four pieces of literature into people's homes. The first would introduce the candidate, laying out broad themes of their platform. The second would be a longer piece, a microcosm of the manifesto. The third might focus on a specific local issue. The fourth would be a reminder of the polling day and a call to action. These need to be designed, printed and distributed. There will need to be social imagery that dovetails with the campaign and securing these images is an important task.

9.2.4 Political Advertising

The role of filmed advertisements for candidates and parties has grown exponentially since Rosser Reeves created the first-ever televised political ad in 1952 (Wood, 1990). It had an earworm song and was one of a series of 30–60 second spots that aired during the campaign. In the succeeding years, there has been a growth in advertisements and they are an important tool of political communication campaigns across the world. A great source of the US presidential election ads can be found at the Museum of the Moving Image's Living Room Candidate website (livingroomcandidate.org).

The impact of online and social media platforms has given a new arena for political advertisements and they are a feature of political communications strategies not just during an election campaign but are used consistently by political representatives and political groups. The production values vary from lavish concept ads to candidates talking to camera. One way of considering what type of video to make is review Diamond and Bates TV advertising typologies (Diamond & Bates, 1993). They catalogue the types of advertising commonly found on political TV adverts. Their list includes as follows: (1) Primitive, (2) Talking Head, (3) Negative, (4) Production/Concept, (5) Cinema Verite, (6) Man in the Street, (7) Testimonials, and (8) Neutral Reporter.

A quick review of the range of political videos on YouTube, Instagram and TickTock in particular will show you the relevance of this list when it comes to deciding what videos fit in with your own communication strategy and budget.

Alongside this, you need to consider ideas of a critical snippet from the videos which can be reproduced on social media as an introduction to the video proper and also the key piece that the news media will centre on. We are familiar with the idea of sound bites. Schill in 2012 introduced the idea of 'video bites' (Schill, 2012) while others had measured TV coverage of political stories. Bucy and Grabe's work in 2007 found that 'Sound bites accounted for 14.3% of election coverage in the US, Image bites 25.1%, with candidate focussed image bites accounting for 25.8 seconds per story'. Armed with this understanding, a communications professional should be able to structure their videos to make them more likely to get news coverage.

Schill also identifies ten functions of visuals in political videos. They are as follows: (1) Image as Argument, (2) Agenda Setting, (3) Dramatisation, (4) Emotional Function, (5) Image Building, (6) Documentation, (7) Identification, (8) Societal Symbol, (9) Transportation, and (10) Ambiguity (Schill, 2012). A practical example of the value of this categorisation is to study where candidates deploy different functions. For example, in the run up to an election, a candidate or party often has a thematic generalised video which would include most of the ten criteria, while a political representative who wanted to highlight a specific issue might rely on the documentation function.

Motta and Fowler (2016) focus on the growth of negative messaging in videos. This tactic is commonly used across the world, but you should only use these methods as part of a wider communication strategy. Seeberg and Nai (2020) note that negative campaigning tends to be focus on three areas. They are 'issue, policy or personal' based (Seeberg & Nai, 2020).

Fowler (2018) notes the rise in digital advertising, even though TV spots are still the most used form of video advertising. She also notes the role of 'third party interest groups' who are increasingly playing a role in US elections with direct appeals to voters (Fowler, 2018). Negative advertising has been in recent years a hallmark of political campaigns in the USA, but also in the Brexit and Scottish independence referenda in Britain.

Despite this focus on video-based political advertising, there is still an important role for print advertising, particularly on billboards and street-level advertising, much of which has a digital option and political posters. There is also striking use of poster-based advertising on public transport networks as this guarantee a mass exposure to the advert. So if the budget allows these are viable advertising methods. As I write this in Dublin, there are adverts supporting Ukraine, often with the hashtag – 'we stand with Ukraine'. These ads are on digital bus shelters, larger billboard displays and digital screens around the city. The council has also erected Ukrainian flags on lampposts across the city.

9.3 Public Affairs: The Role of PR in Government

If getting elected is a challenge from a PR perspective, staying in political office, even in the context of holding your seat, or being returned to power involves another challenge and the formulation of a specific PR strategy to achieve these outcomes.

Also important are the PR strategies employed while a candidate is a member of legislature, whether it is a local council or a state parliament. Common to each case is the need to demonstrate to the key voting public that you are actively at work positively in an ongoing capacity on their behalf while holding office.

It is a longer term version of the strategy created to get elected. The political actor and or the party they belong to need to be able to demonstrate a record of achievement and be able to communicate this to key publics effectively. This is why when political parties enter government they often create a specific PR event transitioning their manifesto into a programme for government.

The first step in this process is to consider how your key publics change when you enter political office. Yes, you have voters to consider and sometimes there might be specific lobby and interest groups that you identified during the election campaign. There are new publics in terms of the personnel involved in running the legislature you are elected to, the institutions that deliver services on behalf of it and your other elected colleagues.

On a national or regional level, dealing with the agencies of government can be complex. The political media take on a new role too as they become active commentators on your effectiveness as a political representative or as a member of government.

Similar to the approach taken to getting elected, there is a need for a planned strategy to be formulated and implemented. At one level, it involves simple objectives such as what are the key three actions or outcomes you want to achieve in your first year of office, and the same question holds for your first term also. An example of this would have been Barrack Obama's commitment to a healthcare act. Boris Johnson in Britain had a campaign slogan that set the theme for his first year in office when he declared the incoming government's key task was to 'Get Brexit done'. These are all examples of a political strategy being communicated to the electorate through an effective credible PR communications strategy.

How will you maintain contact with voters and how will you communicate with them in office? Many politicians around the world use a combination of leaflets, targeted mass letters and local meetings with a matching social media strategy. Social media tools like Instagram and Facebook are excellent platforms to connect with voters. You can give immediate commentary after specific events such as keynote launches of policy or something as simple as what a public representative did in a particular week. These updates communicate concisely and directly to your support base.

Politicians will also seek to get positive mentions and appearances in print and broadcast media. It is the job of the political PR practitioner to plan and organise this. This work ranges from identifying positive photo opportunities to creating press releases on key issues that will translate into positive coverage. It also means seeking to get your political representative on air in a positive way that builds their stature and reputation and enhances their public persona.

The most effective way to achieve these outcomes and optimise the political representative's public reputation is to create a media calendar that identifies key events in the year and matches this with specific media outlets where you will seek coverage. In print, it should identify key reporters on issues relevant to your electorate, as well as opinion writers that are commenting on general politics and relevant issues. For broadcast radio and TV, a similar exercise should be performed. A good political PR practitioner is continually building on their contacts' address book. There is also a need to plan for the potential negatives that challenge political representatives. This though is a topic on its own. Sometimes called crisis communication but for an effective political PR specialist it is known as 'issues management'.

9.3.1 Issues Management

You need to accept that there will be mistakes, accidents and unforeseen events that challenge your candidate, political representative and even their political party. Many of these might be unforeseeable, but are they really?

A prudent PR practitioner contemplates all that could go wrong. This can be broken into the following groupings. Firstly, issues related to the candidate's personal life that might have negative political implications. Secondly are the issues related to the wider political environment. What would be the implications, for example, of a large employer running into business difficulties or seeking to relocate to another area? What are the state of local public facilities such as transport, education and health services? Are there potential conflicts over draft development plans that might involve significant construction or change in the constituency?

In the same way that the political PR practitioner complies a list of media contacts, there is merit in compiling a list of local stakeholders and interest groups, with a rundown of their positions on local issues.

Finally, there are situational contingency issues. How will you deal with the unexpected? These can be best dealt with by preplanning and using traditional PR strategies of crisis communication. One aspect of this that frequently disrupts and can end a politician's career is the failure to deal effectively with a crisis through either a delayed response or an incomplete explanation of their involvement with a particular issue.

Boris Johnson's political legacy is being tainted by the ongoing negative and divisive media coverage surrounding breaches of lockdown in Downing Street. Much of this could have been avoided by a full admission when the breaches were first revealed.

9.3.2 Political Communication as Lobbying

What is sometimes called public affairs is a key aspect of political communications. This is where PR professionals play a role in lobbying elected representatives, political parties, ministers and the wider government. The aim of this lobbying is firstly to convey the views and concerns of your clients. Secondly, its aim is to influence government policies, decision-making and ultimately legislation.

At any given time in its life, a government is in the process of preparing and passing legislation into law. They are also undertaking significant spending decisions in the current time period. The public affairs professional has to have an understanding of both the current decisions and future planning.

Their task is to gain access to the elected representatives and where possible get the opportunity to make their specific case for and against a specific government policy. In many cases, there are powerful funded bodies who take on this role for a specific industry or sector. And so across Europe and other democracies, you will find employers organisations and specific industry groups, that are measured by their members in terms of their effectiveness in influencing government legislation. They are both a membership body and a lobbying organisation.

The PR practitioner in this context has three key tasks. One is developing a comprehensive understanding of the government's spending and legislative agenda. The second is gaining access to politicians. The third is communicating effectively on their client's issues. Presentation and pitching skills are important here. But also vital is leaving the client with clear and effective documentation that makes your case.

9.4 NGO and Outsider PR

There are other political groups that benefit from bringing a PR focus to their work. In this broad spectrum, we can move from NGOs and charities to lobby groups, activist-based organisations such as are prevalent in the environmental issues sector, trade unions and a range of protest-based and single-issue groups whose goals, membership and organisation are fluid and seem ad hoc compared to the regimentation of political parties.

What they have in common often is limited resources both in terms of people and finance to commit to the PR function, and so more planning and strategizing are necessary to optimise their PR output. These groups are fundamentally different from the powerful industry and employers groups already mentioned.

These groups can successfully create media events and a temporary positive or open focus on their mission, but like any other PR strategy or plan, they must identify their publics and hone a message that can land successfully with them.

Examples of effective outsider groups from the late 20th century who have successfully used PR strategies to grow not just their organisation's profile but the group itself would be Amnesty International and Greenpeace. In each case, these groups grew from an idea into an activist-based movement. In the 21st century, examples include Gretta Thunberg's school strikes protests and the emergence of Extinction Rebellion. All of these groups used simple PR strategies to promote their activities and most are activist event-based groups.

Cox (2010) and Cox and Pezzullo (2021) outline some possible strategies used by environmental advocacy groups many of which are relevant to all NGOs and outsider groups. There are as follows: (1) Political and legal channels, (2) Direct appeals to public audiences, and (3) Consumer-orientated actions. Cox in 2010 describes these as 'modes of advocacy', which would include political lobby, entering elections or litigation in the case of the political and legal channel. Direct appeals include, 'community organising, education, media events and direct action' (Cox, 2010, p. 228). Consumer actions would include 'consumer boycotts, shareholder actions, consumer spending campaigns' (Cox, 2010, p. 228).

Cox introduces another key tool for the PR professional here that of 'critical dialogue', epitomised succinctly by the work of Bob Hunter, one of the founders of Greenpeace. Cox writes that a critical rhetoric 'may include the articulation of an alternative policy, vision or ideology' (Cox, 2010, p. 229). This is sometimes characterised by the phrase 'mind bomb'. Hunter's vision of Greenpeace was situated in this sphere. Even the name of the organisation juxtaposing two terms into one brand is an example of critical rhetoric. Greenpeace deployed mind bombs by creating highly visual direct action events such as disrupting whale fishing and occupying nuclear test sites in the Pacific Ocean. Filming these actions and at times embedding journalists within the crews of Greenpeace ships maximised the media coverage they received, while bringing the issue of whaling into the international news media.

In recent years, the Thunberg school strikes and the Extinction Rebellion actions are examples again of using critical rhetoric with direct actions as a form of successful critical advocacy. These strategies can be deployed in a range of environments. The Yellow Vest movement in France would be an example, as would be farmers' protests in Ireland and Netherlands over the last three years, where farmers used their tractors to slow and block traffic. The action got them into the news cycle where their civil disobedience offered an opportunity to educate a much wider section of the public on the grounds of the problems that had led to the protests.

Most NGOs and outsider organisations are trying to build awareness of their issue, grow membership and raise funding for their organisation, so their PR strategies should reflect these needs. The more loosely organised groups in this sector usually just want to build awareness around an issue and this typically means using direct action as their key communication strategy. They still need to organise press releases and photo notices. Events are still planned and organised to optimise media exposure and coverage.

Finally, the key challenge for these groups is the diminishing media interest in their actions and campaigns. This is what makes the activities of groups such as Amnesty or Greenpeace merit further study as they have transitioned successfully from newly formed group to established long-term activism.

9.5 Political Media

A specifically mass political media has been a feature of communications since the printing revolution instigated by Guttenberg's printing press. The social outcomes of a mass reading public have been replicated around the world.

The idea of news, the reporting and discussion of new events is a feature of society since the emergence of writing. Consider Caesar's account of the conquest of Gaul written in 58 BCE or Gerald of Wales' Topographia Hiberniae text on Ireland from 1188 CE. Both of these texts, despite their bias and errors, became for a time the definitive accounts of these places. Modern news is often a continuation of this process where the content creators play an explanatory and educational role for audiences on the current issue in focus.

Printing provided a new mass audience for news, and initially, in Europe, the news sheet emerged, developing into the newspaper we see all around the world today. What had been the preserve of political leaders was now accessible to a wider audience. One European example of this would be the decision to print Martin Luther's 95 Theses in October 1517. Originally written in Latin, a German version was printed in December and with subsequent reprints, thousands of copies were distributed in the following months (Economist, 2011).

By the 17th century, newspapers were established all over Europe and played an important role in the articulation of the politics of dissent and rebellion that were a key factor for example in the United States and French revolutions. Newspapers had become part of what Habermass terms a public sphere, where the role of private citizens discussing and deliberating on political issues had become a key societal process (Habemass, 1989). It marked the beginning of a period where governments and institutions of authority had to accept the conditional nature of their public support and develop strategies of persuasion and propaganda to grow and bolster that support. The widening electoral franchise that became a feature of Europe and the United State of America in the 19th century drove the growth of political media, and so a new phase of political communication was born.

9.5.1 Political Media Online

The processes of political communication have been transformed in the 21st century by the impact of social media platforms and the accompanying unrelenting torrent of communication that streams online daily. This impact has been felt in three areas.

1 The operation and structure of traditional legacy political media.
2 The creation of a new form of public sphere with tens of millions of mass communicators.
3 The creation of new channels of political communication.

9.5.2 Political Media Today

Political media today encompasses a range of content outlets including hourly news bulletins on the radio, longer broadcasts including documentaries and investigative-based shows on TV, as well current affairs programmes on radio, TV and now online. Political media has also spilled over into light entertainment broadcasts such as chat shows, where political guests are commonplace. The hosts of these programmes often build political themes into their opening monologues, and other guests including journalists and writers often raise political themes. In many media markets there are wide-ranging news media outlets including 24-hour TV and radio stations with news and talk show formats.

The primary roles of political media are to:

1 Report on events.
2 Comment and interpret on these events.
3 Conduct investigations in the political arena.

In this context, media can have an important agenda-setting role (McCombs & Shaw, 1972). This means in practice that the gatekeeping role of news media is critical here. It is the process of how the owners and editors of news media form decisions about what events to cover and report on, and how much resources to devote to a particular issue. It means selecting interview subjects and deciding how will political parties, their representatives and the issues they want to highlight be dealt with. In practice day to day, it means how many column inches, how many headlines and how much air time on radio, TV or online.

An example of this process in action would be the decision by US news organisations to devote a disproportionate amount of coverage during the 2016 US presidential election campaign to the candidacy and campaign of Donald Trump. In 2022, it was shown by the focus the news media gave to the Russian invasion of Ukraine compared to other conflicts.

A political PR practitioner has to consider their candidate or party in the context of this gatekeeping process. How are different news media outlets disposed to the candidate or political party? It means developing a strategy of navigating the political media in their specific region, deciding which specific papers, radio stations or TV stations and within this which specific programmes, producers and journalists would have a more positive attitude to the political message you are promoting. Often it is the case that political representatives bypass journalists, media outlets and specific programmes they believe are biased against them.

In this process, it is imperative for a political PR practitioner to continually build and develop an address book of media personnel, identifying their interests and specialisms, which are particularly important when pitching ideas for coverage.

At a basic level, it means deciding when and in what context should a political representative or their spokesperson appear in the media, and what format is best suited for a particular scenario.

There is a range of commonly used routes to achieve this, each has its own strength and value:

i A press conference, designed to provide content and visuals that will optimise the message being communicated.

ii A wider membership-based event where political supporters are present, such as a party conference or political rally.

iii A deliberately truncated short event, often called a doorstep, specifically designed for broadcast media, where a political representative makes a statement and answers questions for a short period of time. Events like this often coincide with another event the political representative is entering or exiting. It can create a segue into longer coverage of one of the other events. It is a platform for creating sound and video bites.

iv A longer set piece interview, usually one on one. It can be for either broadcast or print media.

v Debate formats, usually used in broadcast media where there is a panel of political representatives.

vi Secret briefing of a select journalist allowed a 'scoop' on the basis that other news outlets will have to follow up coverage.

9.5.3 Adversarial Journalism

An example of one specific challenge political parties and their candidates have in the broadcast environment is dealing with the practice of Adversarial Journalism. Oxford Reference defines this as, 'A model of reporting in which the journalist's role involves adopting a stance of opposition and a combative style in order to expose perceived wrongdoings. This style is sometimes criticized as being aggressively antagonistic or cynically divisive' (Oxford, 2022).

This is the modus operandi of broadcast journalism in many countries. It is a challenge for a political representative in this environment, because no matter how good or relevant an answer or interjection is the host will never concur. For the audience, this can be bewildering. But for the political communication adviser, it is a very difficult environment to have your candidate or political representative involved, yet it is the default broadcast news position.

9.6 Propaganda and Persuasion

Propaganda is probably one of the least understood tools of political communication yet one of the most used by strategists. In this section, we will look at definitions of propaganda and consider its application in a political communications context. We will juxtapose the idea of propaganda with persuasion and discuss both, exploring the contexts of use in contemporary political communication, from a practical and ethical perspective. We will also consider the impact that social media has had on political communication, creating a potent tool of considerable scale compared to previous methods of propaganda and persuasion.

Jowett and O'Donnell (2018, p. 1) describe propaganda as, 'a form of communication that attempts to achieve a response that furthers the intent of the propagandist'. Persuasion is 'interactive and attempts to satisfy the needs of both persuader and persuade' (Jowett & O'Donnell, 2018, p. 1). When describing propaganda often the focus is on what is called 'black' propaganda or 'agitprop' and a lot less on 'grey, white, deep and sub propaganda' which all merit consideration. Even if you decide not to deploy a propaganda strategy, there is still a need to understand when your components are deploying it against you.

At its foundation level today, propaganda is understood as 'spin' where a political communications source attempts to redefine or repackage an event or an issue that is more palatable or more positive for the group represented by the source. This can be achieved at a range of levels and methods.

For example, when writing a press release, you are not just relaying information that might be used in a media article, you are suggesting a headline and the order of which a story should be covered. This is the beginning of spin and also propaganda.

Propaganda is a method of communicating with an audience to get them to do something. It could be to vote for a particular party or candidate, or more negatively to convince someone not to vote. Agitprop is intentional agitation. Soules (2015, p. 7) describes it as propaganda that, 'stirs up its target audience to participate in revolution, war' or 'rapid social change', it is 'highly visible and short lived'. Recent examples would include the actions and communications of former US President Donald Trump in the days before the January 6 insurrection in 2021.

The 2022 campaign to support Ukraine after the Russian invasion is another powerful example as this agitprop would not be seen by many to be negative and so people have marched, donated money, food and other supplies, offered shelter for refugees and supported the supply of military equipment and ordinance to Ukraine. They have used hashtags supporting Ukraine in their social media posts and in general adopted a position of active support for the Ukrainian government.

Compare this to the lack of active support for the people of Hong Kong, Palestine or Yemen, and other numerous places of conflict or depravation around the world. One conclusion is that the Ukraine invasion has had a much more effective communication strategy at the centre of the political campaign to build support for their cause.

Soules uses the work of Ellul (1965) to build his definitions of propaganda. And so he writes of: (1) Political versus social propaganda, (2) Agitation versus integration propaganda, (3) Vertical versus horizontal propaganda, and (4) Irrational versus rational propaganda (Ellul, 1965). Political propaganda has a centralised source such as a political party or a government. It is deliberate and intentional. Sociological propaganda arises out of the interactions of society and is seen in trends and fashions. The media in all its forms plays an important role as a conduit for sociological propaganda. For political propaganda, the challenge is to access the media successfully to have your message communicated.

The political communications specialist will invest time in understanding these processes, especially examples of sociological propaganda, as these provide valuable insight into the wider political environment their candidates or party are competing in.

Agitative propaganda is self-explanatory. You want the receiving audience to take action, to do a particular thing. In integrative propaganda, the intention is acceptance and conformity with the outcomes promoted by the propagandist. Vertical propaganda originates in the elites of society, while horizontal propaganda spreads through populations in a very different way, ad hoc, through communal and social interactions. Irrational propaganda is characterised by events like moral panics, where emotion, sentiment and shared fears provoke an action. Rational propaganda involves erroneous use of research and science to promote false beliefs.

We already provided examples of agitprop, but what of integrative propaganda? One example from the Covid pandemic experience was the widespread public acceptance in the early months of strict lockdowns, and then in some communities, the significant take up of vaccines. The messages from government and the justification for lockdowns or shelter in place orders were an example of vertical propaganda, while the panic buying of toilet roll and other household items was an example of horizontal propaganda. Rational propaganda is shown in some of the arguments of the vaccine refusers and the supposed 'research' based arguments they made against being vaccinated.

The term 'black propaganda' is often used in political communication discussion. Jowett and O'Donnell (2018, p. 18) define black propaganda as 'where the source is concealed, or credited to a false authority and spreads lies, fabrications and falsehoods'. White propaganda on the other hand 'comes from a source that is identified and the information in the message tends to be accurate' (Jowett & O'Donnell, 2018, p. 17). 'Grey propaganda is somewhere between, we are not sure of the source or the accuracy of the information' (Jowett & O'Donnell, 2018, p. 20).

Examples of white propaganda would be government ads on healthy eating or safe driving. Black and grey propaganda have found a new provenance in social media and have begun to be documented particularly well by governments concerned about the infiltration and impact on elections by foreign agents (DiResta et al., 2019).

That being said there is a range of propaganda tactics commonly used by politicians. Johnson-Cartee and Copeland provide a comprehensive list of these. It includes a range of simple and viable strategies including 'name calling, propaganda slinging where you accuse your opponent of propaganda, asymmetrical definitions where you use phrases that evoke shared feelings, glittering generalities, positive and negative testimonials, over generalising, false analogies and bandwagon appeals' (Johnson-Cartee & Copeland, 2004).

9.6.1 Persuading the Political Audience

Where this leaves us is with the idea that the political audience can be persuaded and propagandised. Rather than offer a 'how to' guide for this, a more ethical step would be to study the voter. A good political communications professional takes the time to understand their audience. Indeed, it is a key PR strategy: Identify and categorise your audience. So how do we go about this? Well, it can be achieved qualitatively and quantitatively.

But first a theoretical pause. Today's voter does not wake up daily full of political ideas, beliefs and attitudes. They are usually latent and it is only through the events of the day, the week and the year that these beliefs manifest themselves. Consider the amount of terms we have to describe the voter. We can look at them demographically by age, gender, occupation, education and geographical area. This can often be an accurate determination of political perspective. However, alongside this, we talk about a person's values and beliefs, their ideological anchors. Finally, there are the views, opinions and attitudes that are the actual demonstration of a person's political ideologies in a practical sense.

It is the task of political communication professionals to navigate these factors and influence the voter ethically. Robert Worcester, one of the founders of Market Opinion Research International, and Irving Crespi, a long-term pollster with Gallup in the United States, both addressed the question of the links between a voter's beliefs and their persuadable attitudes. Worcester characterised a person's values as being like 'the deep tides of public mood, slow to change, but powerful'. Opinions, he believed are 'the ripples on the surface of the public's consciousness – shallow and easily changed'. Worcester describes attitudes as 'the currents below the surface, deeper and stronger' (Davison, 2022). Perloff describes 'attitudes and their close cousins, values and beliefs', as being the 'stuff of persuasion', the 'materials persuaders try to change' (Perloff, 2014, p. 69).

Crespi described public opinion as being 'multi-dimensional, interactive and continually changing' (Davison, 2022). The Pew Research Center has theorised on other effects on opinion formation which included period, lifecycle, cohort or generational effects (Doherty et al., 2015).

In the United States, the Values and Lifestyles approach has been used in academia and business as a means of understanding audiences, particularly in the context of consumer behaviour. It was created by Arnold Mitchell while working for SRI International (Berger, 2019). Nielsen's Prizm approach segments US households into 66 groupings (Nielsen, 2009, 2022). These are both considered to be psychographic approaches to understanding audiences based on the ideas of 'motivational research' theorised by Ernest Dichter (Dichter, 1960, 2004).

There are multiple theories and tools to aid the understanding of the voter. The political communications practitioner needs to devote time to study these and build an effective toolbox for their political strategizing when it comes to planning and implanting a campaign on behalf of a client.

9.7 Conclusions

We have introduced the key concepts of political communication. Where possible we have outlined the theories and research underpinning the ideas here and provided practical examples of the ideas at work. We have shown how to build a political campaign and explored the more complex principles of formulating a successful strategy. We have looked at the core tasks of PR in government, the idea of public affairs and lobbying. Also touched on were the key elements of NGO and outsider PR. The role of the political media in all of this was discussed as was the environment of propaganda and persuasion.

References

Berger, A. A. (2019). Six marketing typologies in search of a customer. *Consumer Cultural Studies*. Available at: https://journal.poligran.edu.co/index.php/libros/article/download/1535/1426/4207.

Cox, R. (2010). *Environmental Communication and the Public Sphere*. 2nd Ed. Sage Publishing.

Cox, R. and Pezzullo, P. C. (2021). *Environmental Communication and the Public Sphere.* 6th Ed. Sage Publishing.

Davison, W. P. (2022). Public opinion. Available at: https://www.britannica.com/topic/public-opinion/The-Middle-Ages-to-the-early-modern-period#ref258755.

Diamond, E. and Bates, S. (1993). *The Spot: The Rise of Political Advertising on Television.* 3rd Ed. MIT Press: Cambridge, MA.

Dichter, E. (1960, 2004). *The Strategy of Desire.* Transaction Publishers.

DiResta et al. (2019). The tactics and tropes of the internet research agency. *Congress of the USA.*

Doherty et al. (2015). The whys and how of generations research. *Pew Research Center.*

Economist. (2011). How Luther went viral. Available at: https://www.economist.com/christmas-specials/2011/12/17/how-luther-went-viral. [Accessed 18 March 2022].

Ellul, J. (1965). *Propaganda: The Formation of Men's Attitudes.* Vintage Books: New York.

Fowler, E. F. (2018). The big lessons of political advertising in 2018, the conversation. Available at: https://theconversation.com/the-big-lessons-of-political-advertising-in-2018-107673.

Habemass, J. (1989). *The structural transformation of the public sphere: An inquiry into a category of bourgeois society (Translated by Burger T. with the assistance of Lawrence F.).* Polity Press: Cambridge.

Johnson-Cartee, K. and Copeland, G. (2004). *Strategic Political Communication: Rethinking Social Influence, Persuasion, and Propaganda.* Rowman and Littlefield.

Jowett, G. S. and O'Donnell, V. (2018). *Propaganda & Persuasion,* 7th Ed. Sage Publishing.

Laswell, H. (1948). The Structure and Function of Mass Communication in Society. In Schramm, W. and Roberts, D. F. (1971). *The Process and Effects of Mass Communication.* University of Illinois Press: Urbana, pp. 84–99.

McCombs, M. E. and Shaw, D. L. (1972). The agenda setting function of mass media. *Public Opinion Quarterly* 36, no. 2, 176–187.

Motta, P. M. and Fowler, F. E. (2016). *The Content and Effect of Political Advertising in U.S. Campaigns.* Oxford Research Encyclopedia of Politics.

Newman, B. I. (1999a). *The Mass Marketing of Politics: Democracy in an Age of Manufactured Images.* Sage: Thousand Oaks, California.

Newman, B. I. (1999b). *Handbook of Political Marketing.* Sage: Thousand Oaks, California.

Parks, M. and Weiner, C. (2022). How to run for office. Available at: https://www.npr.org/2019/10/15/770332855/how-to-run-for-office. [Accessed 5 May 2022].

Perloff, R. M. (2014). *The Dynamics of Persuasion.* Routledge.

Schill, D. (2012). The visual image and the political image: A review of visual communication research in the field of political communication. *Review of Communication* 12, no. 2: 118–142.

Seeberg, H. B. and Nai, A. (2020). Undermining a rival party's issue competence through negative campaigning: Experimental evidence from the USA, Denmark, and Australia, Political Studies.

Soules, M. (2015). *Media Persuasion and Propaganda.* Edinburgh University Press.

Wood, S. (1990). Television's first political spot ad campaign: Eisenhower answers America. *Presidential Studies Quarterly* 20, no. 2, Eisenhower Centennial Issue (Spring, 1990): 265–283.

Websites Used or Mentioned

Amnesty International. Available at: https://www.amnesty.ie/
Greenpeace. Available at: https://www.greenpeace.org/eu-unit/
Living Room Candidate. Available at: http://www.livingroomcandidate.org/
Nielsen. Available at: https://global.nielsen.com/
Oxford Reference. Available at: https://www.oxfordreference.com/
Pew Research Center. Available at: https://www.pewresearch.org/

10 The Roles of PR Practitioners

Chapter Contents

10.1 Learning Outcomes

On completion of this chapter, the reader will be able to:

- Demonstrate a critical understanding of the varied roles of public relations (PR) practitioners.
- Understand the differences between agency and in-house PR.
- Identify how PR agencies are structured and how the client/agency relationship is managed.

10.2 Introduction

In the PR census carried out by the US Public Relations Consultants' Association in 2022, it was found that 43% of those surveyed were working in agency, 30% 'in-house', 18% as freelance consultants and 5% in education with the remaining 4% working elsewhere.

DOI: 10.4324/9781003253815-10

In the English-speaking European markets of the United Kingdom and Ireland, many more of those surveyed were working in-house. In the UK, it was found that 69% of those surveyed in the industry in 2021/22 worked 'in-house', 18% in consultancy and 3% as independent practitioners. In Ireland, the Public Relations Consultants' Association's census found that, 53% of the approximately 3,000 respondents worked 'in-house' while 35% worked in agencies and 10% were self-employed (Slatter, 2022).

These results could be skewed by the respondents who participated. Possibly many more of those working in-house responded compared to those working in an agency, for example. However, taking the figures at face value and we assume there are more PR professionals working directly for companies than for agencies in Ireland and in the UK, the question is then, why is this the case? Butterick (2011) proffers that the growth of 'in-house' PR has been driven by the need for better communication across the public sector in addition to the private sector in the UK. Regardless, the results demonstrate the varying roles that PR professionals take across continents and the two main forms that PR roles take – either in-house or consultant. The third role is a freelance one which is a role that is growing in popularity possibly made more popular with the recent COVID-19 pandemic when many professionals began working remotely.

Broom and Smith (1979) outlined the four roles of a PR practitioner within an organisation as follows:

1 **Expert Prescriber:**

- Researches and defines the communications problem.
- Devises the PR programme.
- Assumes responsibility for its implementation.

2 **Communications Facilitator:**

- Provides information.
- Develops a process for communication.

3 **Problem-Solving Process Facilitator:**

- Plans and coordinates PR activities with senior management.

4 **Communications Technician:**

- Implementation – writing, editing, event management.
- Concerned with delivery and not a strategic role.

In an ideal situation and as is often the case in large companies with substantially sized PR departments, there would be a different individual to perform each of these tasks. However, very often communications departments are under-resourced and all these tasks can fall to one or two people (Broom and Smith, 1979).

These roles are either carried out by an 'in-house' PR profeesional or by an external PR consultant. The difference between these areas is now explained using a hypothetical situation to describe a week in the life of a PR professional for a large multinational telecommunications company. In addition, we will also reference freelance roles and the roles of the Press Officer and the Publicity Agent.

10.3 In-house PR

Assume that the company is a major multinational telecommunications organisation. I am the 'in-house' PR officer and my official title is Communications Director. I oversee a team of four people including myself. On a Monday morning, I arrive at the office early and check all media (national, international and regional) for news relating to the brand I work for and related topics on telecommunications. This news is all collated and delivered to my inbox by a specific media monitoring agency that we work with. I also quickly check my own favourite news and social media sites to keep up to date with developments.

Next, I attend a weekly meeting of all the directors at the firm to review the previous week and plan the week and months ahead. I then chair the weekly meeting of my team in which the communications manager updates the team on any relevant news and all communications activity for the week. This could include events, news stories being issued to media, meetings – both internal and external and/or reports being compiled for senior management. The Communications Manager is assisted in their role by a Communications Executive and an Administrator. There is also a communications' student working with the team this week on work experience from one of the universities.

This is a big week for the organisation as we are launching a new product. The Communications Manager is organising a large event in the City Centre and the team is inviting business and technology media, influencers and personalities from the entertainment world. There is a huge amount of pre-launch activity taking place in terms of consumer media coverage in the mainstream media and influencer activity on social media. An external agency is assisting with the media relations.

A significant internal communications strategy is being implemented in tandem with the external communications in order to inform all members of the company of the launch. Staff are dispersed throughout various locations around the country so its important to keep them up to date. The Communications Manager, assisted by the Executive, is visiting locations around the country to make a presentation to staff on the product launch. The Communications Executive is drafting content for the monthly newsletter to announce the product launch also.

In addition, it is approaching the end of the first quarter and a report on the communications activity of the firm is due at the end of the week. The team has compiled the information and the Communications Director is drafting a report to present at the following week's meeting.

One of the key differences between in-house and consultancy PR is internal communications or two-way communications between management and staff. As you see from this example, internal communications forms a large part of the in-house PR's role. A consultant will rarely get involved in internal communications.

10.3.1 Internal Communications

Internal communications is the name given to communications within an organisation.

The objectives of internal communications are as follows:

- To communicate the organisation's 'culture' to its employees.
- To communicate and build relationships between an organisation's management and its employees.
- To work with the Human Resources department in change management situations which are common during mergers and acquisitions.

Theaker's 'Relationship Onion' which we discussed in an earlier chapter had employees at the core of an organisation's ability to protect its reputation. This explains why it is so important to encourage a free flow of two-way communication between employees and employers. Employees have the potential to become the organisation's best ambassadors. They can contribute to word of mouth marketing which is invaluable for an organisation.

The means or tools for communicating with internal audiences are the same as the external ones as discussed in later chapters. However, the channels are very different. In external communications, the main channel is media (mainstream print, broadcast, online news and social media). In internal communications, the channels are the internal mediums those available in the organisation. Examples of such channels are as follows:

- Internal newsletter – online/print.
- Internal marketing material – e.g. fliers.
- Loyalty Schemes – usually developed by the marketing department and communicated through internal PR.
- Email.
- Meetings.
- Conference Calls.
- Blogs.
- Videos.

As the media used in internal communications is generated in-house, there is no requirement for the PR professional to have an extensive database of media contacts. The knowledge required for the role is very specific as it realtes to one company and one industry only. An external consultant will often be required to have a wide knowledge of media and industries to manage the various companies and sectors that they are working on and in.

10.4 PR Consultancy

Let us assume that I am the Account Director for the PR consultancy that has been hired to work with the telecommunications company described.

I arrive at the office early on a Monday morning and check all the media coverage relating to this client and all my ten clients. The clients are in a diverse range of industries including telecommunications, healthcare and hospitality. I need to make sure that I am up to date on any developments relating to them including mentions of the client directly in the media, competitor activity and policy issues that might impact them.

Next, I lead my team in an agency meeting where all teams across the agency provide an update on their activity. I head up the Corporate Team and the information I provide on our activity relates directly to the Consumer and Public Affairs teams who are also working on the same accounts. We each give an account of our work for the week and detail any meetings that might be taking place.

At the end of each meeting, the Account Director on each team discusses any new business opportunities that might arise. Each director has a target to bring in a certain percentage of new business every quarter. This target must be met and a certain percentage of time each week is spent chasing leads, meeting with new prospects and working with the team to develop proposals following successful new business meetings from the previous weeks. It is vital for an agency to keep this pipeline of new business very active.

There is some restructuring taking place in the agency presently as two team members, including one from my team, are being promoted from Account Executive to Account Manager. Meetings will need to take place during the week also with the new team members to help assist them in the transition to the new role. The Junior Account Executive will take the place of the Account Executive and an advertisement has been placed with the professional body for PR to advertise the junior roles.

Agencies in the PR industry are generally structured in this way. Most teams will have an Account Director, an Account Manager, an Account Executive and Junior Account Executive working on each client. The number of team members on each client largely depends on the size of the agency as well as the value of the account to the agency. The Account Executive and Junior Account Executive will generally take responsibility for the day-to-day activity with the responsibility for and interaction with clients increasing as the professional progresses through the ranks.

An outline of the structure and its roles is seen in the table as follows.

10.4.1 Agency Structure

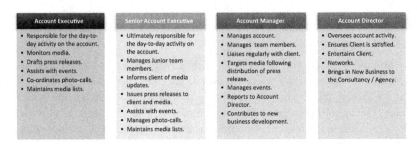

Account Executive	Senior Account Executive	Account Manager	Account Director
• Responsible for the day-to-day activity on the account. • Monitors media. • Drafts press releases. • Assists with events. • Co-ordinates photo-calls. • Maintains media lists.	• Ultimately responsible for the day-to-day activity on the account. • Manages Junior team members. • Informs client of media updates. • Issues press releases to client and media. • Assists with events. • Manages photo-calls. • Maintains media lists.	• Manages account. • Manages team members. • Liaises regularly with client. • Targets media following distribution of press release. • Manages events. • Reports to Account Director. • Contributes to new business development.	• Oversees account activity. • Ensures Client is satisfied. • Entertains Client. • Networks. • Brings in New Business to the Consultancy / Agency.

At Account Director level, there is a huge onus on the professional to bring in new business to the firm which may or may not suit an indiviual. It is often at this point that an agency executive may make the decision to make the transition to an in-house role. An external consultant with this level of experience would be a valuable asset to a company as they would have a wealth of experience and contacts to bring to an in-house role. For the professional, there is less pressure on them to secure new business in an in-house role.

Just as internal communications is a very distinctive part of the in-house public relations PR practitioner's role, pitching for new business is unique to the agency role. Agency PR consultants may be required from time to time to engage in internal communications but an in-house representative will not be required to pitch for new business. However, they may be required to invite agencies to pitch for business and to develop a brief for prospective agencies. The pitching for business aspect of public relations PR is covered in the chapter entitled, 'Making the PR Pitch'.

10.4.2 PR Consultancy Fee Structures

Agencies can either charge their clients a project fee for a particular project or an agreed monthly retainer. A monthly retainer is usually the preferred option for the consultancy as it offers security for the agency. It can also offer peace of mind to the client who can be assured that they have PR support available to them whenever it is required. This can be quite useful to clients who require PR support predominantly for media relations to handle day-to-day media queries. This may be the case with companies that tend to be in the news quite often.

Retainer fees are usually calculated based on an hourly rate for the team involved. For example, in Ireland, an Account Director might charge €200 per hour, an Account Manager €105 (note that these figures are examples only) and an Account Executive €95. The Account Director would generally spend less hours on the activity than others, as they should really be required only to oversee the account. The Account Manager and the Account Executive would be most active on the accounts on a daily basis.

In the case of an organisation possibly, in the consumer sector that may only need support for a particular project such as an event or a product launch, they might hire a PR consultancy to manage this project only for them. In this case, a project fee would be established based on the number of hours required as outlined above. In the case of a project, a payment plan would be agreed (for example, 50% at commencement and 50% on completion of the project) and a small discount could be applied in return for upfront or prompt payment.

10.4.3 Other Costs

In addition to the fee for professional services, most clients, unless they are exempt, will be charged taxes as applicable to the market they are operating in.

Often PR campaigns will require the hiring of third parties such as photographers for events, for example, videographers or media monitoring services. These relationships are often managed by the PR agency and a handling fee is applied to the overall fee billed to the client.

10.5 Other PR Roles – Freelance and Publicity

PR practitioners also commonly work as freelance PR executives. In this role, they may work on a project basis where they are contracted by an organisation and sometimes by an agency to manage or assist with a particular project. Often freelance PR practitioners are hired by the hour by organisations to write material such as annual reports, press releases or to attend and write up conferences for media consumption.

Publicity is an area that can sometimes find itself included in the PR remit. However, it is a completely different role to that of a PR professional working for a business. A publicity representative for an artist, sports person or an entertainer these days, for example, is usually referred to as an agent and would predominantly be tasked with booking appearances for the celebrity rather than managing their PR. The crossover most likely occurs as often the purpose of the media appearances is to gain positive publicity for the celebrity. PT Barnum is thought to be the first example of such a practitioner and his story is discussed in more detail in Chapter 1 (History of PR).

10.6 For Discussion

The following are some discussion points to consider for further learning. These topics can be considered on your own or discussed in a tutorial setting, with peers or with colleagues.

- Think of a large corporation or brand you are familiar with.
- Draw up a list of tasks for their in-house PR officer.
- Draw up a list of tasks for their external consultant.
- Explain how an external PR consultant might work with the organisation and what value they could bring.
- Explain the fee structure that you think would work best for this client/ agency relationship.

References

Broom, G. M. & Smith, G. D. (1979). Testing the practitioner's impact on clients. Public Relations Review.

Butterick, K. (2011). *Introducing Public Relations*. Sage: London.

Slatter, L. (2022). Public relations sector needs more men, says professional body. https:// www.irishtimes.com/business/2022/09/22/public-relations-sector-needs-more-men- says-professional-body/

11 Developing a PR Strategy

Chapter Contents

11.1 Learning Outcomes

On finishing this chapter, the reader should be able to:

- Think strategically and have an in-depth understanding of the core components and tactics involved in the development of a public relations (PR) strategy.
- Research, plan and develop a PR strategy that has clearly defined objectives and demonstrates knowledge of communications skills and a competency in business acumen.
- Assist an organisation in demonstrating the success of and value in PR through the use of appropriate and relevant measurement tools.

11.2 Introduction

In 2021, the communications agency, *'3 Monkeys Zeno'* and its client Lenovo won the coveted *'Best International Campaign'* at the PR Week UK Awards for the campaign entitled, *'New Realities'*.

DOI: 10.4324/9781003253815-11

'*New Realities*' aimed to help Lenovo to be recognised as a creative force and driver of empathy and change. The '*New Realities*' campaign was a creative campaign that focussed on women around the world who were considered to be '*breaking gender norms*' (McCorkell, 2021). The company collaborated with female directors and producers as well as NGOs in ten countries to source ten impressive women who came from a diverse range of fields such as education and music.

The campaign went live virtually during the COVID-19 pandemic. 400 attendees tuned into the live event across 3 continents. It achieved 3,035 pieces of global media coverage as well as 28 million total film views. Brand favourability was reported as rising by double digits across 10 key countries, and finally, the organisation's revenues reportedly rose by 3.6% year on year in the final quarter of the 2020 year.

In another campaign in the US, Dove and Joy Collective won '*Campaign of the Year*' in the PR Week US Awards for their campaign entitled '*The CROWN Act*'. CROWN stands for Creating a Respectful and Open World for Natural hair and the campaign aimed to address the problem of hair discrimination amongst black people.

It featured a targeted, two-pronged approach from the CROWN group involving a significant stakeholder communications programme to reach out to legislators and influential leaders in black community organisations in order to garner support and drive legislative change.

The activity succeeded in gathering over 200 thousand petition signatures in support of the change in legislation and in 2020, the CROWN Act bill, which aims to protect against hair discrimination, was passed in seven key states in the US (PR Week, 2021).

These campaigns described are a demonstration of excellence in PR strategy. For example, in Lenovo's and 3 Monkeys Zeno's strategy, Lenovo seeked to be recognised as an empathetic driver of change. Its campaign was a reputational one. Its objective was to establish and build its reputation as an organisation that cared about its public with women identified as core to achieving this objective. The organisation was able to demonstrate that it had achieved its goal as 'brand favourability' rose by double digits and revenues rose by almost 4%.

The Lenovo campaign could be classed as a corporate communications campaign (see Chapter 8, PR for Business) as it was concerned predominantly with reputation. The CROWN campaign was aligned more closely with the Public Affairs category of PR (see Chapter 9, Public Affairs and Political Communication). Public Affairs campaigns generally seek to change or enact policy and in the case of the CROWN campaign, it was successful in garnering support for a change in legislation and at the time of writing, for the passing of the associated bill in seven states in the US. Both strategies are successful and could be deemed as excellent as they can very clearly demonstrate tangible results that are aligned to the original objectives. Setting specific objectives that can be clearly measured at the end of a campaign are key to developing a successful PR strategy and should be the core around which the strategy is built. A good strategy will be strategically aligned with the organisation's goals, will be well researched and planned and can clearly demonstrate to a client or an employer, what success will look like on completion.

11.3 The Strategy: 'Visit Italy'

'Good, effective PR does not just happen. At the heart of any successful campaign is research, planning and strategy' (Butterick, 2011).

At the commencement of a PR campaign, the PR consultant's role is to research the organisation itself and the environment in which it operates. Most organisations will be working towards their own strategic objectives and the PR campaign should aim to assist the organisation in achieving these objectives. These could be, for example, to increase its profit by x%, to gain market share from competitors or, for example, to successfully launch a new product on the market. The PR consultant will be required to research the brief and think strategically to develop a suitable and relevant PR plan that will assist the organisation in reaching its goals. The final element of a successful PR strategy is measurement or evaluation. The strategy needs to clearly explain how it will or can demonstrate a return on investment that will assist the organisation in achieving its strategic business objectives which will in turn demonstrate the success or otherwise of the campaign.

Most models for PR strategy development should have at least three stages: Research, Planning and Evaluation. Alison Theaker (2016) uses four stages in her process for strategy development: Research (understanding the organisation, its challenges and its publics), Planning (objective setting and messaging), Communication (the tools and channels to use to communicate the message) and Evaluation (the measurement of the success of the strategy).

Other models such as the Research, Action planning, Communication and Evaluation (RACE) model or Research, Objectives, Programming and Evaluation (ROPE) model are used frequently by PR professionals as templates to design PR strategies.

In this chapter, the fictional campaign from the Italian Tourist Board to promote Italy and encourage holiday makers to travel to the country in the aftermath of the COVID-19 pandemic, is used as an example of a PR strategy. We will use the RACE model (see Figure 11.1) to demonstrate the strategy development process.

11.3.1 Research

Research is the first step in the development of any PR strategy. Often, with larger organisations, a brief will have been developed to provide the prospective

THE RACE MODEL

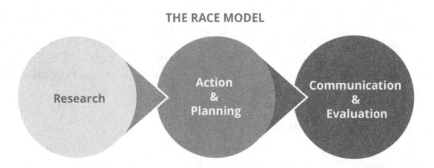

Figure 11.1 Race Model.

PR consultancy with information on the strategic objectives of the organisation and its intended communications goals. However, this is not always the situation, especially in the case of smaller organisations that do not have access to a communications department or a professional to help with the development of the brief. In this case, it is up to the PR consultant to interview the potential new client and identify the business objectives and the required objectives of the communications activity in order to develop a PR strategy that fulfils the organisation's business requirements. In both cases, the PR consultant is required to research the macro and micro environmental factors that will influence the organisation's business and therefore its communications strategy. This is the first stage of development in the compilation of all PR strategies. The research should include an analysis of the brief followed by a Strengths, Weaknesses, Opportunities and Threats (SWOT) Analysis, a Political, Economic, Social and Technological (PEST) Analysis and an audit of media coverage pertaining to the organisation and its competitors.

11.3.1.1 The Brief

When seeking to execute a PR campaign, in an ideal situation, companies or organisations should have assembled what is known as a 'Brief'. This is not always the case however and more often than not, the PR consultant or employee will end up drafting the Brief following a phone call or meeting with the client. If your prospective client has drafted a Brief for this campaign, that shows a clear understanding of commitment on their part and it is likely they may have a good idea of what they hope to achieve from the activity which makes the job of the PR consultant a little bit easier and constructive. Very often businesses aren't really sure what they want but they know that they wish to raise their profile or improve their reputation and drafting a Brief for them can help put structure and shape on this.

The Brief should give a short background on the company's history, followed by an outline of its reasons for requiring a PR strategy along with the strategic objectives that it aims to achieve from implementing the PR strategy. This is the most important part of any PR strategy as the objectives will tell you what the organisation wants and allow you to devise your strategy specifically to meet those objectives. It is against these objectives that you will identify the Key Performance Indicators (KPIs). The KPIs will enable you and your client or employer to measure the success or otherwise of the strategy so it is important that these are clear and concise as discussed later in this chapter.

11.3.1.2 SWOT Analysis

The SWOT analysis (see Figure 11.2) is a commonly used method of analysing businesses. It is a good tool to use in the research stage of the PR planning and strategy process. The SWOT analysis enables a deep analysis of the company, outlining its strengths, weaknesses, the opportunities that it has in the market-place and the threats or challenges that exist.

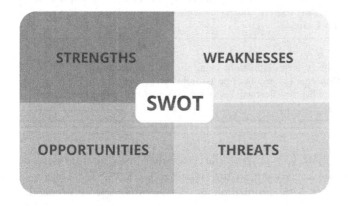

Figure 11.2 SWOT Analysis.

A PEST analysis complements the SWOT analysis to reveal the political, economic, social and technological factors that could impact on the company's communications activity.

The tables in the following text provide an illustration of a SWOT and PEST analyses for a hypothetical campaign strategy from the Italian tourist board to promote Italy as a tourist destination for travellers from outside Italy after the COVID-19 pandemic. The Tourist Board wishes to attract holiday makers and business travellers.

SWOT Analysis – 'Visit Italy'

Strengths
- Geographical position in Europe making it easy for other European travellers to access.
- Italy's reputation for art, history, shopping, scenery, food and wine.
- Fashion.
- Sun and beaches for sun travellers.
- Business facilities.

Weaknesses
- Cost of travelling to Italy.
- Cost of accommodation in Italy.
- Technology infrastructure for business travellers.

Opportunities
- Italy has a long-standing tradition for food, art and culture. This is an opportunity to rebrand Italy, appeal to a new demographic and promote new lesser known destinations within Italy.
- Italy's reputation is strong.
- The country's rich heritage of art, culture food and wine can outlast the damage done by the pandemic.
- Its famous faces across the arts, entertainment and sporting world can help endorse the country and its many festivals and events which are of worldwide interest such as the Venice Film Festival.

Threats
- The numerous other tourist destinations vying for traveller attention.
- The uncertain economic environment post-pandemic.
- Uncertainty about what travellers will be looking for post-pandemic. For example, are party destinations more popular with younger people? Is travel too expensive?

The SWOT analysis will provide the researcher with an overview of the strengths and weaknesses within the organisation. A PEST analysis will provide the researcher with information on the environment in which the organisation operates and will enable a more informed and detailed communications strategy.

Following is an example of a PEST analysis for the *'Visit Italy'* campaign.

PEST Analysis

Political:
- What is the political situation like in Italy?
- Is the Government stable?
- What is the legislation around travelling to Italy? Visas? Passports? COVID tests?

(Continued)

PEST Analysis
Economic: • Where are travellers most likely to come from? • How has the economic situation changed in various target markets? • What is the economic situation in Italy? Have prices gone up or down since the pandemic?
Social: • Attitudes and behaviours to travel due to fear as a result of the pandemic. • Climate change concerns – are people cutting down on travel due to fears over environment?
Technological: • How easy is it to book a holiday to Italy? • What is the infrastructure like there if people need to get health treatment? • What is the technological infrastructure like in Italy? Will people be able to access work meetings easily, for example?

Once this initial body of research is complete, the PR consultant will have a good idea of the macro and micro environment in which the campaign could be launched. The next step is to perform an audit on the image of the *'Visit Italy'* brand through an analysis of media coverage across traditional and social media.

11.3.1.3 Media Audit

A good media audit consists of a detailed analysis of the Paid, Earned, Shared and Owned (PESO) model (see Chapter 12 and 14) and the organisation's use of media within it. This involves analysing the advertisements, the earned media coverage, the social media activity including content posted both by and about the organisation and finally the organisation's own website.

All media dating back over a designated time period should be examined and the results grouped into positive, neutral and negative categories. The media audit will give an indication as to the current image of the organisation and inform the strategy as to the angles that are required and the direction it should take. The media audit will also indicate if the company has a reputational issue as a result of negative media coverage occurring as part of a crisis. In this instance, a reputational management campaign should be implemented prior to the launch of the promotional strategy.

Figure 11.3 demonstrates the results of a media audit. In this audit, media was analysed and results were grouped under a variety of headings to determine if the article was positive or negative, if an interview with the client was included in the media coverage – in this case, this would be an interview with the brand

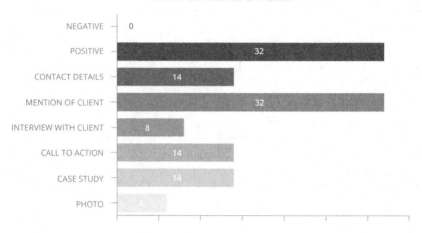

MEDIA COVERAGE CRITERIA

NEGATIVE — 0

POSITIVE — 32

CONTACT DETAILS — 14

MENTION OF CLIENT — 32

INTERVIEW WITH CLIENT — 8

CALL TO ACTION — 14

CASE STUDY — 14

PHOTO —

Figure 11.3 Media Audit.

ambassador for or the head of the 'Visit Italy' campaign, if there was a mention of the client directly, if a photograph was used and whether or not there was a call to action included. A call to action in this instance would be the inclusion of a website or contact details to instruct readers as to how to book a trip to Italy. The media audit also seeks to identify if there was use of a case study. A case study in PR terms involves a feature with a person who had used the service or product in question. In this case, the case study would be a person or a family or any representative from the target market who had visited Italy as part of this campaign and subsequently shared their experience in the media.

11.3.2 Action and Planning

Once thorough research activity has been completed, the next stage of PR strategy development is the 'Action' stage. This is the stage in which the research is analysed and an appropriate plan of action is recommended that combines the results of the research with the appropriate PR strategy.

A PR strategy should aim to map out the campaign, clearly explaining the objectives and setting out a plan as to how the organisation can achieve its objectives through its communications activity. The objectives and projected results should be clearly aligned.

Mind maps are simple visual tools that can be used to visually plan out a PR strategy and assist in strategically aligning the objectives with the desired outcomes. In a mind map, the ultimate campaign objective itself should feature at the core – in this case 'Visit Italy' (see Figure 11.4). The objectives of the

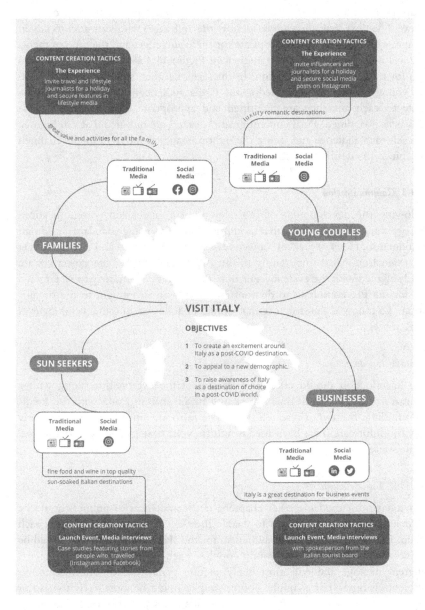

Figure 11.4 Mind Map – 'Visit Italy'.

campaign should be clearly explained and should contain a maximum of three points. The next steps then are to identify the audiences who you wish to target, the messages that are most appropriate for these audiences and the type of media that will most likely reach these audiences. Figure 11.4 is an example of a mind map for the 'Visit Italy' campaign. In this map, families, sun-seekers, businesses and young couples are identified as the target audiences. Key messages appropriate to each audience are identified and appropriate media to reach these audiences is outlined. Final content creation tactics are outlined that can be used to reach each audience and secure the right messages in the right media channels to achieve the desired objectives.

11.3.3 Communication

Following the development of the map or plan, a detailed communications strategy can be developed that comprises the following standard headings: Introduction, target audiences, objectives key messages, tools and tactics, budget and evaluation. Most importantly in the PR Strategy is that the objectives are clearly aligned with the evaluation tactics. This enables the strategy to be targeted and for the PR consultant to demonstrate return on investment to the organisation. To follow is the structure that should be followed in the development of a PR strategy.

11.3.3.1 Introduction

The introduction should offer an overview of the organisation along with a summary of the results of the SWOT and PEST analysis along with the media audit findings from your research stage. The introduction should explain clearly how this information has been used to inform your strategy and identify the goal of the strategy.

11.3.3.2 Target Audiences

As we have discussed in earlier chapters, target audiences or publics should be segmented into various groups to enable messages to be tailored towards each group. For example, the target audiences for the *'Visit Italy'* campaign could be business people, families and young couples. Each of these groups will have a different message and will most likely acquire their news or information via different channels. For example, young couples might be most likely to read or engage with an influencer who posts details of a holiday to Italy on Instagram. A business person might prefer to receive news through the business pages of an online or print newspaper and a 35-year-old mother might receive her information through Instagram and the lifestyle pages in the various publications she follows online.

11.3.3.3 Objectives

Clearly defined objectives or goals that are closely aligned to the tactics and evaluation strategy are the key to the production of an excellent and efficient PR strategy. The Barcelona Principles are a set of international guidelines developed by the PR industry to assist PR professionals worldwide in delivering metrics for their clients or organisations. The principles state that objectives should be specific, measurable, actionable, relevant and time-bound (SMART) (AEMC, n.d.). Key to the formation of a successful strategy is the setting of SMART objectives and it is critical that the objectives are related to communications. For example, an objective such as *'to ensure everyone wants to travel to Italy by the end of the campaign'* would be a very difficult objective to measure. Firstly *'everyone'* would need to be quantified and secondly how would it be possible to demonstrate that this has been achieved? A more specific and measurable objective could be *'to ensure an x% increase in the travellers to Italy in the summer period'*. This is an objective that could be measured by analysing the trends amongst this demographic before and after the campaign. The aligning of ojbectives with measurement tactics is the key to a successful strategy.

11.3.3.4 Key Messages

The purpose of segmenting the publics into various target audiences is to identify and develop messages specific to each audience and to enable that message to be communicated through relevant media channels. For example, one message might resonate with a male audience but not with a female one or a message communicated through social media might reach a younger audience but not a senior group. In a PR strategy, each audience should have a message developed specifically to communicate with the group and to reach the media that this group engages with. Ideally, a PR strategy should have a minimum of three key messages and no more than five to ensure the strategy is clear and concise.

11.3.3.5 Tools & Tactics

These are the content creation tactics you will use to execute your campaign and deliver on the objectives. A PR strategy should be viewed as a holistic communications campaign and should take into account all elements of communications including advertising, PR and marketing. The strategy should outline clearly how the earned media tools and tactics will complement, lead or support the Paid, Shared and Owned media strategies also. Examples of tools and tactics are outlined in Figure 11.5 and are discussed in more detail in Chapter 12 (Content Creation).

In addition to the content generation tools, there are other tactics also available to the PR strategist. This is particularly important to note in the case of

PR TOOLS & TACTICS

Stakeholder Relations

Photocall Notice

Case Studies

Press Conference

Launch

Experiences

PRESS RELEASE

Surveys

Diary Note

Media Drops

Blogs

Statement

Media Pitch

Videos

Speeches

Podcasts

Media Event

Figure 11.5 PR Tools & Tactics.

public affairs campaigns or activity where relationship building rather than media coverage is required to achieve the main objectives.

Such tools include surveys, stakeholder relations and speech writing to name three.

In reputational campaigns in particular, **surveys** are excellent ways to ascertain public opinion and to draw a conclusion on the image of the organisation. They also provide an excellent evaluation tool for the PR practitioner at the end of a campaign enabling the organisation to study public perception prior to the campaign and compare it to the public perception on completion of the reputation building activity. Surveys can also generate content for future use in press releases, for example. Surveys such as these however can be expensive and time consuming to produce and conduct and organisations can be slow to invest in them as a result. Surveys therefore tend not to be performed as often as they perhaps should be.

Focus Groups can be an effective method of two-way communications to ascertain public opinion. They are commonly used in communications to analyse public opinion on a topic or a public's reaction to a new product or service. Focus groups are generally conducted by an independent facilitator and can be conducted in person or virtually. Questions are compiled and results are analysed and provided to the organisation in question to inform their communications activity.

Many PR professionals will have developed relationships or contacts for political representatives or civil servants working within government. These professionals may also have a good knowledge of the workings of the systems and processes of local government. They are often hired by organisations to help with relationship building campaigns or campaigns that aim to effect policy change. This activity is referred to in PR as **stakeholder relations**. Stakeholder relations involves the briefing of policy makers on the issues affecting the organisation involved. It is a common tactic, for example, if a brand is entering a new market in which they wish to try and communicate with local officials or if an organisation is seeking to influence policy.

Speech writing is another tactic of the PR professional that is also common in public affairs campaigns. Often political representatives may call on an organisation to send briefing notes to them for a speech they might be making as part of a launch campaign in corporate or consumer communications or as part of a public affairs campaign. In this instance, the PR professional can weave in the key messages of the organisation and ensure consistency of message throughout all communication.

Figure 11.5 details all the tools and tactics available to PR practitioners, including the content creation tools. For more details on tools and tactics for content creation, see Chapter 12 (Content Creation) in which the tools and tactics specific to content creation for PR purposes are outlined in greater detail.

11.3.3.6 Budget

Obtaining the budget for PR activity can be a constant source of struggle for the PR practitioner. Often PR practitioners find themselves competing with the marketing department for the budget to spend on a campaign, particularly if the campaign is a reputational one which can be harder to justify to the finance department. Often, particularly in the case of NGOs or not for profit campaigns, PR professionals will be tasked with delivering optimal results with minimal financial resources.

PR activity can be billed on either a retainer or a project basis. A retainer involves monthly payments to cover activity based on the hourly input of team members. Retainers tend to be the preferred choice for agencies as they offer financial security and certainty. A project fee is a generally a once off fee that is paid in one lump sum or in instalments to cover a specific campaign. This can be a preferable option for some organisations and particular smaller ones as there is less commitment involved by all parties.

The strategy should provide an estimate as to the cost of the PR activity and identify the payment options that are available to the potential client. In an ideal situation, the prospective client or organisation will have provided a budget guideline in the brief to assist the consultancy in compiling the brief.

In addition to consultancy fees, the strategy should provide the prospective client with an indication of third-party costs that they might expect. Third-party costs are costs that the consultant may have to incur on behalf of the client such as the hire of a photographer, a videographer or a venue, for example. In these instances, agencies generally would pay these suppliers out of their own revenues and add a handling fee or a mark-up to the cost and rebill it to the client. Figure 11.6 is a sample of a basic PR agency budget.

PR Strategy Sample Budget				
Campaign to launch a new car on the market over a 6-month period				
Payment options				
1. Project fee (in Euros)				
	Account Executive	30 hours	100 per hour	3,000
	Account Manager	15 hours	120 per hour	1,800
	Account Director	5 hours	200 per hour	1,000
Total Project Fee		**5,800 paid in one lump sum or in 2-3 instalments**		
2. Retainer Fee (in Euros)				
	Account Executive	10 hrs per month	100 per hour	1,000 per month
	Account Manager	5 hrs per month	120 per hour	600 per month
	Account Director	3 hrs per month	200 per hour	600 per month
Monthly retainer		**2,200 per month or 13,200 for six months**		
3. Third-party costs (in Euros)				
	Videographer hire			5,000
	Photographer hire			1,000
	Venue hire			5,000
Total third-party costs				11,000
Handling fee of 17.5%				1,925
Total third parties				12,925

Figure 11.6 Budget Example.

11.3.4 Evaluation

For years the PR profession justified its existence by quantifying media coverage achieved and in some cases this practice is still commonly used. In mid-2021, the Asia-Pacific Association of Communication Directors conducted a survey on in-house communications executives in the region and found that the most commonly cited method of evaluating return on investment of PR expenditure was 'media clippings' (Nicholls, 2021).

The media clippings method involves gathering the media coverage achieved, analysing the coverage and comparing it to its advertising equivalent. The value of the coverage would be estimated based on the advertising rate card for the same coverage multiplied by an agreed multiple. This was called the Advertising Value Equivalent (AVE). Although never a scientifically sound approach, the AVE methodology probably made more sense when PR first came into being as a profession and was predominantly concerned with media relations. However, as media has evolved and online media in particular offers more transparency when it comes to demonstrating metrics, the pressure intensified on the PR sector to demonstrate its worth in a more tangible and scientific way. In addition, the remit of PR has become more diverse and it is now common for PR professionals to work across PESO media platforms. It is vital therefore that PR activity can demonstrate clear and tangible results in its own right.

The Barcelona Principles were introduced in 2010 to address the need to create a valid and reliable measurement structure for the PR industry. The principles offer a detailed guide to practitioners as to how to structure campaigns and identify clear metrics that can effectively quantify the success or otherwise of a campaign. The key element of the principles is the alignment of desired outcomes with the goals set for the campaign and the requirement to use quantitative and qualitative analysis to demonstrate impact, including website analytics, social media engagement and surveys to assess changes in attitudes and behaviours or assess the effectiveness of reputational campaigns. Most importantly, the principles rule out the use of AVE as a reliable measurement tool. The Barcelona Principles have been regularly updated since their inception to reflect the changing media landscape (AEMC, n.d.).

The International Association of Measurement and Evaluation in Communication (AMEC) has built on the Barcelona Principles to develop the Integration Evaluation Framework to assist PR professionals in evaluating activity. The framework is outlined on the AMEC's website and offers an easy and free to use interactive format. According to the AMEC, the framework takes users on a clear measurement journey from planning and setting SMART objectives, defining success and setting targets through to implementation and the measurement and evaluation itself (AEMC, n.d.).

Measurement in the PR industry should ideally be considered in both a short-term and long-term manner. For example, metrics such as website traffic, social media engagement, bookings for a product or service and media coverage can offer clear evidence of a campaign that is having an impact. However, if one of the core objectives of the campaign is to maintain or improve reputation or to change attitudes and behaviours, the measurement tools may differ. In this case, measurement cannot be performed immediately as it may take at least six months for results to become evident. Reputational campaigns such as this can be measured with more comprehensive tools such as surveys or by linking in with international reputational analyses programmes such as the Global Reptrak

Awards that perform annual measurement of large global brands. Longer term evaluation techniques could also be linked back to the research performed at the outset of the strategy.

Long-term meaningful measurement remains a challenge for the PR industry and is likely to do so for years to come until organisations are willing to invest in regular and detailed analysis of the attitudes and behaviours of their publics before and after PR strategies have been implemented. As Mark Pinsent, Managing Director Hoffman Europe Limited states in his blog on the UK's PRCA website: *'To undertake primary research amongst a representative set of customers to establish current perception and to do the same 12 months down the line to see how the needle has shifted, isn't a cheap task. As a proportion of the overall PR budget, it is too big a pill to swallow so it never gets done'* (Pinsent, n.d.).

11.4 For Discussion

A leading car manufacturer is launching a new electric car on the market. Focussing on a country of your choice, please draft the following, ensuring it is specific to the market in this country.

- A SWOT analysis for the car manufacturer in advance of the launch. Ensure your SWOT analysis is focussed on communications.
- A PEST analysis – what are the political, environmental, societal and technological issues that will affect the communications strategy.
- A media audit – perform a media audit of the new electric car market using an existing electric car as an example. Consider PESO media.
- Design a mind map to illustrate the results you would like to achieve, your target audiences, key messages and media that you will target.
- Develop an outline strategy for the launch of the car using the headings provided in this chapter and using the AMEC toolkit to ensure your objectives are closely aligned with the desired outcomes.
- Develop a budget to launch this strategy that includes an estimation of third-party costs.

References

AEMC. (n.d.). *AMEC's integrated evaluation framework.* https://amecorg.com/amecframework/
AEMC. (n.d.). Barcelona Principles 3.0. Available at https://amecorg.com/2020/07/barcelona-principles-3-0/
Butterick, K. (2011). *Introducing Public Relations.* Sage: London.
McCorkell, A. (2021). https://www.prweek.com/article/1730712/prweek-uk-awards-2021-winners-revealed

Nicholls, A. (2021). https://www.prweek.com/article/1727790/industry-gets-wrong-pr-measurement

Pinsent, M. *PR Measurement, it's you, not me.* https://www.prca.org.uk/PR-measurement-Its-you-not-me

PR Week. https://www.prweek.com/article/1709560/prweek-us-awards-2021-winners

12 Content Creation

Chapter Contents

DOI: 10.4324/9781003253815-12

12.1 Learning Outcomes

On finishing this chapter, the reader should be able to:

- Identify and effectively use the appropriate public relations (PR) tools and tactics to generate earned media engagement.
- Understand the role of various content creation tactics in both social and news media and competently incorporate the appropriate tools and tactics into multi-media campaigns to reach different demographics.
- Effectively use PR tools and tactics to create content as part of a holistic communications strategy incorporating paid, earned, shared and owned media.

12.2 Introduction – Content and Angles

The tactics of PR could be described as the art of content creation. One of the core duties of the PR professional is to create content that can generate media interest and attract public attention. The public can be segmented into various groups based on the demographic that the organisation involved is seeking to communicate with. The creation of content in PR can relate to the tools and tactics used to generate owned, shared and earned media coverage that will reach these publics. The paid media activity is usually the responsibility of the advertising department but a good integrated PR programme should ensure that paid media also is communicating the same messages, albeit in a slightly different way.

Most importantly when creating content for earned media, the organisation wishing to communicate should establish an angle that is of interest to the media and to the organisation's demographic. A skilled PR professional can marry this angle with the requirements of the organisation involved to develop a story that will be in the public interest while also meeting the needs of both the media and the client.

An angle is a news story that is developed by analysing the messages that the organisation wishes to deliver and the context in which these messages will be delivered. For example, the department of public health in Nigeria may take a very different approach to the communication of the launch of a new vaccine programme to that of a Western European country such as Ireland. Although the message to encourage people to get vaccinated will be the same, when developing the angle for media, the department in each country will take into account the context including the attitudes of the people in each country to vaccines and their responsiveness to government messaging. This will influence the language used in the messaging, the channels through which the messages are communicated and the tactics used to generate this content.

An angle is much more than a hashtag and it is important that the angle that is capable of generating earned media coverage is identified first prior to the development of a hashtag or a social media campaign. If the campaign is capable of generating earned media coverage, it can be seamlessly rolled out through social media using various hashtags and social media-specific content to extend its reach. However, a hashtag, or poorly thought out isolated social media content will not have the power to generate earned media coverage. This is often a mistake that those without PR knowledge may make.

In some cases, social media coverage only is required by the client and in this instance, it is important to develop a strategic social media content development strategy using hashtags to communicate the angle. For example, in 2018, the Kentucky Fried Chicken company experienced a crisis when it ran out of chicken forcing its restaurants in the UK to close. As news of the closure of its outlets began to circulate on social media, the company responded immediately through a clever social media campaign which became a positive reputational campaign in itself. The organisation took to social media to immediately apologise to its customers. It then set up a webpage and pushed out humorous content on social media using hashtags such as #wheresmychicken. This was an immediate, transparent and humorous response that worked well for this company. It is important to note that this type of response would not be suitable in a more serious situation in which the crisis involved a loss of life, for example, or a major environmental disaster. The example illustrates however that there are various tools and tactics available to organisations to develop content. In this particular instance, shared media (social media) and owned media (KFC's website) were the desired media channels and the content creation tools used were hashtags, videos and images. It is up to PR practitioners to identify the most appropriate content creation tools to use to communicate with the intended audience for a given organisation or campaign.

12.3 Examples of Content Creation

In 2017, the Irish Food Board won an award at the annual Public Relations Consultants' Association's and Public Relations Institute of Ireland's PR Awards that recognise outstanding achievements in PR in Ireland. This campaign is discussed in detail in Chapter 8 (PR for Business). The campaign aimed to try and encourage the public to consume more eggs and to grow the sales of eggs by over 26 million.

At the cornerstone of the campaign was the acquisition of **brand ambassadors** who could generate a likeable, human dialogue around the egg across multiple media channels. This was one of many content creation tools they used. The Olympic rowing champions, Paul and Gary O'Donovan, were selected. The brothers had been hugely successful in the recent Olympic Games, and as athletes and students, they represented the epitome of the campaign message and resonated with the target audience. The acquisition of the pair as brand ambassadors allowed the brand to develop a whole range of content for the campaign.

Firstly a series of **videos** was created in which the two brothers took part in a race with one cooking an omelette and the other rowing a distance of 500 metres. The videos were distributed on social media and received two million views. One video generated almost 200,000 organic views in less than 24 hours.

A selection of **media interviews** was set up for the brothers across print, online and broadcast media with prime-time interviews taking place on radio, television and news media. **Photographs** of the brothers wearing branded merchandise and taking part in the omelette challenge were taken and published across media channels.

In another example of content creation from the awards in the same year, the supermarket giant, Lidl, won an award for its campaign to improve its reputation as a supplier of Irish products. This campaign is also discussed in more detail in Chapter 8 but here we are focussed on the content creation tools used.

Firstly, the brand selected various Irish suppliers of products to act as **brand ambassadors** for the Lidl brand. Suppliers were selected who had an interesting story to tell and a narrative was developed around them to secure media features in print and broadcast media.

The company issued a **press release** announcing its commitment to deliver a fair wage to all its staff, thus furthering its reputation as a good employer. It also made an announcement regarding its economic contribution to the Irish economy and set up **profile interviews** with its managing director and key publications across online, print and broadcast media.

Lidl then partnered with the government department of enterprise to issue another press release to announce the creation of an additional 600 jobs in order to demonstrate confidence in and support for the Irish economy. To announce this, a **photocall** with the government minister and a representative from Lidl was issued to the media with a press release announcing the jobs. Widespread national print, online and broadcast media coverage was secured as a result.

Both the preceding examples have been extracted from the Public Relations Consultants' Association's 2017 Awards winners (PRCA, 2017). The examples show the wide range of content creation tools that are available and how they can be used by organisations to achieve various objectives and to reach a wide range of demographics.

12.4 Tools and Tactics of Content Creation – External Communications

As social media and online media world began to explode in the early 2000s, Gini Dietrich developed the PESO (Paid, Earned, Shared and Owned) model to assist in categorising media in the newly evolved and crowded media landscape. The model is a vital tool for public relations professionals in developing a media relations strategy and in implementing appropriate communications methods and creating content (See Figure 12.1).

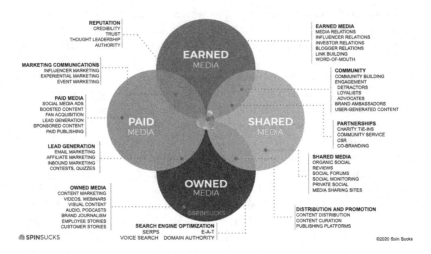

Figure 12.1 PESO Model (Dietrich, 2021).

In the PESO model, **Paid Media** is simply as it states, any media that has been paid for, such as ads on social media or online. **Shared media** is any media that has been shared such as news stories that have been shared with others on Twitter or photos and videos that have been shared on Instagram. **Owned media** is any media that is owned by the organisation such as its own website or its own blog.Earned media is the most important category for public relations. Although PR has an impact on all areas, it is earned media that PR is mostly concerned with. Earned media means any media that has been acquired due to the merit of the story in question. Therefore the story has earned its place because it is newsworthy, not because it has paid to be there. In the PESO model, the idea is that the organisation or campaign in question will be successful if all these areas are working in tandem with one another.

There are a variety of tools and tactics that can be used to generate content that can be published on earned, shared and owned media. The type of content generation tools used depends on the objectives and context of the communications strategy in question. PR strategists can select from a wide range of tools and tactics, including photoshoots, statements, blogs, videos and media interviews amongst others. The cornerstone of content creation in PR is the press release.

12.4.1 The Press Release

The press release forms the main communications tool for a campaign, enabling newsworthy information to be distilled into an easily digestible format that informs the reader as to what the story is, who the story is about, when the event is happening or has happened, where it is taking or took place and why it is important. The construction of a press release should follow the 'inverted pyramid' structure, which is used extensively in journalism.

The inverted pyramid reportedly came into being with the invention of the telegraph by Samuel Morse c.1845. Because telegraphs were expensive to produce with the communicator being charged per character, the communicator was required to be clear and brief in their messaging. As a result, and combined with the technological advancements of the day, news writing evolved to become less verbose and more factual (Scanlan, 2013). There are other theories that suggest that the inverted pyramid evolved out of the American Civil War when communications were required to be brief and to the point in case the wires were cut (Scanlan, 2013). Regardless of how it initially emerged, the inverted pyramid has stood the test of time and is commonly used today by journalists and by public practitioners around the world when developing press releases for media consumption.

In the inverted pyramid, a story is turned upside down and starts at the end with the headline or angle. It takes the opposite format to a good story in a book or a long-winded joke, for example, that might commonly begin by setting the scene and building interest. A PR story starts at the end with the punchline and works backwards from there. For example, an announcement about new jobs for an organisation might lead with a heading like *'300 new jobs announced at X'*. This would be followed by a first paragraph explaining where the jobs would be based when they were being created, what positions were being created and why. This would be followed in the next paragraph with the finer detail on how the new jobs will be created and most likely then a quote from the spokesperson from the company. Finally, the press release would include the superfluous information on the company that might help explain its business to a journalist and provide some additional information for the journalist to flesh out an article if needs be. This information may include detail on where the company is based, for example, how many people work there now, how many employees it has worldwide and what its core business objectives are.

The key point to remember when writing a press release is as follows: **What** is your angle? **Why** is this important? **Why** does it matter to the public? It's important to note also that a journalist is unlikely to delve any deeper into the press release than the first two paragraphs. Journalists are busy and are receiving news and press releases from numerous PR consultants by the hour; therefore, it is important that your press release has a clear angle to attract attention and identify the importance of your story quickly. This is why the information on the **Who, What, Why, When, Where** and **How** is contained in the opening two paragraphs of the press release.

Although there may be slight variations between styles of press releases between agencies and organisations, on the whole, a press release will follow a generally accepted and recognised press release format. This is what is referred to as a *'House Style'* and is extremely important as the reading journalist will be familiar with this layout.

Likewise, attention to detail is vital when writing a press release. The press release is a representation of the company or organisation and it is important that the journalist who reads it has a good impression of the organisation on reading the release. Clients are generally paying good money to their PR consultancy to manage their image and the press release is a demonstration of how the PR consultancy treats that responsibility. Accounts have been and will be lost because of grammatical errors or spelling mistakes on press releases. There is therefore zero tolerance towards grammatical errors and spelling mistakes in a press release. To ensure that this is avoided, it is best practice to ensure that every release that is issued from an organisation or consultancy is read and proofed by at least two people to ensure it is accurate and mistakes are picked up.

In addition to grammar and attention to detail, language and tone are extremely important in a press release. A press release should be written in a factual manner and cliches and superlatives that cannot be substantiated should be avoided. For example, a new product should not be described as *'top drawer'* or *'the best in the world'*. Similarly, cliches such as *'the early bird catches the worm'* should not be used to describe a product that is first to market. Also, personalised language such as *'we think'* or *'we are'* should be replaced with terms such as *'research reveals'* or the *'company is'*. Company jargon should also be avoided as it leads to confusion as the general public are unlikely to understand them. In every industry, acronyms or abbreviated terms can be commonly used in day-to-day communications. However, these terms mean little to people outside of the organisation and therefore should not be used in a press release that ultimately is intended to communicate with the public.

12.4.2 Media Pitch

Generally, once a press release has been written and signed off on by all parties involved, the process begins of pitching the news contained in the release to the media. The content from the release is copied and pasted into the body of an email. It's important not to attach a document to the email but to make sure to copy the content from the release directly into the email. The reason for this is that, firstly, a journalist may not have the required package on their computer to download an attachment. Secondly, journalists receive hundreds of emails a day from numerous PR consultants and the news that you are sending to them needs to be available for them to access quickly without the requirement to open a number of documents.

In a demonstration of this fact, a journalist from Ireland recently commented on Twitter:

'I lose hours of my life every year because people attach press releases instead of simply pasting the copy into email'.

To ensure the press release is noticed, the angle needs to be immediately evident to the journalist and the best way to achieve this is to summarise the news angle in the subject line of the email. Tell the journalist in question in that subject line why the readers or viewers of their media outlet will be interested in this story.

Once the press release has been correctly set up and formatted in the email, it can be sent in two ways: To every relevant journalist on the media list at once or as individual emails to selected journalists. If the email is being released to every journalist in the media list, it's important to insert their email addresses in the BCC field. This ensures that one journalist cannot see the names of the other journalists to whom the press release has been sent and it also ensures that email addresses are not being randomly disclosed to one and all. Those issuing press releases should ensure that all meda data that is stored and used is compliant with GDPR regulations.

To demonstrate this point, in a recent Twitter poll, journalists in Ireland were asked to express their likes and dislikes about working with PR professionals. One journalist commented:

'They [PR professionals] should never ever (like ever) send me a mail with 78 other journalists' email addresses in the cc field. Straight to the junk folder'.

If the press release is being issued to a select number of journalists only, then there is the choice to offer exclusive interviews to certain channels or journalists. In this case, the press release should be emailed directly to the journalist and he or she should be referenced by name. Caution should be taken that journalists working for competing titles are not approached. This can cause conflict and/or reputational damage to the PR practitioner. An answer should ideally be gleaned from one journalist before approaching another in a competing platform.

The final item to note when issuing a press release is the date and time that coverage is ideally required. Often a press release is issued with the words *'embargoed until … xx hrs'* at the very top of a press release. An embargo means that the news in the press release will not be made public until the date and time specified in the embargo. This was a more common practice in the days before social media when access to news was less immediate and organisations wished to control the time and day that a story broke. However, an embargo can still have a function in today's instant media world in various situations. For example, in the case of a news story that may be breaking on a Monday morning, a journalist could receive an advance copy of the press release on a Friday afternoon for reference to prepare for media interviews. Journalists tend to be very respective of embargoes and it is unlikely that an embargo will be broken if used.

12.4.3 Media Lists

Compiling and maintaining an up to database of journalists and influencersis really important in PR. It is vital to understand the style of the communications channels for which they work and the topics that they cover. For example, a technology journalist will have a very different requirement when it comes to the content they require then a business correspondent or a fashion journalist. Every PR company or consultant will keep a regularly updated media list for this reason. The media list is a comprehensive database of journalists' names, titles and contact details. As with many other industries, journalists will change roles regularly and many move between media outlets so it's important that this list is updated regularly. Thankfully, there are many tools available that PR professionals can use to monitor media and assist them in managing media databases, issuing press releases and analysing coverage.

12.4.4 Media Interviews

A pitch to media may or may not result in a media interview with the spokesperson referenced in a press release. Media interviews with the selected spokesperson can be pitched to journalists as exclusive opportunities for their audiences to hear or read the news first. Generally, if the news story is a good one, various media and channels will be vying for it and it's important to approach those most suitable first in terms of type of medium (broadcast, online, print) and audience demographic. It is important to know the journalists and the channels for which they work as discussed in Chapter 14 on Media Relations. If the story is a very basic story with minimal news value, it can be issued to all media in the hope that one or two might run with it. In other instances, media interviews can be performed in a one-to-one fashion which allows for a more in-depth interview to take place. In the case of very large stories, a group interview can be set up in the form of a press conference.

12.4.5 Case Studies/Real-Life Stories

A key tool in the public relations toolbox is the use of real-life stories from people who have experience of the product or service. Media are constantly seeking a way to relate features to their readers or viewers and there is no better way to do this than to relay the stories of others. Often PR campaigns will acquire the story of a customer or a client and pitch this person to the media to tell their story. It is a common tool, for example, in the case of healthcare patient information campaigns when people who have experienced a condition or a disease tell their story on radio, television or online in order to raise awareness of the condition in question or to increase funding for an associated not for profit organisation.

12.4.6 Press Conference

A press conference usually takes place when a story breaks that is of significant public interest. For example, as the COVID-19 pandemic spread throughout the world, public health departments and governments held regular press conferences to communicate rapidly with a wide audience through mass media. Press conferences are common occurrences in times of crisis or in the context of major events such as sports. They are designed to allow the subject to address common questions from mass media at once rather than the time consuming and less effective process of organising numerous one-to-one interviews where the same questions are asked and answered repeatedly.

12.4.7 *Statements*

A statement is most commonly issued to media in response to a crisis or a query from the media on an issue within the company. Statements, therefore, are generally reactive in nature and are designed to protect the reputation of an organisation and to keep the media satiated. An ideal statement is generally a brief one. However, organisations may choose to issue longer statements in some instances, particularly if the issue is of a serious nature.

For example, in 2018, when Facebook was embroiled in a scandal after being accused of sharing user data with a third party, Mark Zuckerberg released the following statement on Facebook:

'I want to share an update on the Cambridge Analytica situation – including the steps we've already taken and our next steps to address this important issue'.

We have a responsibility to protect your data, and if we can't then we don't deserve to serve you. I've been working to understand exactly what happened and how to make sure this doesn't happen again. The good news is that the most important actions to prevent this from happening again today we have already taken years ago. But we also made mistakes, there's more to do, and we need to step up and do it.

Here's a timeline of the events:

In 2007, we launched the Facebook Platform with the vision that more apps should be social. Your calendar should be able to show your friends' birthdays, your maps should show where your friends live and your address book should show their pictures. To do this, we enabled people to log into apps and share who their friends were and some information about them.

In 2013, a Cambridge University researcher named Aleksandr Kogan created a personality quiz app. It was installed by around 300,000 people who shared their data as well as some of their friends' data. Given the way our platform worked at the time, this meant Kogan was able to access tens of millions of their friends' data.

In 2014, to prevent abusive apps, we announced that we were changing the entire platform to dramatically limit the data apps could access. Most importantly, apps like Kogan's could no longer ask for data about a person's friends unless their friends had also authorised the app. We also required developers to get approval from us before they could request any sensitive data from people. These actions would prevent any app like Kogan's from being able to access so much data today.

In 2015, we learned from journalists at The Guardian that Kogan had shared data from his app with Cambridge Analytica. It is against our policies for

---

developers to share data without people's consent, so we immediately banned Kogan's app from our platform and demanded that Kogan and Cambridge Analytica formally certify that they had deleted all improperly acquired data. They provided these certifications.

Last week, we learned from The Guardian, The New York Times and Channel 4 that Cambridge Analytica may not have deleted the data as they had certified. We immediately banned them from using any of our services. Cambridge Analytica claims they have already deleted the data and has agreed to a forensic audit by a firm we hired to confirm this. We're also working with regulators as they investigate what happened.

This was a breach of trust between Kogan, Cambridge Analytica and Facebook. But it was also a breach of trust between Facebook and the people who share their data with us and expect us to protect it. We need to fix that.

In this case, we already took the most important steps a few years ago in 2014 to prevent bad actors from accessing people's information in this way. But there's more we need to do and I'll outline those steps here:

First, we will investigate all apps that had access to large amounts of information before we changed our platform to dramatically reduce data access in 2014, and we will conduct a full audit of any app with suspicious activity. We will ban any developer from our platform that does not agree to a thorough audit. And if we find developers that misused personally identifiable information, we will ban them and tell everyone affected by those apps. That includes people whose data Kogan misused here as well.

Second, we will restrict developers' data access even further to prevent other kinds of abuse. For example, we will remove developers' access to your data if you haven't used their app in three months. We will reduce the data you give an app when you sign in – to only your name, profile photo, and email address. We'll require developers to not only get approval but also sign a contract in order to ask anyone for access to their posts or other private data. And we'll have more changes to share in the next few days.

Third, we want to make sure you understand which apps you've allowed to access your data. In the next month, we will show everyone a tool at the top of your News Feed with the apps you've used and an easy way to revoke those apps' permissions to your data. We already have a tool to do this in your privacy settings, and now we will put this tool at the top of your News Feed to make sure everyone sees it.

Beyond the steps we had already taken in 2014, I believe these are the next steps we must take to continue to secure our platform.

I started Facebook, and at the end of the day, I'm responsible for what happens on our platform. I'm serious about doing what it takes to protect our community. While this specific issue involving Cambridge Analytica should no longer happen with new apps today, that doesn't change what happened in the past. We will learn from this experience to secure our platform further and make our community safer for everyone going forward.

> *'I want to thank all of you who continue to believe in our mission and work to build this community together. I know it takes longer to fix all these issues than we'd like, but I promise you we'll work through this and build a better service over the long term.'*
> (Zuckerberg, 2018)

In 2019, when a Boeing aircraft was involved in a fatal crash, the company issued the following statement:

> **Boeing Statement On Lion Air Flight 610 Investigation Final Report**
> *25 October 2019*
> *CHICAGO, 25 October 2019/PRNewswire/ – Boeing (NYSE: BA) issued the following statement regarding the release today of the final investigation report of Lion Air Flight 610 by Indonesia's National Transportation Safety Committee (KNKT):*
> *'On behalf of everyone at Boeing, I want to convey our heartfelt condolences to the families and loved ones of those who lost their lives in these accidents. We mourn with Lion Air, and we would like to express our deepest sympathies to the Lion Air family', said Boeing President & CEO Dennis Muilenburg. 'These tragic events have deeply affected us all and we will always remember what happened'.*
> *'We commend Indonesia's National Transportation Safety Committee for its extensive efforts to determine the facts of this accident, the contributing factors to its cause and recommendations aimed toward our common goal that this never happens again'.*
> *'We are addressing the KNKT's safety recommendations, and taking actions to enhance the safety of the 737 MAX to prevent the flight control conditions that occurred in this accident from ever happening again. Safety is an enduring value for everyone at Boeing and the safety of the flying public, our customers, and the crews aboard our airplanes is always our top priority. We value our long-standing partnership with Lion Air and we look forward to continuing to work together in the future'.*
> *Boeing experts, working as technical advisors to the US National Transportation Safety Board, have supported the KNKT over the course of the investigation. The company's engineers have been working with the US Federal Aviation Administration (FAA) and other global regulators to make software updates and other changes, taking into account the information from the KNKT's investigation.*
> *Since this accident, the 737 MAX and its software are undergoing an unprecedented level of global regulatory oversight, testing and analysis. This includes hundreds of simulator sessions and test flights, regulatory analysis of thousands of documents, reviews by regulators and independent experts and extensive certification requirements.*
> *Over the past several months, Boeing has been making changes to the 737 MAX. Most significantly, Boeing has redesigned the way Angle of Attack (AoA) sensors work with a feature of the flight control software known as Maneuvering Characteristics*

Augmentation System (MCAS). Going forward, MCAS will compare information from both AoA sensors before activating, adding a new layer of protection.

In addition, MCAS will now only turn on if both AoA sensors agree, will only activate once in response to erroneous AOA and will always be subject to a maximum limit that can be overridden with the control column.

These software changes will prevent the flight control conditions that occurred in this accident from ever happening again.

In addition, Boeing is updating crew manuals and pilot training, designed to ensure every pilot has all of the information they need to fly the 737 MAX safely.

Boeing continues to work with the FAA and other regulatory agencies worldwide on the certification of the software update and training programme to safely return the 737 MAX to service.

Contact
Boeing Communications
(Boeing, 2019)

By contrast, when KFC experienced its less serious chicken crisis, it released a short statement as follows:

'A chicken restaurant without any chicken. It's not ideal. Huge apologies to our customers, especially those who travelled out of their way to find we were closed. It's been a hell of a week, but we're making progress, and every day more and more fresh chicken is being delivered to our restaurants. Thank you for bearing with us'.
(Petroff, 2018)

12.4.8 Photoshoots and Photocalls

Photoshoots and photocalls are tools PR professionals use regularly to try and leverage the news value of a story. The words are often used inter-changeably, but generally, a photocall is a staged photograph that media are invited to and a photoshoot could be classified as a staged photo with no media involved at the shoot. In both situations, the organisation arranging the photo opportunity will organise for a specialised PR photographer to take the shots. This is a photographer who is specifically skilled in taking newsworthy photographs who can identify photographic angles to accompany a news story and has a direct line of communication into the various media outlets for distribution.

Photoshoots for media should ideally feature no more than three people. The people who feature should tell the story of the product, service or organisation that they are promoting. Often subjects in photoshoots like this will use props such as large signs or some sort of visual aids to depict the story or the message that they are trying to convey. Most photographs that are published in the business pages of news sites such as the New York Times or the Guardian, for example, are orchestrated shots that have been set up by PR professionals.

Photocalls on the other hand are similar in nature to press conferences and often take place as part of major conferences or events. These are photographs that are in the public interest and therefore a large number of media outlets are interested in them. In this case, photographers from various outlets are invited to attend the photoshoot and take the same photographs. An example of this situation is at the COP26 Climate Change Conference that took place in the UK in 2021. At this conference and at other conferences similar in nature, photographs are taken of a group of world leaders attending. Usually, this takes the format of the leaders outside in a group and/or perhaps three of the key leaders taking part in some sort of activity outside the venue.

12.4.9 Videoshoot

A videoshoot is often used as a way to support an online story or in the case of a story that is only relevant to online media. A short video interview can tell a story online and communicate with an audience who may prefer to receive their news in an audio–visual fashion. A video as part of a business' story should be short (no longer than 3 minutes) and should be scripted by the PR professional. The press release should guide the script as to the angle of the story to ensure consistency in the communication of the key messages. A video can often be used to support a blog.

12.4.10 Blogs

A blog can be used to ensure publication of a topic on owned media. It can also assist with leveraging the profile of the organisation or campaign on social media. It is a common tool to use when a story is not newsworthy enough to generate media attention or in the case of internal communications when a story is interesting only to employees of an organisation. Blogs are generally stories that are written in an informal style although they are controlled and edited by the internal communications department. They offer an opportunity for an organisation to raise its profile as they can be published on owned media and shared across the organisation's social media sites.

An example of such a blog can be seen on the website of Price Waterhouse Coopers. The organisation hosts a blog page entitled '*A collection of opinions and insights from our people*' where experts on various topics from within the organisation share their experiences and views on topics such as business, industry and technology (Price Waterhouse Coopers, n.d.). Blogs such as these are common practice for today's large global organisations.

12.4.11 Podcasts

Podcasts can be used to assist with the communication of a message from an organisation. Often if a celebrity brand ambassador is involved, they might have a podcast and agree to interview the representatives from the organisation on their podcast. Very often radio shows reproduce interviews also as podcasts on their websites offering additional opportunities for the organisation to promote the interview by sharing the link to the podcast on its social media channels.

Some larger organisations may also produce podcasts of their own to help leverage a specific campaign. For example, in September 2021, the pharmaceutical company, Novartis partnered with the Multiple Sclerosis Society of Ireland to provide *'easily accessible information resources for the MS community' (MS Ireland. n.d.)*. The podcast featured interviews with people affected by MS and also with experts on the condition offering tips and advice for those affected. The podcast was hosted on MS Ireland's own website. This type of podcast would be a common content creation tool in patient information campaigns in particular in the healthcare sector.

12.4.12 Hashtags

Hashtags are effective ways of categorising stories online to increase engagement and generate more interest. Hashtags generally sum up the angle of a campaign message or are simply the name of a particular campaign with a '#' infront of it. They enable multiple people to post stories, videos and photographs online about the same topic and increase online visibility and engagement for a campaign or story. Most news, sports, entertainment events and campaigns would therefore have an associated hashtag. For example, #Cop26, #AusOpen, #COVID-19.

12.4.13 Launch Event

If launching a new product or service, a launch event is a good way to create a focal point to which influencers and media can be invited to. The purpose of a launch event of this nature should be to generate publicity for the product or service that is being launched. Launch events can be pricey to organise and attendance by media is not generally guaranteed which can lead to disappointed clients and wasted budgets. In modern times, due to budget constraints and restrictions, it is more common to send a product to journalists and influencers and invite them to experience a service or a product for themselves. This removes the cost of and uncertainty around organising a media event although media events are still regularly held for items with large appeal.

12.4.14 *The Experience*

The experience refers to the tactic of providing an influencer or a journalist with a product or service in order for them to experience it for themselves in the hope of generating 'earned media' coverage as a result on social or/and in mainstream media. For example, in the event of the launch of a new beauty product, the producer might send a package to a journalist or influencer containing samples of the product accompanied by a short press release or message that explains what the product is and how it would be useful to them. The influencer receives this and publishes an Instagram story about the products. The influencer or journalist is chosen for their style of broadcasting/ writing and the demographic of their audience. As another example, consider an airline that puts on a new flight to a holiday destination. The airline's PR team might invite travel journalists to travel on the flight to the destination to experience the service for themselves. The journalist would then write about their experience and thus motivate readers to book a flight to this destination. It is important to note that this is earned media coverage, in other words, coverage that has not been bought. The influencer or journalist has been invited to experience the service or product in the hope that it is good enough for them to talk about it on their channels but they are not being paid to do so.

12.4.15 *Surveys*

Surveys can provide a content creator with statistical evidence-based information which is ideal for media articles and makes them instantly more relevant and topical to the reader. For example, in the case of a press release from the Cancer Society seeking to increase awareness of a certain type of cancer for National Cancer Awareness Day, it would be useful to include information in the press release about the prevalence of this type of cancer. Surveys can also provide the PR practitioner with a useful evaluation tool which is particularly important in reputational campaigns. In this instance, an audience can be surveyed both prior to and post campaign offering an indication of how the campaign has impacted on public opinion and the reputation of the organisation.

12.5 Tools and Tactics of Content Creation – Internal Communications

Internal communications, which is discussed in more detail Chapter 10 (Roles of PR Professionals), describes the practice of communication within organisations. Its role in the world has become increasingly important when you consider the findings of the most recent Edelman Trust Barometer which found that people were relying on businesses to give them trustworthy information. The report found that trust was local with people looking to their local communities and businesses for information rather than to governments, NGOs and media. A total 60% of employees surveyed wanted CEOs to speak up (Edelman, 2022). The onus is therefore on businesses to provide clear and concise channels of communications between their team members from the CEO to the ground floor and vice versa.

Furthermore, Alison Theaker (2016) demonstrates the importance of good internal communications in maintaining and developing a good reputation. Therefore to communicate trust externally, trust must be present and communicated internally within an organisation. In the 'Relationship Onion' model, Theaker looks at the various relationships that take place within an organisation in order for the business in question to maintain or improve its reputation. At the core of an organisation's reputation are its employees, and the best way of reaching employees is through internal communications.

In internal communications, in general, the media is different and the content creation tactics and mediums on offer are fewer. However, the same tools and tactics of external communications can be used in internal communications where relevant with the addition of a few extra tools and channels as outlined to follow.

12.5.1 Intranet

An intranet is essentially a website or a portal that is designed for staff within an organisation. Most large corporations would have an intranet site where they would upload information about the company, possibly host blogs from staff members and even a forum where staff can interact with each other. Intranet sites usually use a standard operating platform that can be designed and tailored specifically to the requirements of the company in question. Usually contained within intranet sites is information on the company, its values and mission statements which are discussed elsewhere in this book.

12.5.2 Newsletters

A newsletter is the main internal media channel for an organisation. It can commonly be used to communicate with employees and also with suppliers, contractors and members or volunteers in the case of not-for-profit organisations. Content for newsletters should be developed as they would be for external media using the inverted pyramid and using photos and video links (if online) where possible to leverage the stories. Newsletter stories tend to be more personal, highlighting achievements and featuring photographs where possible of staff members. Newsletters can be distributed in print or PDF format or online using an online newsletter creator.

12.5.3 Emails

Emails are most likely the main channel of internal communication in organisations worldwide. In the case of a PR campaigns, employees can be informed of a news story quickly, for example, prior to its external release via an emailed press release to all staff. It is important that an email of this nature is incorporated into an internal communications campaign as part of a targeted and cohesive strategy to ensure the message remains consistent internally and externally.

12.5.4 Internal Events

Often prior to the external launch of a product or service, an organisation will conduct an internal launch to inform employees of the activity. These events can take place in person or as was common during the COVID-19 pandemic, online using online conferencing tools such as Zoom or Microsoft Teams.

12.6 Conclusion

This chapter provides the reader with a comprehensive list of tools and tactics to use as part of a PR strategy, both for external and internal communications. The single most important item to consider when beginning a PR campaign or developing a story is the angle. This will help you to formulate an appropriate strategy and direct you as to the tools, tactics and channels to use in your PR activity. Chapter 14 (Media Relations) delves deeper into angle development, creating a newsworhty narrative and pitching stories to the media.

12.7 For Discussion

Assume the role of a PR consultant for the department of health in a country of your choice. You have been assigned a task to develop and launch a campaign to encourage the take-up of vaccines amongst 18–35-year olds in this country. Using the information contained in this chapter, identify the tools and tactics you would use as part of a strategic communications campaign to communicate with this audience.

- Begin your content strategy by developing a press release using the inverted pyramid.
- **Online Resource: For downloadable templates of press releases, please visit the book's website:** www.routledge.com/aoifeodonnell, **under Support Material.**

References

Boeing. (n.d). Boeing statement on Lion Air flight 610 investigation final report. https://investors.boeing.com/investors/investor-news/press-release-details/2019/Boeing-Statement-On-Lion-Air-Flight-610-Investigation-Final-Report/default.aspx
Edelman. (2022). https://www.edelman.com/trust/2022-trust-barometer

MS Ireland (n.d.) Available at: https://www.nationalmssociety.org/Resources-Support

Petroff. (2018). KFC apologises for chicken shortage with hilarious hidden message. https://money.cnn.com/2018/02/23/news/kfc-apology-ad-shortage-chicken/index.html.

PRCA. (2017). Awards for excellence in public relations 2017 – winners. https://www.prca.ie/prca-award-winners-2017/

Price Waterhouse Coopers. (n.d.). *PwC UK blogs. A collection of opinions and insights from our people.* https://pwc.blogs.com/

Scanlan, C. (2013). https://www.poynter.org/reporting-editing/2003/birth-of-the-inverted-pyramid-a-child-of-technology-commerce-and-history/

Theaker, A. (2016). *The Public Relations Handbook*. 5th Edn. Routledge: New York.

Zuckerberg, M. (2018). Statement on Cambridge Analytica situation. https://www.facebook.com/zuck/posts/10104712037900071

13 Pitching for Business

Chapter Contents

13.1 Learning Outcomes

On finishing this chapter, the reader should be able to:

- Prepare and structure engaging content to present to a potential new client in a business pitch scenario.
- Construct and understand how to incorporate visually engaging presentation slides into a presentation to an organisation.
- Understand the roles that verbal and non-verbal communication play and the interpersonal factors at play in a pitch situation.

13.2 Introduction

In 2016, neuroscientist Uri Hasson revealed details of research he had conducted on communication and the brain. In the study, Hasson analysed the

DOI: 10.4324/9781003253815-13

human brain using MRI scans. His research revealed that communication is a *'single act performed by two brains'* in a process he referred to as *'coupling'*. In this process, the speaker generates speech and this causes a response in the brain of the listener that brings it into alignment with the speaker's brain.

The research is significant for public relations (PR) as Hasson found that a person could recall a story just as easily if it was told to a person as when a person watched the story on a video. Hasson used the TV series, Sherlock to test this theory. In the study, participants lay in an MRI scanner while watching an episode. Then a participant recounted what they had watched while being scanned again. People who hadn't seen the shows were then scanned while they listened to the recording of those recounting the episode.

The study revealed that the brain patterns that occurred in people who watched the episode and in those who listened to the person recounting the story were similar, regardless of whether they were watching, remembering or imagining the scene (Hobson, 2018).

Hasson's study emphasises the role that memory and story-telling play in effective communication. As discussed in Chapter 1 (The History of Public Relations), story-telling is a technique that humans have used through the ages to transmit information from generation to generation. Story-telling in all its modern forms is hugely powerful as it has the ability to resonate with people, enabling them to connect to one another and to form memories.

Story-telling has very much become a 'buzz' term in recent years, as it is at the very core of what PR does. Whereas advertising tells people about a product or service and offers them a window to purchase, PR tells the story of the brand, product or service, generating trust and motivating people to take action or to change their attitudes or behaviours.

The story begins with a PR proposal and if good enough, the PR consultant will be invited to present the proposal to the prospective client or organisation in what is called a business pitch. The pitch presentation allows the consultant or employee to present their strategy and to tell the story of the strategy in a way that resonates with the audience.

This is achieved through a well-structured brief that outlines the strategic business objectives of the organisation. The next step is the production of the visual aids that can be used to support the main theme of the pitch rather than to drive the pitch itself. Next is the selection of the pitch team who will deliver the presentation and the final step is the engagement and interpersonal re-lationships that develop during the pitch, which usually happens in the more informal questions section at the end of the presentation.

13.3 The Business Pitch Process

The 'Forgetting Curve' (see Figure 13.1) is a memory model formed from study of memory from the late 19th century by scientist, Hermann Ebbinghaus (1885/1962).

In his study, Ebbinghaus found that memory declined rapidly within a month. His study and later subsequent studies found that the vast majority of what people learn is lost within a month.

However, there are methods that can be used to assist with memory retention such as reinforcement of the message repeatedly over a period of time, increasing the clarity of the message being communicated, ensuring the message being communicated is relevant and making the message interactive, for example through the use of videos and story-telling.

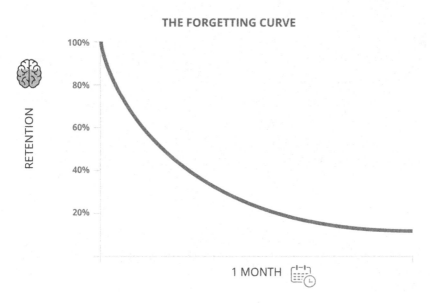

THE FORGETTING CURVE

Figure 13.1 The Forgetting Curve.

In the context of a business pitch, making a memorable pitch is extremely important. Often, on the presentation of a strategy to a company, a number of PR agencies are invited to present their strategies and pitch for the business. All agencies will be provided with the same information by the company in question and will likely be arriving with the same knowledge and skills in the pitch. What will make a winning pitch will be the energy generated by the pitch team, their enthusiasm for the business involved and the content of the pitch and how well it resonates with the audience. Pitches are therefore won by developing well-structured content, attractive visual aids and through the delivery style of the presentation team and their engagement with the audience.

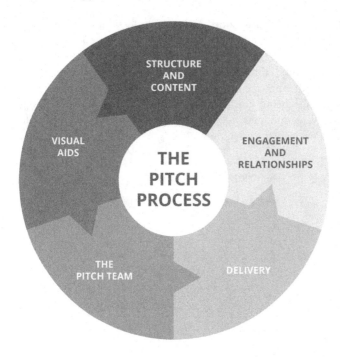

Figure 13.2 The Pitch Process.

Figure 13.2 illustrates the five elements involved in the pitch process.

a   Structure and content.
b   Visual aids.
c   The pitch team.
d   Delivery.
e   Engagement and relationships.

13.3.1 Structure and Content

As Dale Carnegie stated many years ago in his famous book *'How to Win Friends and Influence People'*, when talking to an audience, *'tell 'em what you're going to tell 'em,' 'tell 'em'* and then *'tell 'em what you've told 'em'* (Carnegie, 2010). In a business pitch, the PR agency should follow this structure and should try and tell a story to the prospective new client. The story should aim to bring the strategy or proposal previously submitted to the organisation to life, helping them to visualise and to really understand how this PR strategy will help them to deliver on their objectives and add value to their business.

Pitch presentations should have a beginning, a middle and an end. They should bring the audience through a journey, outlining what the objectives of the communications project are, how these objectives can be achieved and what success will look like.

Very important in the presentation is the creative idea. Every PR consultancy that will be presenting to the client is likely to have the same knowledge, experience and information when presenting for their pitch but the creative idea is unique to each. Therefore, one unique creative idea should be included in the pitch presentation and it is important that this idea is both creative and practical. In other words, it should demonstrative innovation and thought on the PR consultant's part but it should also be something that can easily be put into practice and that demonstrates some business acumen on the PR consultant's part.

13.3.2 Visual Aids

The importance of visual aids is often over-estimated in a pitch situation with the presenter relying more on what the slides look like and the content rather than the points that they want to make. This is frequently the biggest mistake that presenters pitching for new business make and can be corrected by clearly working out and rehearsing the key points of the presentation before the preparation of the visual aid.

The visual aids or 'deck' is most commonly prepared using a presentation tool such as PowerPoint™. Although tools such as these offer ideal ways of illustrating a point in visual form, there are many issues with its use, the main one being an over reliance on the visual aids and not enough focus on the key points of the strategy. This is a common issue with corporate tools such as these that have become ubiquitous in presentations both in the corporate world and in educational worlds. For example, Donovan and O'Connor (2017) studied the use of PowerPoint as a teaching tool and found that its use may result in the reduction of the analytical quality of presentations and the inhibition of presenter–audience interaction. This could partly be due to the design of PowerPoint slides or how they are delivered by the presenter. For example, in his TED Talk entitled *'How to Avoid Death by PowerPoint'*, David Philips states that poorly designed PowerPoint slides can result in 90% of what the presenter says being gone from the audience's memory in 30 seconds (Philips, 2014).

The presenter should not therefore be overly reliant on the visual aids to drive the presentation. The reverse should be the case. The slides or visual aids should provide an aid to assist the presenter in attracting the audience's attention and help them to remember and recall what is being said. Text on the slides therefore should be minimal and merely act as prompts with further detail delivered by the speaker and made available in the written strategy document and verbally in the questions and answers segment at the end of the pitch process.

Images are important visual aids but it is vital that only images that relate to the topic in hand are used and that permission is sought to use images. Images that are limited for use under copyright law should not be reproduced. There are many websites where 'free to use' images can be acquired without the requirement to purchase.

A video is a useful interactive tool to include in a presentation and can often assist with audience engagement and recall. The video should be sourced from a reputable provider and the presenter should be able to reference its origins. The video should support the topic and should not be longer than 3 minutes to avoid audience disengagement.

13.3.3 The Pitch Team

A common mistake that pitchers make when presenting for a PR contract is to take many team members to the presentation to demonstrate scale or power. This can be a mistake unless each team member has a role of some description. It's important when presenting that all team members have a role in the presentation and have something to say. It's also important to bring the team that is intended to work on the business to the presentation as these people may form relationships with the prospective new client at this initial meeting.

13.3.4 Delivery

A study by Dr Albert Mehrabian on likeability and first impressions found that when communicating, the audience will make the decision on whether to like a speaker or not based predominantly on non-verbal communication (body language, gestures and facial expressions). A total of 55% of the impression is based on this communication, 38% is based on the tone of voice used and only 7% is based on what is actually said (Mehrabian, 1972).

Mehrabian's study is used regularly in the business world. Although it is quite limited, it does highlight two points which are worth noting in a business pitch: The vital role that non-verbal communication plays in first impressions and the importance of having a small number of clear concise messages that are repeated regularly throughout the pitch to ensure that they are noticed and retained in the audience's memory.

In his video for Forbes, Carmine Galo (2012) discusses the success of former President of the United States, Barrack Obama's non-verbal tactics that he used in his speeches. Galo describes Obama's use of repetition in his 2004 Democratic National Convention speech where he repeatedly uses the term 'I believe'. Galo also discusses the power of Obama's hand gestures. For example, when he talks about 'the bonds that hold us together', he clenches his fists in an empowering way. Another example of the use of gestures and facial expressions comes from Obama's successor, Donald Trump. In a video for Sky News, body language expert, Peter Collett states that Trump's body language is designed to position him as 'the ultimate alpha male'. To do this, he uses tactics such as the firm and forceful handshake, the puckering of his chin and the use of small, controlled hand gestures (Collett, 2018).

People in high-profile powerful positions, particularly in politics, receive training on verbal and non-verbal delivery in to maximise their use and to ensure that one complements the other in the communication of their messages.

Some further pointers on non-verbal communication delivery and presentations are contained in Figure 13.3.

13.3.5 Engagement and Relationships

Once the didactic part of the presentation process has been completed, the audience should be thanked and offered the opportunity to pose questions. It is during this questions and answers section when pitches can be won and lost. The questions and answers session offers the group the chance to discuss items of interest in more depth. It is also a more informal process in which non-scripted information is relayed. This can be an opportunity for relationships to be formed or on the other side, it can reveal potential personality clashes and in which case the organisation is unlikely to select the pitchers to work on the account.

13.4 What Makes a Winning Business Pitch?

Like any good relationship, a client/agency relationship is built on good chemistry. According to a survey conducted by the Harvard Business Review, one of the most important things to consider when pitching for business is your audience. The survey revealed that the more senior the audience, the less that the presenter should rely on the 'the deck' and the more they should rely on conversation. The article states that the presenter should show *'your team's authentic passion for the challenge or problem and their resilience for solving it creatively, together'* (Quinn, 2020).

Creativity, energy and passion are key factors to demonstrate if you want to win a pitch. These factors are quite often displayed in the less informal questions and answers section at the end when the pitching team is less reliant on the formal structure of the presentation they have created. Presenters should factor this into their presentation planning therefore and make sure they have identified potential questions and considered how they might answer them. This is another reason why also the pitch team should be considered carefully with everyone attending having a role and a passion and enthusiasm for the business. This will come across in the informal section at the end of the pitch. The most important point to make for all pitches is preparation and practice. Prepare your content, your slides and your answers to potential questions, particularly difficult ones and then practice your delivery and timing.

Following a pitch, the prospective new client will usually make contact within a day or two to inform the successful candidates or their winning pitch. Following the acceptance of the business by the successful pitcher, the other unsuccessful candidates are contacted and a contract is drawn up for the successful

NON-VERBAL COMMUNICATIONS TIPS

Keep calm and
breathe.

Speak more slowly and clearly
than you would normally.
Most people are nervous and
tend to speak faster than
normal.

Stand straight - Open
chest and arms - helps
breathing.

Make eye contact if
possible.

Use positive facial
expressions.

Use small stiff hand
gestures.

Dress for your
audience.

Keep clothes simple.

Don't stand in one
spot, cross legs or
arms!

Figure 13.3 Non-Verbal Communications Tips.

pitcher. Negotiations usually take place around fees and then once agreement is reached, contracts are drafted and signed by all parties and dates are agreed for the commencement of activity.

13.5 The Elevator Pitch

Another type of business pitch that might fall under the remit or require the input of a PR professional is the elevator pitch. An elevator pitch takes the format more of a sales pitch and is usually conducted by a start-up organisation seeking investment or the format can sometimes be used by a graduate at an interview. It should ideally take the form of a short summary of the business or yourself, what it is that you offer, why you are going to be successful and how you're going to make that happen.

According to an article in Forbes, an elevator pitch should be delivered ideally within 60 seconds and tailored to the specific audience to whom it is being delivered. The article states that *'the best pitches are the ones that are prepared and perfected in advance with memorable anecdotes'*.

Regardless of the type of pitch, whether it's for a job interview, to win new business, or to secure investment, the keys to a successful presentation are preparation and practice.

13.6 Conclusion

This chapter has explained the role that the business pitch plays in the PR professional's world. If working as an in-house consultant, you will be the person drafting the brief and interviewing the agency. If working as the consultant, you will be the pitcher and presenting to the company alongside your team. This is the moment to bring your carefully constructed PR strategy to life and to secure the business for your agency. Generating and securing new business is an integral part of the PR consultants role and understanding how to make a pitch for new business is a vital skill to have in PR.

13.7 For Discussion

Using the strategy developed in the previous chapter, create a PowerPoint presentation to pitch to the client or organisation.

Record yourself pitching this presentation using an online platform such as Zoom and taking no longer than 30 minutes to present.

Rate your presentation from 1 to 5 (with 1 being poor and 5 being excellent) using the following metrics:

- Structure and content – was it clearly structured and was the content easy to follow?
- Use of visual aids – were they engaging and attention grabbing?

- Delivery – Verbal – were you clear and understandable in the delivery?
- Delivery – Non-verbal – were you happy with your non-verbal communication and if so why/why not?

References

Borton, T. (1970). *Reach, Touch and Teach*. McGraw-Hill Inc: US.

Carnegie, D. (2010). *How to Win Friends and Influence People*. Ebury Publishing: London, UK.

Collett, P. (2018). Donald Trump, the alpha male. Available at https://news.sky.com/video/body-language-trumps-presidency-power-play-11181124

Donovan, P. and O'Connor, C. (2017). The PowerPoint free classroom: Passivity, engagement and student perceptions. Available at http://icep.ie/wp-content/uploads/2017/05/donovan_and_oconnor.pdf

Ebbinghaus, H. (1885/1962). Memory: A contribution to experimental psychology. New York.

Galo, C. (2012). Barrack Obama, A masterclass in public speaking. Forbes. Available at https://www.youtube.com/watch?v=HKv9wYO5a9s

Hasson, U. (2016). *This is your brain on communication*. Available at https://www.ted.com/talks/uri_hasson_this_is_your_brain_on_communication?language=en

Hobson, K. (2018). *Clicking: How our brains are in sync*. https://paw.princeton.edu/article/clicking-how-our-brains-are-sync

Mehrabian, A. (1972). *Nonverbal Communication*. Taylor and Francis: New York, USA.

Philips, D. J. (2014). *How to avoid death by PowerPoint*. Available at https://www.youtube.com/watch?v=Iwpi1Lm6dFo

Quinn, M. (2020). What makes a great pitch. https://hbr.org/2020/05/what-makes-a-great-pitch

14   Media Relations

Chapter Contents

14.1 Learning Outcomes

On finishing this chapter, the reader should be able to:

• Understand media relations and the role it plays in public relations (PR).

DOI: 10.4324/9781003253815-14

- Evaluate the requirements of the media when pitching a spokesperson for media interviews and understand the importance of marrying news angles with the key messages of an organisation.
- Have a critical understanding of the symbiotic relationship between PR professionals and journalists.

14.2 The Role of Media Relations

Media relations is the name given to the fundamental core of a PR professional's role, which is to liaise with the media to secure favourable media coverage on behalf of a client. This media relations can be proactive where the PR professional approaches a journalist or it can be reactive, for example, in times of crisis, when a journalist may contact the organisation in question to verify information or to answer questions pertaining to a story.

To understand media relations, it is important to understand first of all to have a clear idea of the desired outcome from a media relations strategy. PR professionals will proactively pitch a story to news journalists with the aim of generating news coverage in the media. This is the purpose of media relations. If you log on to an online news channel or pick up a newspaper in your country, you will note that the channel or paper is full of stories and advertisements.

Advertisements generally come in two forms: Clear ads that are designed to generate a click or tap through to the purchase of a product or service, or an advertorial which is a sponsored article that is designed to look like an editorial. These should be easy to identify as they will generally look like an ad, include a logo and have a call to action such as *'book'* or *'buy now'*. Advertorials or sponsored content will generally announce itself as such.

News articles also appear in two formats: Soft and hard news. Hard news is generally a topic that is in the news and is generating column inches in the news channel because it is in the public interest. For example, news relating to COVID-19 or an outbreak of war will generate news articles as they are current topical stories that are in the public interest.

Soft news stories are harder to identify. These are stories that are newsworthy but not as immediately pressing and may be of interest to a niche audience. Using the example of a broadsheet newspaper, these types of stories would generally be confined to the pages after page four leaving the cover and subsequent pages for the hard news of the day. Similarly using the example of an online news channel, the hard news stories would be published at the top of the home page with the softer, less urgent news stories contained further down the page and within the navigational links at the top of the page, for example, in *'business'* or *'lifestyle'*. The majority of these stories are generated through a media relations campaign as part of a PR strategy.

To tell the difference between hard news stories, soft news stories and advertising, it is useful to look at the following aspects of the feature. Firstly, does this article or feature contain a byline? In other words, has it been written by a journalist? If the answer is no, this is most likely an advertisement and you should look for signs of that such as the use of a logo within the ad or the use of the words *'sponsored'* or *'advertorial' which should be* detailed at the top of the feature. In the case of a social media post, the influencer or organisation involved should disclose that it is an ad or sponsored content in the post.

To differentiate between hard and soft news is a little more difficult. Firstly, the reader should consider the byline and note who the journalist is. For example, is this person a business or political correspondent, and therefore can it be assumed that they have sourced this story themselves through their contacts? Thinking about the journalist in question and how they might have sourced the story should answer the question relating to hard or soft news. Consider the example of an article on the business page of a national news channel such as the New York Times. A general news journalist, for example, is not going to arrive at his or her desk and suddenly think to themselves, I wonder what this certain fitness company is doing today but yet there is an article there with a picture of the gym owner in his/her new gym launching the service and talking about the merits of keeping healthy and fit. How then did this journalist get access to the story? By contrast, consider the example of the home page of the New York Times that contains a story of the war in Ukraine. How did the journalist get this story? In this case, the journalist probably did arrive at their desk and think, what is happening in Ukraine and made contact with their correspondent there to get the latest update. In the first example, it is unclear how the journalist would have heard about this story and therefore you could assume that they were told about the story by the organisation itself and this is media relations.

To follow are some examples that demonstrate media relations in action.

14.2.1 Facebook

In early 2018, Cambridge Analytica, a data analytics firm that was working in partnership with Facebook, used the personal information of more than 50 million Facebook profiles without users' permission. The information was allegedly used to target US voters with personalised political advertisements in the US presidential election. When the information was revealed to the media by a whistleblower, it emerged that Facebook had known about the data breach for a number of years prior to it being made public. It also emerged that hundreds of millions of further users were likely to have had their private information accessed in the same way. A #deletefacebook movement was founded and billions of dollars were wiped off Facebook's stock market valuation, making it the first major crisis Facebook had experienced in its 14 years in business.

In the days following this crisis, Facebook's renowned Chief Executive, Mark Zuckerberg was nowhere to be found. He remained silent for five days until he eventually came forward in a Facebook post in which he acknowledged that the misuse of data was a *'breach of trust between Facebook and the people who share their data with us and expect us to protect it'* (Wong, 2018). In a follow-up interview on CNN in the United States, Zuckerberg apologised and stated that Facebook was making changes to ensure there was no repeat of the data breach (Wong, 2018).

When it came to this seminal time of crisis for Facebook, its response in the media was key to its short-term and long-term reputation. In its response, Facebook firstly chose to make a statement through social media and its own social media channel. Secondly, the CEO took part in media interviews, including one relaxed style interview with CNN. No doubt Mark Zuckerberg used his media contacts and knowledge of the media to devise a clear strategy for his response in order to control the message along with his own and his brand's reputation.

This was not the last crisis however to befall Facebook. Over the following years, the organisation was repeatedly associated with hate speech and of playing pivotal roles in serious events such as the storming of Capitol Hill in the United States on 6 January 2021 (Wagner, 2021). In October 2021, Frances Haugen, a former Facebook employee testified before a Senate Committee hearing in Washington following the leaking of documents to the Wall Street Journal (WSJ) in which it was claimed that Facebook *'put astro-nomical profits before people'* (Milmo, 2021) and that it failed to act on evidence that demonstrated that the Instagram app was damaging to the mental health of teenagers. According to the WSJ, the documents demonstrated *'how the com-pany's moderation rules favor elites; how its algorithms foster discord; and how drug cartels and human traffickers use its services openly'* (McKinnon & Tracy, 2021). The testimony made worldwide news. Zuckerberg refuted the claims in a blog post in which he said: *'I'm sure many of you have found the recent coverage hard to read because it just doesn't reflect the company we know. We care deeply about issues like safety, wellbeing and mental health. It's difficult to see coverage that misrepresents our work and our motives. At the most basic level, I think most of us just don't recognise the false picture of the company that is being painted'.*

Frances's claims renewed calls for the strengthening of regulation for the tech industry. However, in the article in the WSJ, senator Amy Klobuchar high-lighted the power of the tech industry when she said: *'There are lobbyists around every single corner of this building that have been hired by the tech industry. Facebook and the other big tech companies are throwing a bunch of money around this town and people are listening to them'* (McKinnon & Tracy, 2021).

In the immediate aftermath of this crisis, Facebook's share price dropped sharply by almost 5%. It is worth noting at this point, however, the impact that previous crises have had on Facebook's reputation. Reputation as we have seen in previous chapters has a significant impact on profitability of an organisation. The first crisis that befell Facebook however appears to indicate the company bucked this trend. As Wagner (2021) states: *'the gap between Facebook's public reputation and its financial success has never been greater'*. In the New York Times, three years after the first crisis and approximately one year after the outbreak of the Coronavirus pandemic, Ovida (2021) wrote: *'This is a company that's embroiled in a different scandal each week and that people say they dislike, yet its products are used by billions of people, and businesses spent like crazy on ads during a pandemic to reach them'*. In the same article, Ovida writes that Facebook's revenues reached nearly $86 billion in 2020 and the vast majority of this sum came from ads on Facebook and its other apps, including Instagram. Both Ovida and Wagner attribute Facebook's success in 2020/21 to the shift towards online shopping and reliance on apps like Facebook during the pandemic.

The long-term reputational issue for Facebook might be a little different however following its crisis involving the whistleblower, Frances Haugen. In 2020, Reptrak reported that Facebook had *'a bloodied nose and two reputational black eyes'* and attributes this beaten up image of Facebook to its association with *'hate speech'* and its loss of revenues from major corporates such as Starbucks and Pfizer, for example, as a result (Reptrak, 2020). The reputational experts at Reptrak proffered that the association between hate speech and misinformation in the long term may damage Facebook's reputation as advertisers will not want to be associated with this negative activity. Wagner also cautions that new legislation that threatens to make apps like Facebook legally liable for media content could have detrimental effects for the brand and its contemporaries. A strengthening of legislation regulating the tech industry now looks more imminent.

14.2.2 'No Time to Die' – James Bond Film Release

In September 2021, the stars of the newly released James Bond film, 'No Time to Die' stepped out in London for the premier of the film which was finally released over a year late, due to the restrictions imposed on the entertainment industry worldwide by the COVID-19 pandemic. The stars of the film were interviewed by the media who were waiting on the red carpet to photograph them and interview them for online and TV channels. Around the same time, the stars, including actor Daniel Craig, who was playing the part of James Bond for the last time, were interviewed by media all over the world to coincide with the various releases of the film in individual countries. The media activity or media relations for this film would have been managed by the PR or publicity firm for the filmmakers with the objective of ensuring that coverage for this film was achieved in each country as the film launched. The media relations strategy in this case is to achieve blanket coverage and visibility for the film and its stars worldwide in order to create awareness of the film's release and in the long term to secure attendances at cinemas (no doubt with some help from an advertising campaign).

14.2.3 'No Drama' – Switzerland Tourism Board Campaign

In mid-2021, as the Western world started to slowly edge its way out of the restrictions imposed on it by the COVID-19 pandemic, travel started to open up again with free movement of people more possible due to the rollout of the vaccine. With this increased movement, countries around the world started vying for the attention of potential travellers. In Switzerland, the Swiss Tourist Board enlisted the services of one of its most famous natives, the international tennis star, Roger Federer, along with the internationally acclaimed Hollywood actor, Robert De Niro, to promote Switzerland to a wide audience. A clever video ad was recorded with the two celebrities comically discussing the virtues of Switzerland and the ad was distributed across social media platforms and promoted via a media relations strategy that resulted in the campaign being written up by various outlets. For example, in an article in Forbes in May 2021 entitled: *'Watch Roger Federer And Robert De Niro Team Up in Hilarious New Switzerland Tourism Film: No Drama'*, Duncan Madden wrote: ' ... *the Swiss Tourist Board is going the extra mile to inspire you, hiring the big guns and pouncing on the country's natural beauty as a source of contention in a comedy-gold pairing of Swiss tennis legend Roger Federer and Hollywood icon, Robert de Niro'* (Madden, 2021). The media relations for this ad campaign may have involved the writing of a press release to explain the ad campaign and the distribution of this to the media to coincide with the ad campaign launch. Although not privy to the strategy involved in this media relations campaign, it can be assumed that it also involved an invitation to travel journalists and influencers to visit Switzerland and to record their experience for publication/broadcast on various online channels and on social media.

14.2.4 The French Open – Press Conference or No Press Conference?

In May 2021, the then world number two tennis player, Naomi Osaka pulled out of a major international grand slam tennis tournament in France following a row about her media obligations. The organisers of the French Open tournament, Roland-Garros, had fined Osaka $15,000 for refusing to speak to the press during the tournament. Osaka had decided not to take part in the media activity associated with the event because she said that the interaction with the media caused anxiety to her and had a negative impact on her mental health. Her sudden departure caused ripples throughout the tennis world and generated a conversation around the obligatory press conferences in sport and whether or not they are actually still relevant in the social media age. As one journalist said: *'it's not that Osaka isn't a highly effective communicator. She is – whether on social media, posting statements via her Notes app, or via the masks she wore at last year's US Open to highlight the names of black victims of police brutality. But not everyone communicates in the same way'* (Ryan, 2021).

Osaka's issue relates to modern-day media relations and how it is conducted in the social media age. She was not the first to have this problem. Prior to this incident, in the States, NBA star Kyrie Irving was fined up to $35,000 for breaching media rules around a high-profile match appearance (Carayol, 2021). The controversy demonstrates the importance of celebrities, who are brands in their own right, in having good relationships with the media. It also raises the question of how media relations is managed at major events in the age of social media. As the media has evolved, celebrities, including sports stars, have more control over their own image. Through their own social media platforms, they can freely communicate their own thoughts and beliefs and their image without relying on the publicist or a press conference to do this for them. Could this be the beginning of the end of the post-match press conference in sport?

14.2.5 Activism and Anti-Vaccination Campaign

In 2016, the World Health Organisation (WHO) backed a campaign from the Health Service Executive (HSE) in Ireland to raise awareness of the benefits of young girls in taking the HPV vaccine to help prevent cervical cancer. The campaign was developed in response to a sharp drop that had occurred in the uptake of the vaccine from 87% in 2015 to only 50% in 2016. The drop-off is thought to have been caused by a campaign of misinformation from an 'anti-vax' activist group who claimed their daughters had developed side effects after receiving the vaccine. The high-impact campaign from the group was rolled out predominantly across social media and resulted in a significant drop-off in those receiving the vaccine.

In response, the HSE, backed by the WHO, enlisted the services of activist and cervical cancer patient, Laura Brennan. In the time before her tragic death from cervical cancer, Laura became an advocate for the vaccine and fronted a large-scale nationwide campaign to inform people of the benefits of the vaccine and to explain how her situation and prognosis could have been different had she been given the vaccine. The multi-media campaign ran across multiple channels and succeeded in reversing the downturn in the vaccine uptake and increasing uptake from 50% to 70%, a reversal that in the words of Dr Brenda Corcoran in the HSE, was *'extremely unusual'* (Power, 2017). The campaign demonstrates the powerful role of activism in PR and the role that opinion leaders such as Laura Brennan play when an organisation is communicating with the public through the media.

These different situations demonstrate media relations in action. The Facebook issue was a crisis that required very specific and immediate engagement of a media relations programme. Naomi Osaka's situation was a reputational crisis of her own making but demonstrates the power of a person or sportsperson in this case, as a brand and the critical role that media relations plays in the life or the brand of a sportsperson, while also raising the question of the purpose of some press conferences in the social media age. The launch of the *'No Time to Die'* James Bond film is an example of proactive publicity style communications in which media coverage is sought to raise awareness and to support advertising. The HSE/WHO campaign is an example of activism, both on behalf of the anti-vax group and from the HSE/WHO in the media campaign it ran to dispel the misinformation.

Media relations at its core is the art of engaging with the media and marrying what it is that the organisation wishes to communicate with what is newsworthy or in the public interest. The secret to good media relations is in the creation of newsworthy content that is capable of capturing public attention while at the same time communicating the organisation's key messages which we will come to shortly in this chapter. The creation of newsworthy content is extremely important as it is what secures soft news stories' place in the media and demonstrates the success of a media relations campaign. The creation of content involves using specific PR tools with a press release being the cornerstone of the content creation toolbox. Content creation tools and tactics are discussed in detail in Chapter 12).

14.3 Developing an Effective Media Relations Strategy

PR, according to the Mexico Definition, is concerned with building and maintaining relationships between an organisation (or a political party, or person) and its public. Although many factors are at play in this relationship building and maintenance activity, including stakeholder relations and internal communications, the media is the most commonly used channel through which the PR professional communicates with the public on behalf of an organisation.

Media relations is the name given to the managing of and dealing with the media to generate content that interests the public while at the same time helps to build relationships and maintain the reputation of the organisation involved. As we have seen in Chapter 10, the PR professional has many roles, from content creator to media relations to trainer, counsellor and strategist. However, media relations remains at the core of what PR professionals do. In the PRCA's Census of the PR industry in the UK when PR professionals were asked what their main duties were, media relations featured in the top four main roles or duties undertaken by PR professionals. The duties identified were: Strategy Development (16%), Corporate PR (9%) and Media Relations – both general and strategy planning (22%) (PRCA, 2019).

Media relations can be either reactive or proactive. Reactive is when a story comes to the attention of the media about an organisation and it is required to respond or not as the case may be. This is evidenced, for example, in Facebook's crisis described earlier in this chapter. Proactive is when the organisation approaches the media with a story that it would like to tell in what is commonly referred to as a media pitch. For example, the launch of the James Bond film would have been communicated through a proactive communications campaign from the film company to the media.

In general, media relations involves the following tasks:

- The promotion of the organisation's message to its publics through the media.
- Managing inward media queries and sourcing appropriate spokespeople from within the organisation to speak to the journalists.
- Training the spokespeople in how to conduct themselves and represent the organisation in media interviews.
- Monitoring media for news or stories that may concern the organisation.
- Managing the reputation of the organisation in the media.
- Producing content including video and audio for online and social media.

The real skill in PR is being able to marry the intentions of the organisation in telling the story, with what is in the public interest. This is what will ignite the journalist's interest in the story. The mark of a good, creative PR professional is in how well they can develop this public interest angle, while protecting and communicating the best interests of their client. At the commencement of a media relations PR strategy, a communications professional should therefore always ask themselves the question, *'what is the angle'?* This is discussed further in Chapter 12.

14.4 The Media Pitch and Preparation for Media Interviews

In a proactive communications campaign, that is a campaign for a brand or organisation that is not reacting to a bad news story or crisis, the first step in media relations is the pitch to the media and the main point to consider when pitching to the media is the angle. Good communications professionals as we have mentioned will be able to marry this angle with the business and reputational interests of the organisation in question. For example, in James Bond's case, the aim of the film producers in communicating the release of the film is to encourage people into cinemas to view the film. However, it also seeks to convey a certain image of James Bond as this is the reputation of the brand that is James Bond and this will influence people's decision-making process when it comes to watching the film or not.

If the organisation is in crisis or if the request for a media interview comes from the media or a bad news story, the first task of the PR representative is to screen the request to ascertain if this is a media interview that is in the best interests of the client's reputation or not. If the organisation in question is in crisis, then there is a series of actions that should have taken place as part of the crisis communications planning. Assuming that this has been taken care of and the interview request has been granted, the following actions should be taken when preparing a spokesperson from the brand or organisation for a media interview.

14.4.1 Prepare Potential Questions and Answers

It is important to consider all the questions that your spokesperson may be asked and especially to consider the question/s that your spokesperson does not want to be asked and would rather avoid. For example, in the Facebook situation described at the outset of this chapter, Mark Zuckerberg most likely did not want to be asked the question: *'how long did Facebook know about the data breach and why didn't they take action sooner'?* Naomi Osaka may not have wanted to be asked the question: *'does this mean you will never play tennis again'?* If the question would rather be avoided, it is highly probable it will be asked so it's important to develop an answer. All questions should be considered and answers should be carefully drafted to take into consideration what is in the public interest but also of what it is that the organisation wishes to say.

14.4.2 Key Messages

Key messages is the term commonly used to refer to the main points that the business would like to make in its media interviews. When an organisation is asked to think about their key messages, the points they usually initially make relate to the business's objectives and generally don't tend to give too much thought about what the public want to hear. Often companies can be too engrossed in their own business objectives and unable to look at their messaging objectively. It is the role of the PR professional to understand what it is that the business is seeking to communicate and marry this with the public interest to develop succinct key messages that can portray the company's objectives but that are also topical and of interest to the public.

Two to three core key messages should be developed using this structure. The PR professional should take the points that the business wishes to make and ask himself or herself, how can this be made relevant or why would the public be interested in this? This will assist in the structuring of the three key messages.

For example, in the case of Facebook's CEO, Mark Zuckerberg, prior to his interview on CNN in response to the media furore over the breach of privacy scandal, the three key messages developed by the company could have been as follows:

1 We would like to apologise sincerely for what has happened.
2 Data was used by a third party without the consent of the users and this is not standard procedure.
3 Facebook takes the privacy of its users very seriously. We are conducting an investigation to make sure nothing like this ever happens again.

The first message explains immediately where Facebook stands on the issue. The company has apologised (for more information on apologies in a crisis, see Chapter 7). Secondly, the company is explaining what happened. Finally, Facebook is telling us what they are going to do about it to ensure it doesn't happen again. The development of key messages enables a company to focus its responses. The key messages can be peppered throughout a media interview and the interviewer can revert back to them in response to tricky questions.

14.4.3 *Know Your Angle/Top-Line*

The angle is what the journalist is looking for and not an opinion or an expression of the client's objective. It's important therefore to look at the story from the journalist's point of view, and even better, from a member of the general public's view. What is it that they would want to know? What is it that your brother, sister or friend would want to know if you were talking to them? That is your angle. The job of a communications professional is to take this angle and combine it with what the organisation wishes to communicate in order to meet its own business and reputational objectives as discussed earlier in this chapter.

14.4.4 *Know Your Media*

It is important when preparing and delivering key messages to understand the medium in question. For example, in the event of a crisis such as that that befell Facebook, a radio journalist could make contact for a quick interview with a spokesperson for the hourly news bulletin. Even though a 5–10 minute interview might subsequently take place, the interview that is broadcast may only be a short excerpt of approximately 1 minute or less. This is what is called a soundbite – a short, usually one or two sentences to surmise a point or a news story. It is therefore extremely important that the interviewee gets across the key messages during the interview and is short and succinct as this gives them the best chance of ensuring that the soundbite that is broadcast is relevant. By contrast, if the spokesperson was being interviewed on live television or for a video interview for online consumption, a more detailed interview would be broadcast affording the interviewee with a greater opportunity to get his or her point across. If the feature is being prepared for social media only, the messages might be conveyed in a different manner altogether using images or video. Understanding the medium and the type of interview it is gives the interviewee the best chance of preparing for the interview and ensuring they perform to the best of their ability.

Furthermore, journalists expect the PR professional who is approaching them to be familiar with their style of interview and the type of programme or publication they work for. In a recent poll, journalists in Ireland were asked what they liked and didn't like about liaising with PR professionals. Many of the journalists responded to say that they appreciated it when they were pitched to by PR professionals who were familiar with the medium they were representing and with the style of this medium.

For example, some comments from journalists included:

> 'The best is when they know your product (even as simple as the days of the week it publishes) before phoning. The worst is when they don't: wastes everyone's time'.

> 'The best is when they know what audience I cater for and tailor pitches appropriately'.

> 'I prefer when people have clearly done their research before pitching to me. If it's not relevant to our readership, I'm not doing it'.

It is not always easy to be familiar with every journalist and influencer in a particular area. To assist PR professionals in keeping up to date with their target media, many will keep a regularly updated database on the file of all journalists and influencers working in various target areas. There is usually one person appointed within an agency to ensure this list remains up to date at all times.

In the early days of PR, it was common for PR professionals to forge relationships with journalists through gifts or by inviting them out to an event. However, this practice has largely been discontinued in many markets as it raised questions over the impartiality of journalists and the morals of the PR professional. Many PR professionals would have developed good relationships with journalists over the years as they would have been the source of trusted newsworthy content. There is no doubt that the best relationships between journalists and PR professionals are built over the years and are based on trust. Others would have many contacts in the journalism field due to the long-standing relationship between the professions.

14.5 The Relationship between PR Professionals and Journalists

The relationship between PR professionals and the profession of journalism is a complex relationship, on one hand symbiotic and, on the other hand, conflicted. We have demonstrated in this chapter, how the media plays an integral role in the activity of a PR professional. The media is the channel through which PR professionals achieve their ultimate goal of maintaining and building relationships and reputation. In recent years, PR professionals have become content creators for their clients developing the content of public interest for the media to use across multiple platforms and journalists appreciate this content when it is well-written or presented. Journalists can also work well with PR professionals to verify stories as PR professionals can provide journalists with credible sources for stories in an era of misinformation and fake news. This is the mutually dependent relationship that often exists between journalists and PR professionals.

Another reason for the strong link between the professions is that there is a long tradition, of journalists making the transition from journalism to PR. Cutlip (1994) cites the first official PR agency, the Publicity Bureau, which was established in Boston in the early 1900s as staffed by former journalists (Cutlip, 1994, p.10). When discussing the move of Boston Herald reporter, James Ellsworth to the Publicity Bureau, Cutlip states: *'he [Ellsworth] was one of the first but certainly not the last of newspapermen to be lured to public relations work by higher pay'* (Cutlip, 1994, p.14). The conveyor belt of journalists making their way from media to PR is a recurrent theme in PR that continues to this day. Many of those who work in PR have worked in journalism at some point or may do at some point in the future. The professions are linked but where they veer off the same path is in the relationship between PR and client. This is a relationship that requires not only writing skills and intelligence but also intuition, awareness of the motivators for human behaviour and diplomacy. PR professionals not only need to be able to identify angles and develop the narrative for the organisation but they need to do so while being cognisant of the strategic business objectives of the organisation involved and an awareness of what will motivate and interest the public. This is where the two professions diverge and this is where often there is friction between the industries and their professionals. There is an inherent conflict between PRs and journalists as PRs are very often perceived by journalists as trying to promote their businesses whereas journalists prefer to be impartial and autonomous to communicate news that is in the public interest.

14.5.1 Dos and Don'ts of Media Interviews

As the career of the PR professional evolves from that of a recently graduated junior executive to an account director in an agency, the professional should develop a competency in media relations. The professional should also develop his or her own media contacts and a knowledge of the media. In the meantime, to follow are a few tips on media relations:

DON'T:
- **Don't** conceal information or avoid an answer. A good journalist will find out the truth.
- **Don't** blame another party, unless it's their fault and they have admitted liability.
- **Don't** use Jargon – for example, acronyms or abbreviations used only in your industry or organisation. The general public will not be familiar with them.

- **Don't** allow the crisis to ripple through to other brands/products. Isolate it to the brand in question only.

DO:
- **Do** use the interviewer's name.
- **Do** refer back to your top-line and key messages regularly. Repetition is key.
- **Do** apologise if it is your fault.
- **Do** speak clearly and concisely.
- **Do** remember to answer your first question succinctly and then STOP! This gives time for your point to be digested and for the interviewer to reflect on your answer.

14.6 For Discussion

As social media and the online media world began to explode in the early 2000s, Gini Dietrich developed the paid, earned, shared, owned (PESO) model (see Figure 12.1) to assist in categorising media in the newly evolved and crowded media landscape. The model is helpful for PR professionals in developing a media relations strategy and in implementing appropriate communications methods and creating content for each medium (see Chapter 12).

For further learning or discussion on media relations, consider the following topics:

- Research a news site and a brand from your country and find an example of each of the categories – paid, earned, shared and owned media.
- One of the key roles of a PR professional is to marry the message that an organisation wishes to communicate with the requirements of a journalist to write or broadcast an impartial story that is in the public interest. This is earned media. The story is published or broadcast on its merits and not because it is paid for. This is the fundamental difference between PR and advertising.
- Find an example of an Earned Media article from an online news site that has been generated through PR.
- Find an example of an Earned Media article from an online news site that has been published because it is a topical news story and has had no input from PR or advertising.
- Find an example relating to the same topic of Shared Media.
- Find an example relating to the same topic of Owned Media.

References

Carayol, T. (2021). *Naomi Osaka will not speak to French Open press due to mental health impact.* Available at https://www.irishtimes.com/sport/other-sports/naomi-osaka-will-not-speak-to-french-open-press-due-to-mental-health-impact-1.4576745

Cutlip, S. M. (1994). *The Unseen Power: Public Relations. A History*. Routledge Taylor & Francis Group: New York and London.

Dietrich, G. (2021). *Why communications must (finally) embrace the PESO Model*. Available at https://spinsucks.com/communication/pr-pros-must-embrace-the-peso-model/

Madden, D. (2021). *Watch Roger Federer and Robert de Niro team up in hilarious new Switzerland tourism film* No Drama. Available at https://www.forbes.com/sites/duncanmadden/2021/05/10/watch-roger-federer-and-robert-de-niro-team-up-in-hilarious-new-switzerland-tourism-film-no-drama/?sh=79e5a46b2eea

McKinnon, J. and Tracy, R. (2021). *Facebook whistleblower's testimony builds momentum for tougher tech laws*. Available at https://www.wsj.com/articles/facebook-whistleblower-frances-haugen-set-to-appear-before-senate-panel-11633426201

Milmo, D. (2021). *Mark Zuckerberg hits back at Facebook whistleblower claims*. Available at https://www.irishtimes.com/business/media-and-marketing/mark-zuckerberg-hits-back-at-facebook-whistleblower-claims-1.4692728

Ovida, S. (2021). *Facebook is hated and rich*. https://www.nytimes.com/2021/01/28/technology/facebook-earnings-reputation.html

Power, J. (2017) *HPV vaccine uptake increases following information campaign*. https://www.irishtimes.com/news/health/hpv-vaccine-uptake-increases-following-information-campaign-1.3314148

PRCA (2019). *PR and Communications Census 2019*. P.20.

Reptrak (July 2020). https://www.reptrak.com/blog/what-companies-can-learn-from-facebooks-latest-reputation-challenge/

Ryan, E. (2021). *Can a press conference really get to the heart of sport?* Available at https://www.irishexaminer.com/opinion/columnists/arid-40304570.html

Wagner, K. (2021). *Facebook's critics are riled up, but investors are happy*. Available at https://www.bloomberg.com/news/newsletters/2021-01-27/facebook-s-critics-are-riled-up-but-investors-are-happy?sref=Qk91czAc

Wong, J. C. (2018). *Mark Zuckerberg apologies for Facebook's 'mistakes' over Cambridge Analytica*. Available at https://www.theguardian.com/technology/2018/mar/21/mark-zuckerberg-response-facebook-cambridge-analytica

15 The Post-Truth Era

Chapter Contents

15.1 Learning Outcomes

On finishing this chapter, the reader should be able to:

- Understand how major world events such as the COVID-19 pandemic have shaped the communications landscape.
- Understand the key growth areas and challenges for the public relations (PR) industry and how that impacts on careers in PR.
- Understand the role that technology, diversity and inclusion play in PR and how PR can play a role in counteracting the damaging impact of misinformation.

15.2 Introduction – Before and After COVID-19

In 2016, following the election of President Donald Trump in the United States, The Economist indicated that *'the world had entered an era of "post-truth politics"'* (MacNamara, 2018). The Oxford Dictionaries defines 'post-truth' as *'relating to or denoting circumstances in which objective facts are less influential in shaping public opinion than appeals to emotion and personal belief'*. Harsin (2018) argues that there are

DOI: 10.4324/9781003253815-15

several factors that have contributed to the 'post-truth' world including the fragmentation of media, the pursuit of celebrity and click-bait and algorithms that dictate social media and online activity.

Although these observations relate to the pre-pandemic era, the post-pandemic Edelman Trust which measures the levels of trust in media, businesses, NGOs and governments throughout the world would seem to corroborate this. In its most recent report, it found that fake news and disinformation had contributed to a default feeling of distrust in society. The analysis found that trust had become local with businesses being the most trusted institutions in the world and a large level of trust indicated for scientists, co-workers and CEOs within staff's own companies, health authorities and communities, followed closely by NGOs. Only 42% of those surveyed trusted government leaders and only 46% trusted journalists.

The distrust in media indicated in the Edelman report is attributed to fake news and disinformation. The report states that social media is particularly distrusted in the Western world and traditional media in the East and particularly in parts of Asia. The distrust in government is attributed to the major societal issues which governments around the world are seen to have mismanaged including the COVID-19 pandemic and also climate change.

As a result of the increasingly important role that businesses are now playing in society, the Edelman Trust Barometer concludes that there is a responsibility on companies to act responsibly and to present clear, consistent and fact-based information to break the cycle of mistrust in the world. This is where communications should play a role. However, Macnamara postulated in 2018 that a post-truth communication culture existed which he defined as 'one-way, top-down persuasion, propaganda and spin designed to manipulate and coerce audiences into compliance and acquiescence, rather than dialogue, debate and negotiation' (Macnamara, 2018). He continues to state that public communication requires a humanistic approach rather than an over reliance on data analytics and behavioural insights which can cause a backlash and resistance from the intended audience.

The COVID-19 pandemic was hopefully a once in a generation event that has perhaps escalated this paradigm shift in communications identified by Macnamara. As the disease spread around the world and became a pandemic, countries, governments, businesses and publics worldwide entered into a crisis. All of a sudden businesses and livelihoods were threatened and most importantly health and human life were threatened. There was no room for 'post-truth' as misinformation could endanger lives. Fact-based transparent communications was called for and this is seen in the successful communications strategies of leaders such as Jacinda Ardern in New Zealand whose fact-based empathetic and clear communication led to the successful management of the pandemic in New Zealand and a sharp increase in Ardern's popularity as a result.

The pandemic itself also shone a light on misinformation with people seeing first-hand the detrimental effect that misinformation can have on health and human life. At the height of the pandemic, the prevalence of misinformation in the media, and in particular in social media, led to the use of the term 'info-demic', which is defined by the World Health Organisation as *'too much information including false or misleading information in digital and physical environments during a disease outbreak'* (WHO, n.d.). The WHO goes on to say that an info-demic can cause *'confusion and risk-taking behaviours that can harm health. It also leads to mistrust in health authorities and undermines the public health response'*.

As the COVID-19 pandemic slightly abated in Europe,the Russian invasion of Ukraine took place in March 2022. At the time of writing, the war in Ukraine represents a huge humanitarian crisis with millions of Ukrainian people harmed and displaced throughout the world as a result. As with the COVID-19 crisis, the onset of war generated debate and engagement in mainstream and social media with both facts and misinformation spreading throughout the world rapidly as a result.

Propaganda is a tool of war that was widely used by the Nazis in World War II in an effort to disseminate their racist rhetoric throughout Germany and the world. In propaganda, media is skilfully used to communicate messages that are specifically designed to manipulate and mislead the public. The infodemic that occurred during COVID-19 demonstrated how effective a tool social media was in helping to spread propagandistic messages. By the time the Russians invaded Ukraine two years into the pandemic, the world may have been more savvy and informed and therefore ready to identify propaganda and understand how to counter it. President Zelensky and Western leaders met Russian propaganda head on by announcing it as such before it had a chance to seed. For example, when Putin started pushing out propagandistic messages into the media to say that he was fearful that Ukraine might use chemical weapons, Zelensky used his media profile to inform people that this was Putin's way of justifying his use of chemical weapons himself. He said: *'if you want to know Russia's plans, look at what Russia accuses others of (doing)'*. Throughout the war, Zelensky, other leaders and media repeatedly exposed and fact-checked misinformation emanating from the Kremlin. This effort to build public resilience to misinformation is one of four tactics outlined by the WHO as activities that can help to stop the spread of misinformation. Other tactics include listening to community concerns and questions, promoting understanding of risk and health expert advice and enga-ging and empowering communities to take positive action. All these actions fall under the remit of PR and emphasise the important new role that PR could have in tackling fake news and facilitating the flow of fact-based information through the media in the Post-Truth Era.

This chapter will look at the 'Post-Truth Era' and provide an indication of where the key growth areas and challenges are for the PR industry using the following headings: Technology – Big Data, Algorithms and Artificial

Intelligence, Growth Areas in and Challenges for the PR industry, Diversity and Inclusion and Careers and Internships.

15.3 Technology – Big Data, Algorithms and Artificial Intelligence

Organisations throughout the world have long been using algorithms and big data to target audiences and persuade and manipulate them into a course of action or behaviour. Their short history in operation has already demonstrated to us how these new technologies can be used by organisations in both ethical and unethical ways.

In 2016, technology giant, Facebook was the centre of a huge scandal after a third party, Cambridge Analytica was accused of using the data of Facebook's users illegally. The data was used to provide information to organisations that would influence marketing strategies and political campaigning. The data was allegedly used by the 'pro-Bexit' campaigners to analyse vital information on people's habits, interests and 'emotional triggers', enabling them to target potential voters with propaganda and persuade them to vote leave.

In an article in the Guardian discussing Brexit and the election of President Trump in the United States, Carole Caddwaladr says that there are three strands to the story: *'how the foundations of an authoritarian surveillance state are being laid in the US. How British democracy was subverted through a covert, far-reaching plan of coordination enabled by a US billionaire and how we are in the midst of a massive land grab for power by billionaires via our data. Data which is being silently amassed, harvested and stored. Whoever owns this data, owns the future'* (Caddwaladr, 2017). It was clear at this point in 2017 when this article was written, that big data had emerged as a deeply effective tool that could be very effectively used for propagandistic purposes and threaten democracy as a result.

Many agencies however are using data and artificial intelligence for ethical means to engage with employees, to build online communities for clientsand for intelligent, effective, two-way communications. For example Endersby states that

> Data science and artificial intelligence are areas to watch for PR. In the ICCO report, it states that respondents to the survey expected data science and artificial intelligence 'to be ever more relevant to the world of PR in the years to come (53% and 40% of respectively)' (Endersby, 2022, p. 6). However, it also outlines the importance of PR not getting left behind by failure to adopt new technology quickly.

15.4 Growth Areas in and Challenges for the PR Industry

In terms of the PR industry and how it fared during the pandemic and now stands in the 'After-Covid Era', the indications are that the humanistic approach as outlined by Macnamara may now have its time.

In her blog, Catherine Arrow proffers that we need to look at the world of PR and communications as two distinctive eras: Before Covid (BC) and After Covid (AC). She states: *'in our new AC19 era, trust will be the new oil. Success and the ability to restart operations will be based on your behaviour throughout the pandemic, your redefined operating practices and your genuine concern for people and society'* (Arrow, 2021). Although slightly aspirational, there does seem to be evidence that supports this from the PR industry.

The International Communications Consultancy Organisation (ICCO) represents associations and agencies in 70 countries throughout the world. In its 2021–2022 report on the state of the PR industry, the ICCO found that companies in every region of the world are paying more attention than ever to corporate purpose since the pandemic. The top service area reported in 2021–2022 was corporate reputation, up 27% from the previous year. Purpose and CSR work was reported to be the average agency's second biggest growth service area.

In terms of revenue growth, according to James Endersby, (2021), the second year of the COVID-19 pandemic, was a year of success for the PR industry. Over half of those agencies surveyed in the ICCO were expecting to close off the year with a growth of 52% in client fees. He also stated that two in five PR firms surveyed believed that the pandemic had resulted in new opportunities and a quarter reported experiencing an increase in business as a result (Endersby, 2022). In terms of specific potential revenue streams, the top three listed in order of merit were found to be: IT and technology, healthcare and financial and professional services. PR firms were reporting to be spending in the digital area and also in environmental, social and governance or sustainability, which would indicate that prospective trainees should be honing their skills in these areas.

15.5 Diversity and Inclusion

In his Theory of Excellence, Grunig had highlighted the importance of PR departments in accurately reflecting the societies in which they were operating. Diversity has been a hot topic for the PR industry for many years and a key objective of many firms in ensuring they can attract staff of varying ethnicities, races and genders. Worryingly, however, despite all the evidence that highlights the importance of a diverse workforce, the most recent ICCO report concludes that there is no change in PR reflecting the diversity of society.

Sudha Singh states *'for an industry that aspires to have a seat at the table, and advise clients on purpose and sustainability, this puts us on the back foot. How can we advise clients authentically if we as an industry are not equitable or inclusive?'*.

The positive message however is that there does seem to be an increased awareness in some areas of diversity and inclusion brought about by major societal events such as the Black Lives Matter movement in the United States and the COVID-19 pandemic which highlighted to many, the inequalities in society. The challenge is now to turn this increased awareness into action through authenticity. Being authentic involves getting the buy in from management and ensuring that there is two-way communication with employees and stakeholders followed by a commitment to an inclusive hiring process and equality in salaries. Taking action involves putting the company diversity and inclusion policy into action and being accountable for it.

One of the challenges for the PR industry as discovered in the ICCO's report is the eternal problem of the industry's own reputation. In the report, one out of three respondents believed PR to be unethical. As we have discussed at the outset of this book, this image stems back to the very origins of PR as a profession and its links to propaganda and unethical practices as a result. A change in the right direction in the diversity and inclusion policy of the PR industry as a whole may have a positive impact on the reputational issues suffered by the PR industry.

15.6 Careers and Internships

Recruiting and retaining key talent is referenced in ICCO's report as *'a significant challenge across the board [for the PR industry]'* (Shah, 2022). Shah states that employees are looking for value and key members of staff should be incentivised to stay and recommends that new talent is encouraged to join the industry by strong brands and developmental opportunities for staff.

As highlighted earlier in this chapter, healthcare, technology and financial PR are growth service areas for the industry, and graduates and future employees should be considering how they can develop skills in these areas. One of the ways of doing this is to take on voluntary work for not for profit organisations while studying. Offering to help with the website and social media strategy for a local club or charity is a good way of getting some experience in these areas that can be included on a CV upon graduation.

PR is an extremely practical subject and many of the skills and competencies required to work in the area can best be taught through experiential learning. Competencies such as critical thinking and communication skills are referenced regularly as in demand by the profession (Barnes & Tallent, 2015; Flynn, 2014; Madigan, 2017). In his research published in the Canadian Journal of Communication, Flynn (2014) postulated that 21st-century PR practitioners are required to have a *'different skill set and competencies to their counterparts'* who practised before them. Flynn references a report from the Expert Group on Future Skills Needs (2003, cited in Flynn, 2014, p. 4) which found that *'soft-skills'* such as communications skills were of *'ever-increasing importance in the workplace'* but difficult to train. Business Acumen which is defined as *'the ability to make good judgements and take quick decisions'* (Oxford Dictionary of English, 2010) is another competency required in the industry. In Flynn's article, business acumen is explained as a *'good appreciation of business, business strategy, and business intelligence'* (Gregory, 2008, cited in Flynn, 2014, p. 8). Flynn proffers that business acumen is a competency that has been widely reported in the literature and by industry professionals as important to PR practice. In their article published on the Institute of Public Relations' website and entitled *'Public Relations and Business Acumen: Closing the Gap'*, Ragas and Culp state that *'as the public relations industry evolves, the need for greater business acumen among professionals working in all levels of the field ... has never been more important'*. They add that *'to be a strategic partner to clients requires an intimate understanding of business, and how your counsel can advance organisation goals and objectives'* (Ragas & Culp, 2014).

Present research supports the use of creative teaching methods in the classroom to teach practical skills, such as simulations and what Barnes and Tallent (2015) referred to as *'Constructivist Thinking Tools'*. The word *'Simulation'* can be used to define the *'imitation of a situation or process'* or *'the production of a computer model of something, especially for the purpose of study'* (Oxford Dictionary of English, 2010). An example of *'simulation as the production of a computer model of something'* can be seen in the emerging technologies of virtual reality (VR) and augmented reality (AR). VR allows users, through the use of a headset, to immerse themselves completely in an alternative reality. AR allows the user to bring elements of the artificial world into the real world. Both technologies are being used in education in the STEM disciplines but there is little evidence available by comparison cataloguing their use in the teaching of PR. Research in this area in PR education could offer insight as to whether simulation of this nature could be beneficial in teaching media communication skills and critical thinking by enabling learners to immerse themselves in computer or video-generated common scenarios such as press conferences or media events.

Evidence on the use of simulation in PR pedagogy as an *'imitation of a situation or process'* is more common. In their Australia-based study, Sutherland and Ward (2018) conducted research on the efficacy of using immersive simulation as a pedagogical tool to provide students with a practical experience of a media conference. In the study, they combined simulation tools such as role-play and immersive technology in which scenes from PR scenarios were projected onto the walls. They found that students enjoyed the experience, they felt that it enhanced their learning and analytical skills and the students recommended the use of the pedagogical tools in the future. When it comes to means to assess the specific competencies required by the PR industry, Bartam (2004) links competencies to performance and identifies workplace assessments and simulations as appropriate measurement tools.

Despite the evidence linking experiential learning to PR that supports internships, it has been a common practice not to offer paid internships in the PR industry and trainees are generally expected to work for free in return for experience. Although never an acceptable practice, this may have been something that was less contentious in the days before PR courses were so prevalent. As a recent census from the PR sector in Ireland, for example, reveals, most PR professionals in the industry now hold a qualification. President of the Public Relations Institute of Ireland (PRII) said following the publication of the PRII's 2019 census: *'Public relations has a highly educated workforce. Of those surveyed, 82%*

have a qualification relevant to their work and over half spent time on training or upskilling in the past year' (PRII, n.d.).

As graduates enter the PR industry with more skills and experience, this is a practice that is no longer acceptable and it is time that a standard should be introduced across the industry to ensure the value of the work done by future PR professionals is recognised from the outset. Some progress has been made in this regard. For example, PR Week and the PRCA in the UK launched a campaign called *'Internships for All'* which they state aims *'to end the practice of unpaid internships, as part of the association's commitment to raising standards in all areas of the PR and communications industry'* (PRCA, n.d.). The campaign has been supported by several third-level institutions and the PRCA has published a list of all the organisations that offer at least the *'National Living Wage'* to interns on their website. As well as encouraging payment of interns, the *'Internships for All'* campaign aims to encourage the industry to be more inclusive of people from all ethnicities and socio-economic backgrounds.

In its 2017 report, the Commission on Public Relations Education made recommendations for designing and structuring higher education undergraduate PR programmes at an international level. It stated that PR educational curricula should cover six essential topics including an introduction to or principles of PR, research methods, writing, campaigns and case studies, supervised work experience or internships and ethics. The PR industry worldwide needs to identify the qualifications and competencies required by the PR industry at the entry level into the profession. These competencies and qualifications required by industry could then set the standards and pedagogical approaches used in education to teach PR students and increase their employability. As PR education evolves and graduates emerge more qualified and equipped with the competencies the industry requires, the industry needs to recognise this and set standards for appropriate and fair treatment of its interns and new recruits.

The PR industry is an evolving one that has undergone much change since the profession originated. However, its early years and the actions of some of its professionals since have tarnished the reputation of the industry and ensure that the industry itself requires a reputational makeover. This is occurring organically through the training and education of its newest recruits. However, more attention needs to be paid in educational curricula to the competencies required by the industry and the industry needs to reciprocate with a more professional and standardised process for the recruitment, retainment and training of interns and long-term staff.

Indications are that a paradigm shift is taking place in the 'Post-Covid Era' that is leading to a more humanistic approach in the industry. Purpose and corporate social responsibility are reported to be the biggest growth areas in terms of services in the PR industry. In terms of revenue areas, IT and technology, healthcare and financial and professional services are growing. PR firms worldwide are investing in digital and sustainability. Students and prospective trainees should observe the developments occurring and challenges facing the industry and take note of these growth areas to ensure they are appropriately skilled and ready to take on the roles as the industry evolves for the better into the future.

References

Arrow, C. (2021). https://wadds.co.uk/blog/2020/4/29/the-covid-19-road-to-reform

Barnes, J. J. and Tallent, R. J. (2015). *Think Bubbles and Socrates: Teaching Critical Thinking to Millennials in Public Relations Classes.* Universal Journal of Educational Research. Horizon Research Publishing Corporation: USA.

Bartam, D. (2004). *The SHL Universal Competency Framework,* SHL [White paper]. SHL Group Ltd: Thames Ditton, UK.

Caddwaladr, C. (2017). The Great British Brexit Robbery: How our democracy was hijacked. Available at: https://www.theguardian.com/technology/2017/may/07/the-great-british-brexit-robbery-hijacked-democracy

Commission on Public Relations Education (CPRE). (2018). *Fast Forward: The 2017 Report on Undergraduate Public Relations Education.* p. 17, Commission on Public Relations Education: USA.

Edelman Trust Barometer. https://www.edelman.com/trust/2022-trust-barometer

Endersby, J. (2022). ICCO PR Report, p. 6. Available at https://iccopr.com/wp-content/uploads/2021/12/ICCO-report-2021-v6.pdf

Flynn, T. (2014). *Do They Have What It Takes? A Review of the Literature on Knowledge Competencies and Skills Necessary for Twenty-First-Century Public Relations Practitioners in Canada.* Vol 39, 361–384. Canadian Journal of Communications: Canada.

Harsin, J. (2018). Post-Truth and Critical Communications Studies. Available at: https://oxfordre.com/communication/display/10.1093/acrefore/9780190228613.001.0001/acrefore-9780190228613-e-757;jses sionid=A779683092354D384702539BE1A3EB40

Macnamara, J. (2018). Public relations and post-communication: Addressing a paradox in public communication. *Public Relations Journal.*

Madigan, P. (2017). *Practitioner Perspectives on Higher Education as a Preparation for Employment in Public Relations in Ireland.* University of Sheffield: UK.

Oxford Dictionary of English. (2010). *Simulation.* Available at https://en.oxforddictionaries.com/definition/simulation. [Accessed 6 April 2019].

PRCA. (n.d.). PR and communications employers that pay their interns. Available at https://www.prca.org.uk/campaigns/better-internships/pr-and-communications-employers-pay-their-interns

PRII. (n.d.). PR sector contributes over €1bn to Irish economy. Available at https://www.prii.ie/news/2019/research-into-public-relations-sector-shows-over-€1-billion.html

Ragas, M. and Culp, R. (2014). *Public relations and business acumen: Closing the gap.* Available at https://instituteforpr.org/public-relations-business-acumen-closing-gap/ [Accessed 4 April 2019].

Sutherland, K. and Ward, A. (2018). *Immersive simulation as a public relations pedagogical tool.*

Shah (2022). https://iccopr.com/wp-content/uploads/2021/12/ICCO-report-2021-v6.pdf

WHO (n.d.). Infodemic. https://www.who.int/health-topics/infodemic#tab=tab_1

Index

Printed in the United States
by Baker & Taylor Publisher Services